### Shakespeare's

# WORLD
*of*
# DEATH

# THE DIRECTOR'S SHAKESPEARE SERIES
by Richard Courtney

## SHAKESPEARE'S WORLD OF WAR
*Henry VI, Parts 1, 2 & 3, Richard III, King John, Titus Andronicus*

## SHAKESPEARE'S COMIC WORLD
*The Comedy of Errors, The Taming of the Shrew,*
*The Two Gentlemen of Verona, Love's Labour's Lost,*
*A Midsummer Night's Dream, The Merchant of Venice*

## SHAKESPEARE'S WORLD OF DEATH
*Romeo and Juliet, Julius Caesar, Hamlet*

## SHAKESPEARE'S WORLD OF LOVE
*Much Ado About Nothing, As You Like It, Twelfth Night,*
*The Merry Wives of Windsor*

## SHAKESPEARE'S MASKED WORLD
*Richard II, Henry IV, Parts 1 & 2, Henry V*

## SHAKESPEARE'S PROBLEM WORLD
*All's Well That Ends Well, Measure for Measure,*
*Troilus and Cressida, Timon of Athens, Coriolanus*

## SHAKESPEARE'S TRAGIC WORLD
*Antony and Cleopatra, Macbeth, Othello, King Lear*

## SHAKESPEARE'S MAGIC WORLD
*Pericles, Cymbeline, The Winter's Tale, The Tempest, Henry VIII,*
*Two Noble Kinsmen*

# Shakespeare's

# WORLD
# *of*
# DEATH

## THE EARLY TRAGEDIES

*Romeo and Juliet*
*Julius Caesar*
*Hamlet*

# RICHARD COURTNEY

### Series Editor: Barry Thorne

 SIMON & PIERRE

**General Editor:** Marian M. Wilson
**Series Editor:** Barry Thorne
**Copy Editor:** Jean Paton
**Designer:** Andy Tong

Printed and bound in Canada by Best Book Manufacturers

All quotations from Shakespeare's plays are from the New Penguin edition, except as noted in *End Notes*. Illustrations on pages 247-249 by Richard Courtney. Photographs on pages 8 and 240 courtesy Stratford Festival.

The publication of this book was made possible by support from several sources. We would like to acknowledge the generous assistance and ongoing support of the **Canada Council**, **The Book Publishing Industry Development Program** of the **Department of Canadian Heritage**, and **The Ontario Arts Council**.

*J. Kirk Howard, President*

1 2 3 4 5 • 0 9 8 7 6

**Canadian Cataloguing in Publication Data**

Courtney, Richard
  Shakespeare's world of death : the early tragedies

(The Director's Shakespeare series)
"Romeo and Juliet, Julius Caesar, Hamlet.
Includes bibliographical references.
ISBN 0-88924-261-5

1. Shakespeare, William, 1564-1616. Romeo and Juliet.
2. Shakespeare, William, 1564-1616. Julius Caesar.
3. Shakespeare, William, 1564-1616. Hamlet.
4. Shakespeare, William, 1564-1616 - Dramatic production. I. Title. II. Series.

PR2983.C68   1995   822.3'3   C95-930802-4

Order from Simon & Pierre Publishing Co. Ltd.

| | | |
|---|---|---|
| 2181 Queen Street East | 73 Lime Walk | 1823 Maryland Avenue |
| Suite 301 | Headington, Oxford | P.O. Box 1000 |
| Toronto, Canada | England | Niagara Falls, N.Y. |
| M4E 1E5 | 0X3 7AD | U.S.A. 14302-1000 |

We are such stuff
As dreams are made on; and our little life
Is rounded with a sleep.          *(The Tempest,* IV.i.156-158)

for

G. WILSON KNIGHT, C.B.E.
In Memoriam

# CONTENTS

The Festival Theatre, Stratford, Ontario.

In July 1953, the first Shakespearean Festival at Stratford, Ontario, presented a six-week program of plays in a tent.

The first artistic director was Tyrone Guthrie, and the plays that year were *Richard III*, with Alec Guinness playing the lead, and *All's Well That Ends Well.*

The Stratford Festival moved into its permanent theatre, designed by Canadian architect Robert Fairfield, in 1957. The season of the internationally acclaimed Festival now runs for six months and includes 500 performances.

# PREFACE

his series of books is intended as an introduction to the plays of William Shakespeare. It is written for stage directors, theatregoers and readers who need to find their way about the plays.

As an actor and director of many of the plays, I have taken a rather different perspective on them: first, that they can only be adequately understood as scripts intended for performance by players; and second, that they focus on the greatest of all themes, the nature of life and death. The first allows us to grasp how the plays *work*. The second demonstrates one reason why Shakespeare's plays are regarded so highly: they address the key issues of our own and every other era by showing that they are universal to humanity in all ages.

The series has a common Introduction and End Notes, which provide basic information for understanding the plays. Acts, scenes, and lines are indicated by round brackets. These divisions into Acts and scenes were added by neo-classical scholars years after Shakespeare's death. But Shakespeare did not intend his plays to be chopped up into small segments. In his time they were played on an unlocalized stage, with one scene flowing into the next.

To recapture this undulation, the plays are examined in the large rhythmical Movements so necessary if they are to be performed. In the theatre, each scene is divided into *beats,* or small rhythmic units; groups of beats with similar emotional effects are *rhythms* (of one or more scenes or within a scene); and groups of these rhythms are *Movements*. In addition, *timing* ranges between fast and slow, and *pace* is the way in which elements of timing are put together.

It is forty years since I first began to direct and act these plays, and almost as long since I began teaching students about them. As a result, I owe much to far more people than I can thank here. But I am under the greatest obligation to the late Professor G. Wilson Knight, for his encouragement and help with my early Shakespearean productions, for the warmth of his personal friendship over several decades, and for his inspiration as an interpreter of Shakespeare. I am grateful to the late Professor Bonamy Dobrée, for his enthusiastic support of my work in directing classic and modern plays; Derek Boughton, for his invaluable support as assistant director in several productions; Philip Stone, the late John Linstrum, Zelda Black, Jacqueline Heywood, Jean Terry Robertson, James Curran, Dorothy Chillingsworth, and other members of experimental drama groups who have worked with me in performances or prepared rehearsals to discover practical ways to overcome specific "knots" in plays; the many players and technical artists, young and old (but particularly the young who continually demonstrate how fresh these plays are), for the long hours we have worked to interpret Shakespeare's plays in the theatre, or in practical interpretation in the classroom. Mention must be made of members of audiences in Britain, Europe, and North America, not just for the warmth of their reactions but specifically for their helpful comments. My thanks also to Sandra M. Burroughs, who typed up the notes for these books; to my wife, Rosemary Courtney, for her usual exemplary editing skills; and to Dr. Barry Thorne, for his expertise.

R. C.
*Toronto* and
*Jackson's Point*

# INTRODUCTION

## READING SHAKESPEARE

The plays of William Shakespeare are among the greatest human achievements. His comedies are funny, his tragedies make us weep, his adventures thrill, amaze and provide us with meaningful experiences. But Shakespeare also means to entertain us.

This does not always happen. Too often, in schools and universities, the plays can be boring, when teachers stop the action to seek out the meaning of a word or discuss the plays like novels. They are *not* novels. We can even be bored in a performance if the actors do not relish Shakespeare, or if they speak his poetry as if it were the telephone directory. The *very last* thing we should be with Shakespeare is bored!

## PRINCIPLES

Shakespeare created his plays for *living performance*. They are not "fixed" like a novel, which is the same each time you read it, even if you change. One performance of *Hamlet* is never the same as another. Shakespeare wrote his plays for the players who are to act them, for the stage where the people are to come alive, and for the audience who attends them. When we read his plays or see them in a playhouse, they should excite us. We should be carried along with the action, eagerly waiting for the next thrilling moment. If we are bored in the theatre, we are at a bad performance. If we are bored when we read them, we are reading them badly.

There are two complementary ways of reading Shakespeare's plays: as practical working scripts and as works of artistic meaning. Both ways are complementary. If we read them *only* as working scripts for actors, we may misjudge their significance. If we think of them *only* as great poetry with imaginative meanings, we may miss how they work in practice. But if we read them as living entities we combine both methods.

Shakespeare was the leading dramatist of a working profes-
sional company: the Lord Chamberlain's Men in Queen
Elizabeth I's time, called the King's Men in the reign of James
I. Shakespeare was a part-owner of the company. He acted in
his own plays and those of others; he may have played the
Ghost in *Hamlet*, and he might have "doubled" it with the First
Gravedigger. Perhaps. We will never know for certain. But we
do know that he was a man of the theatre.

When we read Shakespeare, his play is not simply a story,
and we cannot read it as one. We must do what Shakespeare
did: we must imagine "in our mind's eye" the events happening, alive and active, performed by actors on an actual stage.
We should imagine where they stand, or where they move. If
one is to sit on a throne, where will it be? Actors on a stage are
*the medium* through which Shakespeare's genius works. As readers, we must focus on the actors and use our imagination, as
Ben Jonson said in *The New Inne* (1629):

> I imagine all the world's a play;
> The state, and men's affairs, all passages
> Of life, to spring new scenes, come in, go out,
> And shift, and vanish; and if I have got
> A seat, to sit at ease here, i'mine Inn,
> To see the comedy ...
> Why, will you envy me my happiness?      (I.iii.128-137)

This passage, with its echoes of Shakespeare's more famous:

> All the world's a stage,
> And all the men and women merely players ...
>                          *(As You Like It*, II.vii.140-141)

tells us that the stage is Shakespeare's world. Even King Lear
can lament:

> When we are born we cry that we are come
> To this great stage of fools.            (IV.vi.183-184)

If, as we read, we people the stage with actors in roles, we find
out about other human beings: their feelings, their experiences, their manner of living. Then the plays are so engrossing
that we can hardly put them down.

But as we study them, more ideas will dawn on us. Perhaps
we gain more understanding of the crown, or storms and the
sea — always important concepts for Shakespeare. *We must
allow our imagination the freedom to understand Shakespeare's artistic*

*meanings.* We cannot always put these meanings into words, but as Michael Polanyi says: "We know more than we can tell."\* Poetic and symbolic meanings give artistic significance. Putting them into words is the business of criticism. We cannot always use language when we appreciate a play, but we should realize that we are absorbing unconscious meanings.

## FINDING PRACTICAL MEANING

When we read a play, we use imagination. Thinking "as if" is imagining. But in order to imagine well, we must understand the basic issues when a dramatist writes for the stage.

### RECOGNIZING "THE GAP"

Like other great dramatists who are men of the theatre — and we have such examples as Sophocles, Molière, and Goldoni — Shakespeare wrote plays which have *"a natural gap"* between the *meaning the words have in themselves and the meaning which the performers give them.* A great playwright knows the skills of actors and the meanings they can convey. In the same way that a composer creates a score, the dramatist writes a play for others to interpret. The words on the page provide one kind of meaning: they are the skeleton for a performance. When the actors speak the text they provide a meaning that gives the skeleton flesh and blood — and life. But the meaning which one actor conveys is not necessarily the same as that of another actor in the same role. They are different people; they have different thoughts, ideas, feelings and emotions. In my production of *The Taming of the Shrew* (Leeds University, 1954), I played Christopher Sly in the Induction; when we took it to Germany the same year, the actor playing Gremio was not available, so I had to double the two parts. This doubling provided a new balance to the ensemble, and people who saw both thought it emphasized different meanings. We must allow for "the gap" as we read Shakespeare's plays, and imagine the play taking place before us.

---

\* *Personal Knowledge* (New York: Harper, 1964) 6.

## FILLING IN THE MEANING

Then we "fill in" the meanings given to us by the text. We re-create the possibilities of the script within the *play world,* an imagined world in which people (performed by actors) live and breathe. This type of re-creation forms a major contrast with the novel. The printed novel, as we read it, is also a fictional "world," but it is a work of art in itself. The *play world* is not. A great dramatist writes the script so that we can "fill in" the meanings, and only then is it a work of art. We "fill in" the meanings on several levels.

On LEVEL 1 we imagine the events "as if" actors are playing them "here and now," in both space and time. We do so through questions that actors and directors ask. Where does the first scene in *Hamlet* take place? What does it look like? What is the atmosphere? What does each actor do there, moment by moment? Does the atmosphere change during the scene? How do we *feel* "now" in comparison with how we felt a minute ago? *Space and time are the key issues to address in any play.*

These questions lead to LEVEL 2. At this level we reach *questions that are specifically asked by actors,* such as:

- What does Hamlet *think* as he says, "To be or not to be"? "To live" or "not to live" is an important question. Hamlet must be in great personal difficulties to ask himself that. He then asks if it is "nobler" to do one thing rather than another. What does he mean by "nobler"? Actors have to know what people *mean* before they can adequately perform roles.
- Is there a distinction between what the person *thinks* and what he *says?* In some cases there is a difference. When Richard of Gloucester tells his brother Clarence he will help him while he is in the Tower of London, he is lying — he is actually about to arrange for him to be killed.
- Is there a distinction between what the person *consciously thinks* and what he means *unconsciously?* When Olivia asks Viola in *Twelfth Night* what she thinks of her face, or when Claudius tells Hamlet he regards him as a son, what are Olivia's or Claudius' unconscious thoughts?

- What will Hamlet *do* physically when he says, "To be or not to be"? Will he move his arms? Will he stand still or move — and, if he moves, *where* is he moving to, and *why*, and *how?*
- When actors perform together, in pairs or groups, slightly different questions arise. What is Romeo thinking of when Juliet speaks to him from her balcony? How will the nuances of her performance affect Romeo? And how will the players achieve these effects?

On LEVEL 3, *we allow for the "filling in" that specific actors do.* We ask such questions as how would one actor play Romeo in the balcony scene in comparison with another? Or how would different actresses play Juliet in that scene? If the reader has little experience of "live" theatre, then comparisons of performers in film or television might be made — though they perform in a smaller, more intimate way than players on a stage, who act in a grander, larger manner. We might "cast" these performers as the people in the play as we read it.

Finally, we must ask the LEVEL 4 type of question. *What stage objects do the actors use, and how do these objects affect what happens?* Viola in *Twelfth Night* wears the costumes of a woman and of a man. These affect her movement: she can stride about in the male costume, but an Elizabethan bodice and skirt restrict her movements. When Launce enters in *Two Gentlemen of Verona* with his dog, Crab, is it a real dog, or is it imagined (like the rabbit in *Harvey*)? *What is done? Why is it done? And how is it done?* The answers will greatly affect the action of the play. In the Battle of Shrewsbury, Falstaff, a "gross, fat man," is a coward. When I played Falstaff in *1 Henry IV* (Leeds University, 1953; Colne Valley, 1959), I wore armour, a heavy helmet, a sword, a dagger, and heavy padding round my body. During the play I had to fall on the ground and act as if Falstaff were pretending to be dead. Later, I had to carry off the body of Hotspur, a big man also in armour. As an actor, I had to ask in both instances how Falstaff would do it and how it could be done. Such questions illustrate the practical nature of the plays. These questions we do not ask of novels.

## FINDING ARTISTIC MEANING

ACTORS OR CHARACTERS?

Too often, critics discuss the plays as if they were dealing *only* with real people and real events, as if they were happening in real life. Yet people and events change with the actors who are playing them. Here we face a major difficulty: *looked at practically, stage roles are actors, but looked at artistically, stage roles are people.* When we read a play we should look at roles in both ways. Unlike novels, plays are simultaneously both practical events and works of art.

Are some dimensions more important than others? This problem was faced by Shakespeare in the late 1590s when the leading comic actor, Will Kempe, left the company and was replaced by Robert Armin. Shakespeare could no longer write the type of part he had created for the quick-witted Kempe, when the role was to be played by the slower Armin. His plays had to be changed. But what happened when the King's Men revived a play in which Kempe had created the role? Armin now had to act it, and the dramatic events changed practically and artistically. A Shakespearean play is always new on stage. With new actors, we in the audience have a different experience from the one we had with other actors.

Readers, like actors and audience, approach the people within a play in two stages: *we go THROUGH the actor to the role, and THROUGH the role to the person.* That is to say, when acting Macbeth about to murder Duncan, the actor asks *what* does Macbeth do? *Why?* And *how?* Will he see a real dagger, or will he imagine it? He has to settle these questions as himself, the actor; as himself in role; and artistically as Macbeth. Similarly in comedy, the actress playing Portia in *The Merchant of Venice* dresses as a male lawyer to defend Antonio in court. At each step in the scene, the actress must ask of Portia *what* she does, *why*, and *how*. The answers to such questions throughout the play make up the total person of Macbeth or Portia.

Readers must also "discover" a text both technically *and* artistically. If you read *The Taming of the Shrew*, you will have to ask the questions I asked when playing Christopher Sly: What does the *actor-in-role* do? (He stays on the chair in which he has been placed.) Why? (Because the Lord is playing a trick on him.) How? (With eyes open as if in a daydream, slurred speech, drunken gestures.) What does the *person* do? (He thinks he dreams.) Why? (He's drunk.) How? (With bewilderment and pleasure.)

## POETIC, IMAGINATIVE, AND SYMBOLIC MEANING

Why are Shakespeare's plays so important to humanity? They convey enormous meaning. *King Lear* is not just about an old king who stupidly gives away his kingdom to two of his three daughters, who treat him so badly that he goes mad and dies. That is the broad storyline, which sounds almost like a "soap opera." But there is much more to the play.

First, much of it is in verse. Prose conveys ordinary meaning, but poetry gives us *extra*ordinary meaning. In *King Lear* the old king, turned out of doors by his ungrateful daughters, is caught in a raging storm. If he were going to convey ordinary meaning, he might say:

> Listen to that thunder, and that awful wind. It's raining
> so hard that the churches will get wet, and many chick-
> ens and cockerels will drown.

But he does not. What he says is:

> Blow, winds, and crack your cheeks! Rage! Blow!
> You cataracts and hurricanoes, spout
> Till you have drenched the steeples, drowned the cocks!
> (III.ii.1-3)

Say that aloud as if you are shouting at the storm (with no pause between "spout" and "Till"). Now that is *not* ordinary! Nor is it "natural"; kings in ancient Britain did not talk like that. Shakespeare takes the language to a new and higher level and gives it richer and more complex meanings.

Poetry helps Shakespeare to expand his imaginative ideas. What Lear says to his daughter, Regan, when she turns against him, is:

> You nimble lightnings, dart your blinding flames
> Into her scornful eyes! Infect her beauty,
> You fen-sucked fogs drawn by the powerful sun,
> To fall and blister. (II.iv.160-163)

Say that, spitting it out in fury and contempt (with no pause between "flames" and "Into"). Now *that* is how to curse! Look at the images Shakespeare uses. "You fen-sucked fogs" has fogs being sucked up from wet fenland by the sun. You can only speak that phrase clearly by emphasizing the "ked" at the end of "sucked" with the "d" as a "t" (thus, "suck't"). Try it once more. Remember the lightning flames blinding Regan's eyes, infecting her beauty and blistering her. It sounds harsh and bitter.

Shakespeare also gives us imaginative meanings: the great storm that buffets Lear is also the storm of life we all must face. It destroys him. How can we stop it from destroying us? His daughters have been warped by the power of kingship, symbolized as a crown. Often to Shakespeare, "crown" signifies temporal power, contrasted with love for others and humanity as a whole. Such ideas extend our thoughts beyond the mere words.

## WHAT IS REALISM IN SHAKESPEARE?

The people and the events of a Shakespearean play are *not* "real life." They are dramatic fictions. Yet Shakespeare's works are "life-like," or "true to life." No other dramatist gives us such an accurate picture of human life. But it is a "picture," *not the reality of life itself,* that occurs within the nature and conditions of the stage. This is the kind of experience we try to capture when we read a Shakespearean play. It is grander and more profound than the so-called "reality" of television. Each drama creates a *play world* of its own.

## WHAT IS SAID AND DONE

When we read a play by Shakespeare, we create our own reality: we compare the practical with the imaginative. We read the words on the page in two ways, and our comparisons make the script "live" in our minds.

But one particular danger we must notice: *what is said* (the words on the page) does not always easily reveal *what is done.* The reader must treat the script like a detective story: hidden within the text are many clues about *what is done* on the stage. Sometimes the solution is easy, like most stage directions. *Enter Hamlet* is quite simple, except that we must ask *why? Where?* And *how?* But *Exit pursued by a bear* is not as simple as it seems. When we reach the stage implications of the dialogue, sometimes the problem would daunt the most brilliant sleuth. When the old, fat Falstaff is teasing Bardolph about his huge red nose:

BARDOLPH:   'Sblood, I would my face were in your belly!

FALSTAFF:   God-a-mercy! So should I be sure to be heart-burnt.

*Enter Hostess.*

FALSTAFF:   How now, dame Partlett the hen...

*(1 Henry IV,* III.iii.48-51)

Why does Falstaff call the Hostess "Dame Partlett the hen," when her name is Mistress Quickly, and there is no other mention of chickens? Is this a hint that her laughter as she enters sounds like a hen's cackle?

When the shrew Katherine is wooed by the brash Petruchio:

KATH:   I knew you at the first
You were a movable.

PET:   Why, what's a movable?

KATH:   A joint-stool.

PET:   Thou hast hit it. Come, sit on me.

*(The Shrew,* II.i.196-198)

What acts does Shakespeare imply here? Much will depend on the players, but Katherine could thrust him away on "movable" so that he sits suddenly on a stool and then pulls her onto his knee with "come sit on me."

As another example, on the battlefield, Lear carries in the dead Cordelia and puts her down:

LEAR:   Lend me a looking-glass;
If that her breath will mist or stain the stone,
Why then she lives ...
This feather stirs — she lives!

*(King Lear,* V.iii.259-263)

To see if a person was still breathing, Elizabethans used mist on a mirror or the movement of a feather. Even if someone finds a mirror for Lear on a battlefield, where does the feather come from? Probably from nowhere. The others know Cordelia is dead and give Lear nothing. In his distress, Lear imagines both mirror and feather.

## KINDS OF REALITY

Shakespeare knew two kinds of reality. One was the reality of Renaissance England in which apprentices, burghers, and aristocrats were an audience watching a play. They lived in a world of ordinary experience: the *actual world*. Reality was what everyone with common sense knew it to be, and those who did not were dreaming or were "mad."

But within that ordinary, commonsense reality was another: the *play world*. Similar to the "world" of the child at play, which children believe to be as "real" as the everyday, the *play world* was on a stage that Shakespeare's audience knew was not actual, not "real" as the world they lived in was real. But a play performed on a stage might *appear* to be real. Then the actors were not actors but flesh and blood persons who laughed and cried like people in the actual world. The reality of the *play world* was imaginative: created in the mind of the playwright, the actors, and the audience together. When Jaques in *As You Like It* says, "All the world's a stage," Shakespeare compares the two realities in a double metaphor: life is like a theatre, and theatre is like life. And this is the metaphor Shakespeare uses throughout his plays.

But the Renaissance audience was not *quite* sure of the difference. They did not, for example, clearly separate the actual (the natural) from the *super*natural, nor the supernatural from the dream. Thus at the end of his life, Shakespeare creates for Prospero the lines:

> We are such stuff
> As dreams are made on ...      *(The Tempest,* IV.i.156-157)

Here, it is not that life is like theatre, or that theatre is like life, but that life *is* a play, and that people are created from such dreams.

The complication comes when we, today, are part of an audience for one of Shakespeare's plays. If there were two realities in Shakespeare's time, the ordinary Renaissance actuality and the *play world* of, say, *Hamlet* on the stage, are we in a modern audience, then, another reality? And what reality does the reader have?

You, the reader, must answer that for yourself ...

# SHAKESPEARE'S WORLD OF DEATH
# THE EARLY TRAGEDIES

D ead bodies on stage, murder, suicide, graves, corpses: Shakespeare's first tragedies create a world of death. Medieval morality plays often featured an abstract character called Death, a Christian theme that never lost its hold on the imagination of Elizabethan playwrights. But Shakespeare used his characters themselves to portray Death, and his tragic heroes take on the characteristics of Everyman. His tortured souls are prototypes of humanity. He combines this idea of personified types with the medieval notion of "the fall of princes," a phrase of Boccaccio used by Chaucer and Lydgate, and with the Latin traditions of Seneca who used various sensational elements that were basic to the Elizabethan stage: adultery, incest, murder and revenge, ghosts and other supernatural visitants, and madness, real and false. All these elements are found in *Hamlet* and may have reached Shakespeare through the plays of Thomas Kyd, notably *The Spanish Tragedy* (c. 1589).

*Romeo and Juliet, Julius Caesar* and *Hamlet* were written as Shakespeare came to the middle of his career. *Romeo and Juliet* was first, and *Julius Caesar* and *Hamlet* about four years later. Earlier he had used the tragic mode within other plays: *Titus Andronicus* becomes a bloodthirsty melodrama; *The Merchant of Venice*, a comedy, is distorted by the tragic figure of Shylock; and the end of *Richard II* manifests tragic elements later used in the figure of Hamlet.

In the early tragedies, however, the tone is tragic, and death is a central theme. It contrasts with life, but it does so differently in each play. In *Romeo and Juliet*, death is centered in society: the two main families manipulate the world of Love, the passionate love of the hero and the heroine whose death redeems Verona. In *Julius Caesar*, the world of death is carried in the "honour" of the conspirators; its contrast is human friendship. In *Hamlet*, the theme is doubled; it is transferred from Claudius to Hamlet. Before the play, the world of death wins when Claudius poisons his brother, the king, and takes his crown and his wife. But in the play proper, Claudius is an effective king, and it is Hamlet who represents the world of death. Only after he has killed Claudius, and been killed himself, can goodness return to Denmark.

In these three plays we are always conscious of the idea of death and the state of being dead. That is why the symbol of Yorick's skull in the graveyard is so important. The first half of *Julius Caesar* focusses on the plans to bring about Caesar's death; in the second half, the death of the conspirators results from the assassination of Caesar. In *Romeo and Juliet*, the play naturally concludes in the tomb.

How do Shakespeare's three early tragedies fit A.C. Bradley's criteria in his penetrating analysis, *Shakespearean Tragedy*? *

- A tragedy presents a tale of suffering and calamity: true of all three plays.
- A tragedy leads to the death of an exceptional man: true of *Julius Caesar* and *Hamlet*; Romeo and Juliet die, but they are young more than exceptional.
- In a tragic play, misfortunes arise from acts or omissions for which the hero is responsible: true of all three.
- A tragedy conveys "the sense of causal connection of character, deed and catastrophe": true of *Julius Caesar* and *Hamlet*; in *Romeo and Juliet* many of the links are accidental.
- The plot in a tragedy hinges on an external conflict, but we are caught up in a moral struggle in the hero's soul: true of all three plays.
- In a tragedy, there is a grave threat to the natural order by the protagonist(s), who must be destroyed: true of all three plays, though in different ways.
- In a tragedy, the evil the protagonist(s) embodies is purged: true of *Julius Caesar* and *Hamlet*; in *Romeo and Juliet* the world sacrifices good in order to be redeemed.
- A tragedy must bring about the ruin of much good that the protagonist also embodies: true of all three.
- In a tragedy, an impression of waste lends poignancy to the

---

* Bradley (1978).

hero's down-fall: true of all three plays.
- A tragedy exemplifies a painful and all-encompassing mystery in the hero's defeat: true especially of *Romeo and Juliet* and *Hamlet*, less so of *Julius Caesar*.

As shown, the three early tragedies obey most of Bradley's criteria.

In a Shakespearean tragedy, the death of the hero closes the action. While his death signifies great loss, it is also partly redeemed by feelings of triumph. *Romeo and Juliet, Julius Caesar* and *Hamlet* provide the hero with a tragic world where action produces reaction. When an action is begun it does not necessarily end as planned. The attitude to death in these plays is different from that in the later tragedies. It is not implanted in the minds of the other persons, as is the consciousness of evil in *Macbeth* and *Othello* and the consciousness of suffering in *King Lear*.

In the worlds of the early tragedies, the heroes are provided with tragic worlds where action produces reaction; and the idea of victory in defeat and the sacrifice of a scapegoat render death as much an entrance as an exit, a triumph rather than a failure.

# ROMEO AND JULIET

**R**omeo and Juliet is a romantic masterpiece known by lovers everywhere. But its ideas and its poetry are thicker and more clotted than is often assumed. Perhaps this is why comparatively few stage productions are as successful as theatre artists expect them to be.

Despite the family feud between the Montagues and Capulets in Verona, Romeo, a Montague, falls in love with Juliet, a Capulet. They secretly marry but are crushed by society. The warring families are united in grief. The play presents a love union in opposition to family hostility and civil disorder.

## THE WORLD OF DEATH AND LOVE

The Prologue tells us that there are three major themes in the tragedy: *love-death*, *fate* and *society*. Shakespeare requires us to grasp these before anything else. Stage directors in particular should carefully follow his guidance.

Love shaped by death underpins the plot and the imagery. Death causes hate: the bloody feud is destroying life in Verona, infecting the noblest and the humblest people. Hate also brings forth a monstrous character: Tybalt, whose rage makes him seek revenge. He becomes the catalyst for doom: he forces Romeo to kill him, which hastens the lovers to their deaths.

The love of Romeo and Juliet embodies hope. Their frank acceptance of their feelings is highly positive: it might even bring the warring parties together if it has the chance. The lovers' intensity is most memorable when Romeo's family name is seen by Juliet as her enemy:

> O, be some other name!
> What's in a name? That which we call a rose
> By any other word would smell as sweet. (II.ii.42-44)

The lovers' superb poetry expresses the moral core of the play: *love transforms lovers*. But the death-bound world of Verona dooms them.

Parallel to the love-death polarity is that of light-dark. The Light is that of Christian Truth, and the Darkness is that of Sin — a strong hint of the morality tradition. Modern theatregoers, however, may not see Romeo and Juliet as sinners.* In fact, they are both saints and sinners. Romeo wears a pilgrim's costume when he first meets Juliet, and they speak to each other as saints (or pilgrims) throughout. The lovers become saints in the *play world*: they overcome death when they spiritually transform Verona. Yet their love is also a tragic passion: it is immediate, violent, and final. What kills their love is also partly of their own making — why, we wonder, do they not elope?

The Friar raises moral questions, like what is the value of love? Shakespeare's answer is relative. The views of people change: Juliet, before and after she has fallen in love; Romeo, both while in love with Rosaline and then with Juliet; Mercutio, whose light-hearted sensuality turns passion into sex; Friar Laurence, who thinks that love is an accompaniment to life; old Capulet, who says love must be arranged by a prudent father for his daughter; Lady Capulet, who thinks love is worldly wisdom; and the Nurse, who believes love is natural and pleasurable. Moral views about love are also given poetically:

Too like the lightning, which doth cease to be
Ere one can say 'It lightens.'                    (II.ii.119-120)
Love is explosive like the flash of lightning or of gunpowder.

Although Romeo and Juliet are little more than children, their torment is real: Romeo's at Friar Laurence's cell (III.iii) parallels Juliet's when she hears that Romeo is slain — a profound mental disturbance brought on by their passion. His isolated individualism is absurd. The positive forces are simple goodness and the unity between human beings. *The aim of the human condition is the interdependence of people.*

Ideal love in the Renaissance was neo-Platonic.** Romeo is

---

* But conservative Elizabethans thought the lovers were at fault. This judgment is closer to an Aristotelian tragic flaw than the accident of fate, and brings *Romeo and Juliet* nearer to Bradley's view of tragedy.

** In the "ladder of love," loving the single body of the beloved finally led to embracing the universal love of the One, or God. Love began with sexual intercourse; as it grew, according to Spenser and Sidney, a moral and spiritual element could truly transform a person.

a moping Petrarchan lover until the power of ideal love transforms him. His is a religious change. He boasts of "the devout religion of mine eye" (I.ii.87). When Juliet calls "My Romeo!" he comments: "It is my soul that calls upon my name" (II.ii.163-164); Juliet is for him "my soul" (III.v.25). The Friar condemns Romeo for contemplating suicide because this would "slay thy lady that in thy life lives" (III.iii.117). Because it has been overused, Neo-Platonic love-language may seem trite today.

Through the play runs the image of death as Juliet's bridegroom. When Romeo is banished, Juliet cries "And death, not Romeo, take my maidenhead" (III.ii.137).

Fate appears in the play as a series of premonitions and through Shakespeare's use of speed in the dramatic action. The Prologue says that Providence uses fate (accident) to end the power of love. Yet the play really emphasizes chance. An Elizabethan audience accepted astrology: Romeo worries about "some consequence, yet hanging in the stars" (I.iv.107), he cries "I defy you, stars" (V.i.24), and he finally shakes off "the yoke of inauspicious stars" (V.iii.111). In this sense, *the play is a tragedy of "bad luck."* Romeo is fortune's fool.

*Romeo and Juliet,* like all Shakespeare's tragedies, is social because it is public. Elizabethan stage convention demanded it: tragedy *is* social; the private is never tragic. Yet violent death in the play is not only social. Romeo is responsible for five deaths. We may, therefore, ask other questions: is sexual passion a deadly force in the hands of naive young people? Sexual passion without love becomes, as the Friar says, "The unreasonable fury of a beast" (III.iii.111).

Thus the play poses many questions entwined with highly complex ideas. This makes the task of the stage director a formidable one.

## FROM THE STAGE TO THE MOVIES

The script is also a problem. The young Shakespeare may have created *Romeo and Juliet* in 1596. If written earlier, it was later revised at roughly the same time as *Richard II* and *The Dream;* if *Romeo and Juliet* is parodied in "Pyramus and Thisbe," 1595 is a possible date. The feud of the Montagues and Capulets is first mentioned by Dante, and the story is outlined in Matteo

Bandello's novella *Romeo e Giulietta* (1554). This was adapted into French (1559) and into English (1567). But Shakespeare's main source was Arthur Brooke's *The Tragical History of Romeus and Juliet* (1562).

It is unlikely that we have the script as Shakespeare wrote it. The "bad Quarto" of 1597 (Q1) was reconstructed from memory, probably by an actor. Q1 is valuable for providing details of how Shakespeare might have staged it. For example, in the Friar's cell, Romeo offers to stab himself, but the Nurse snatches the dagger away.

The second Quarto (Q2) was perhaps printed as it left Shakespeare's hands; it is our principal text for the words of the play. This "good Quarto" was reprinted in 1609 (Q3), in 1622 (Q4), and in 1637 (Q5). The script in the First Folio (F1) of 1623 was derived from Q3. In none of these scripts is the play divided into acts; Nicholas Rowe supplied them in the Augustan age.

*Romeo and Juliet* has been loved by theatre audiences ever since it was first performed. But it suffered from adaptations.* Thomas Otway's version (1680) was given an "improvement" which became the usual theatrical version of *Romeo and Juliet* from Garrick's time until the nineteenth century. In September 1750, there was a famous rivalry when the play was staged simultaneously at Drury Lane, with Garrick and George Anne Bellamy, and at Covent Garden, with Spranger Barry and Mrs. Cibber. Macready made his debut as Romeo in 1810, and two great Juliets followed: Eliza O'Neill in 1814 and the nineteen-year-old Fanny Kemble in 1829. Henry Irving and Ellen Terry were too old for the main roles in 1882. That production was sumptuous but mortally slow, and Mrs. Stirling was a fine garrulous, humorous, immoral Nurse. Strangely, Irving inserted a Rosaline into the play.

Between the two World Wars, John Gielgud and Laurence Olivier alternated the parts of Romeo and Mercutio, as Richard Burton and John Neville did at the Old Vic many years later. Peter Brook's Stratford revival of the play (1947), a sunny production, was much abused.

---

* For stage history see Sprague (1944, 1953), and Sprague and Trewin (1970).

Franco Zeffirelli's *Romeo and Juliet* (Old Vic, 1961), probably the most famous production of the twentieth century, was overpraised. His direction was fussy, he treated the play like an ardent Italian who could not hear English verse, and his cuts were ill-judged. But his hot, dry Verona became quite modern with sexually virile lovers whose impulsive affair contrasted with a small-town, closed society baking in the sun. Mercutio enjoyed calling Tybalt a cat:

> MER: Tybalt, you ratcatcher, will you walk?
> TYB: What wouldst thou have with me?
> MER: Good King of Cats, nothing but one of your nine lives. That I mean to make bold withal, and, as you shall use me hereafter, dry-beat the rest of the eight. (III.i.74-78)

Accordingly, in the duel Mercutio cried "Puss! puss!" derisively — a happy invention. The Zeffirelli movie of his stage production (1968) was incredibly slow: at the gala preview attended by the greatest performers, as a real rabbit hopped very slowly by the Friar's cell Sir Donald Wolfit's voice rumbled across the audience with, "Ye gods — Harvey!"

## PASSION AND IMMATURITY

Despite Zeffirelli, we can ask how passionate is the lovers' passion? For *Romeo and Juliet* is one of Shakespeare's more sexually explicit plays. This is particularly evident in the *double entendres,* of which there are many: "come" and "die" also mean to experience orgasm.

Romeo's idealism contrasts with Mercutio's hearty realism towards sex. Each idealistic statement of Romeo brings an erotic response from his friend that hides a lesson Romeo needs to learn:

> 'Twould anger him
> To raise a spirit in his mistress' circle
> Of some strange nature, letting it there stand
> Till she had laid it and conjured it down.
> That were some spite. My invocation
> Is fair and honest. In his mistress' name,
> I conjure only but to raise up him. (II.i.23-29)

Mercutio and the Nurse have a practical awareness of the physiology of sex which Romeo ignores.

Shakespeare's Juliet is even younger than the Juliet of his sources, and Romeo is immature. Romeo does not mention any explicit physical desire for either Rosaline nor Juliet. Rather, he unwittingly represents immaturity and sexual inhibition. His poetic sentimentalism contrasts with Juliet's practical nature. Juliet is eager to gain the fullest sexual consummation, to which Romeo seems oblivious. Her problem is that she falls in love with the immature aspects of Romeo's passion. Despite the eroticism in the play, however, the passion of the lovers includes a spiritual dimension as well.

## TRAGIC CHANCE

How much of a tragedy is *Romeo and Juliet?* It is a *tragedy of mischance,* and chance does not fit the tragic mode for Bradley and many other critics. This raises two fundamental issues for the stage director. First, while the kind of tragedy is of great concern to the actors and director, it is of no interest whatsoever to the audience. The players must persuade them that all the events are natural and logical, that the whole is satisfying from first to last. How do the players do that?

This leads us to the second major issue. The characters are bound by the story. Shakespeare is content to be guided by the story line. The players must not be otherwise. Shakespeare's medieval inheritance gives him a tragedy of fortune. But he begins to experiment with a play of character here; this experimentation eventually leads him to his final tragedies. When action is determined by accidents it is not tragic. So Shakespeare tries to shape his characters in order that events become likely. Accordingly, the players must stress their verisimilitude. This applies to two accidents in particular. First, it is pure bad luck that Friar John cannot deliver the letter of Friar Laurence to Romeo at Mantua before Balthasar reaches Romeo with the news of Juliet's death. But it is Romeo's recklessness that prevents Friar Laurence from correcting the mistake. And secondly, Juliet's false repentance of her "disobedient opposition" allows Capulet to "have this knot knit up tomorrow morning" (IV.ii.24). The change of one day is the difference between life and death.

People make wrong decisions that are only partly related to their characters, and the players must show that such decisions are not always inevitable choices. Mercutio's challenge to Tybalt, Romeo's vengeance, the Nurse's advice to Juliet to abandon Romeo and to marry Paris — each decision might have been different. The players should also stress the irony which binds the plot together; people frequently say things which, unknown to them, have a deeper and more cruel meaning.

## STRUCTURE

Although *Romeo and Juliet* is an immature work, Shakespeare's command of all kinds of dramatic effect is masterly. This is particularly the case with the highly complex structure.

### SURPRISE CHANGE

Things are not all that they seem to be. Individual actions constantly begin well and turn out badly. The play as a whole initially promises to be a comedy but becomes a tragedy. At first the feud seems a rough and bawdy exchange between Montague and Capulet servants, with both sides too cowardly to draw blood. Only later do we realize that it is deadly.

### REALITY AND ILLUSION

All Shakespeare's plays deal with reality and illusion; sometimes, as in this play, he uses the play metaphor both for internal effects and for structural purposes. In most cases, the metaphor is deeply embedded in its context. As Juliet, the night before her marriage to Paris, looks at the Friar's potion and thinks about what she is to do, she tersely comments: "My dismal scene I needs must act alone" (IV.iii.19) — which is at once part of death and night, the smell of earth, and the horror of the charnel house, as well as part of the theatrical world.

In the same scene, Shakespeare also gives the play metaphor a striking theatrical effect. Indeed, it can only be realized in the Elizabethan theatre for which it was designed [see *End Notes*]. The curtains of the inner stage are drawn back to show us Juliet's bed (IV.iii). The Nurse and her mother leave her; she drinks the potion, and *She falls upon her bed within the curtains* (i.e., the curtains are closed). At once Capulet, his wife, the Nurse and servants enter to prepare for the wedding (IV.iv), but when the Nurse opens the curtains she finds Juliet's body. The illusion of Juliet's death is emphasized in a brilliant *coup de théâtre*.

The play metaphor is also inherent in the structure of the play, when the lovers' roles make Shakespeare's play into a double drama. Their love story becomes an unannounced play-within-a-play. The lovers refuse to suppress their love in their family roles; rather, they fulfil their roles as lovers in their own love drama. This playlet is a world within a world. There is a constant transfer of experience from the real world to the dream world and vice versa. In Capulet's orchard, Romeo is

> afeard,
> Being in night, all this is but a dream,
> Too flattering-sweet to be substantial.      (II.ii.139-141)

One kind of play constantly slips into another as one course of action is thwarted by the other. How does this happen?

- At first, Romeo mentally acts a melancholy lover with Rosaline but is a character in search of a play.
- Once he falls in love with Juliet, he creates the role of an ideal lover, and, in Juliet's response, they jointly create a playlet.
- Their family roles interfere with their playlet in two ways: they force the lovers to be part of the feud, and the family roles prevent them from fully acting out their roles in the love drama.
- In their created playlet they first go through a secret marriage, the killing of Mercutio and Tybalt, and the banishment of Romeo; they alter the shape of the playlet and give its plot new twists.
- In a parallel way, the performance of their playlet leads the lovers to change *Romeo and Juliet*; from the light and comic mood of the first two acts, it moves to the tragic mood that governs the rest.
- Juliet emphasizes the double nature of Shakespeare's play by seeking help from the Friar. His scheme with the potion has two purposes: to be another kind of playlet to counter Capulet's scheme and to be the final act in a triumphant love drama.

- Shakespeare now introduces the coincidence of the mixed messages, and the result is the double death. This action also has a play-like structure because of the great emphasis on coincidence.

When old Montague describes Romeo's conduct at dawn, he says:

> Away from light steals home my heavy son
> And private in his chamber pens himself,
> Shuts up his windows, locks fair daylight out,
> And makes himself an artificial night.      (I.i.137-140)

In a sense the play is about the "artificial": it is not only about young love but about love — and they are not quite the same. Romeo has an idealized love for Rosaline; he is in love with love. When he first sees Juliet, he loves more profoundly. Yet even so there is a touch of the artificial: both lovers self-consciously posture in the "pilgrim" sonnet they speak at their meeting; and in the balcony scene there is an element of artificiality that permeates the imagery.

## ANTITHESIS

Shakespeare uses antithesis to isolate the lovers, finally driving them to the point of complete isolation, death. He uses antithesis on four main levels:

- Love-death

    The love of Romeo and Juliet is a public event. It must struggle with the feud of their families, which brings death.

- Youth-age

    The youth of the lovers emphasizes speed, an instrument of fate. It is out of place in a world ruled by old people.

- Ideal-real love

    The sexual realism of Mercutio, the Nurse, and the servants contrasts with the love of Romeo and Juliet. This heightens the meaning of both; one makes the other believable.

- Fate-free will

    The lovers (falsely) see themselves as "stars": as creatures with free wills who can shape their own fate. But the "stars" of fate are immutable; the lovers face the forces of chance.

A remarkable achievement of this early play is the balance which subsumes all the antitheses.

## SPACE

The tragedy takes place in a real place in a real time: in the "here and now." Although Shakespeare uses historical time, he gives the action a setting that is "here" with a powerful sense of the present tense.

The setting is Verona, Italy, in the early Renaissance or possibly the High Middle Ages. As the locations are simple interiors and exteriors, the play is easy to arrange on any unlocalized stage. Even the final tomb offers no serious difficulties. It has also been effectively staged on a *scène Italienne*: a house with a door either side and the sky at the rear, before which the tomb is placed. On a proscenium stage, the play risks returning to the decorative Victorian traditions, and the wise director will construct a large forestage.

## TIME

No play of Shakespeare's has such an overpowering sense of time as *Romeo and Juliet*. Time is related to heat: it is late July in Verona, a very hot time in a very hot place; and a hot July night enhances the audience's awareness of love in the Capulet garden. But most overwhelming is the general impression of speed; we feel that there is not enough time for anything.

Our awareness of time is not fixed or absolute. Time is *felt* in this play. Before Juliet is united with her lover, time works as it does for the older characters: "Unwieldy, slow, heavy and pale as lead" (II.v.17). Old people reminisce while they talk; they carry the audience beyond the framework of the play; but simultaneously they put Juliet and her Romeo in perspective. There is a challenging contrast between age without maturity and youth that is immature. Old Capulet and his cousin discuss the past rather like Justice Shallow and Justice Silence in *2 Henry IV*. "'Tis gone, 'tis gone, 'tis gone" (I.v.25) also runs through *Romeo and Juliet*.

Juliet's invocation to the "fiery-footed steeds" that will bring her love to her is fulfilled. Time is revenged when the separated Romeo and Juliet find "in a minute there are many days" (III.v.45). Now and again the rush and hurry, the dread and the confusion stop, and there comes a tender beauty, most appropriate in scenes of still moonlight: "That tips with silver all these fruit-tree tops" (II.ii.108). But Romeo and Juliet's all-consuming love brooks no delay: "from nine till twelve Is three long hours" (II.v.10-11). Love is always in a hurry, and its symbol is the flash of lightning or the destructive flash of gunpowder, echoing the headlong speed with which love's action proceeds.

The lovers defy time: "love-devouring death do what he dare" (II.vi.7). This is not, however, a tragic error. Rather, their youth reaches beyond time. They are limited not by nature or the divine but by mortals who, as pseudo-dramatists, create playlets for the lovers; they try to bend the lovers to their designs and leave them to be the victims of chance.*

The play also has a "double time": it seems that two clocks are running, which do not agree with each other. Shakespeare makes dramatic use of time when he needs to.

CAP:   But soft! what day is this?
PAR:         Monday, my lord.
CAP:   Monday! Ha, ha! Well, Wednesday is too soon.
        A' Thursday let it be. A' Thursday, tell her,
        She shall be married to this noble earl.
(III.iv.18-21)

The marriage looming only three days ahead is dramatically important; to intensify it, Shakespeare even lessens the interval by a day.

Extraordinarily, Shakespeare, in using Brooke's tale, doubles the dramatic value of time by turning its months to days. The sense of urgency experienced by the lovers and the audience becomes breathtaking.

LINEAR STRUCTURE

Rehearsal makes it obvious that originally there was probably no act or scene division in *Romeo and Juliet* at all. Sometimes two actions become almost simultaneous, as when Tybalt pads about the streets sniffing out Romeo just as the Friar is marrying him to Juliet.

---

* This differs from the later tragedies where Shakespeare uses a purposeful evil. For example, with Iago and Macbeth evil seeks both the downfall of others and the extinction of all that is different from itself.

The four days of the play are framed by the echoes of the many years discussed by the older people.

FIRST MOVEMENT: EXPOSITION (I.i-I.v)

| | | |
|---|---|---|
| *Sunday* | Morning | The servants fight. The Prince restores order. |
| | Afternoon | Romeo reads the guest list of the Capulet feast. |
| | Night | Juliet and Romeo meet at the ball. |

SECOND MOVEMENT: THE CONFLICT (II.i-IV.v)

| | | |
|---|---|---|
| *Sunday* | Night | Later (balcony scene) they agree to marry. |
| *Monday* | Dawn | Romeo and the Friar plan the wedding. |
| | Afternoon | Romeo and Juliet marry. Mercutio is killed. Romeo kills Tybalt and is banished by the Prince. |
| | Night | Capulet agrees Juliet is to marry Paris Thursday morning. Romeo and Juliet's wedding night. |
| *Tuesday* | Dawn | Juliet hears she must marry Paris on Thursday. |
| | Morning | The Friar tells Juliet how she can pretend death and then flee with Romeo to Mantua. |
| | Afternoon | Capulet accelerates the marriage to Wednesday. |
| | Night | Juliet takes the sleeping potion. The Capulets' wedding preparations. |
| *Wednesday* | Dawn | Juliet is found and thought dead. |
| | Morning | Juliet is taken to her tomb. |

THIRD MOVEMENT: THE CATASTROPHE (V.i-V.iii)

| | | |
|---|---|---|
| *Thursday* | Morning | Romeo learns of Juliet's "death" and buys poison. |
| | Afternoon | Friar Laurence learns of Friar John's mishap. |
| | Night | Romeo enters the tomb, kills Paris and himself. Juliet awakens, kills herself. |

## ACTION

### First Movement: Exposition

> *A chorus prologue explains that two families in Verona,*
> *the Capulets and Montagues, have a blood feud. Juliet of*
> *the Capulets and Romeo of the Montagues will fall in love*
> *and meet their deaths (I. Prologue).*

The Chorus enters and speaks the celebrated Prologue:

> Two households, both alike in dignity
>> In fair Verona, where we lay our scene,
> From ancient grudge break to new mutiny,
>> Where civil blood makes civil hands unclean.
> From forth the fatal loins of these two foes
>> A pair of star-crossed lovers take their life;
> Whose misadventured piteous overthrows
>> Doth with their death bury their parents' strife.

$$(1-8)$$

Dignity is given by an Elizabethan sonnet: fourteen lines —
three quatrains and a final couplet. The chorus summarizes the
plot, the "death-marked love" (9) of Romeo and Juliet: to atone
for the feud, a sacrifice brings civil justice to Verona — marked
by three forces (fate, society, and love-death) and a grim foreboding. The stage director must lead the audience to see that
the love-sacrifice is creative.

> *In a street brawl Capulet and Montague servants quarrel;*
> *it becomes a skirmish and Prince Escalus orders peace on*
> *penalty of death. Benvolio and the Montagues play an*
> *elaborate word game about Romeo's love for Rosaline (I.i).*

The low comedy opening derives from Roman plays that
provide broad humour and comic relief. Sampson and Gregory
are two cowardly Capulet servants. They fantasize exploits with
the Montague women: Sampson will "cut off their heads ... the
heads of the maids, or their maidenheads" (22-25). They give
one view of the male-female relation: a brutal male dominance
expressed in sadistic quibbles, which opposes the romantic idealism of Romeo and Juliet.

Prince Escalus stops the swordplay. He directs the law, but
ironically he is not very good at it. The wives of the old men

who head both families easily restrain them. When the tetchy, eager Capulet calls for his long sword, his wife retorts "A crutch, a crutch! Why call you for a sword?" (76).

Shakespeare turns the focus to Romeo. Prior to Romeo's entrance,* the verse slips into a typical cadence as Lady Montague interrupts the men:

> O where is Romeo? Saw you him today?
> Right glad I am he was not at this fray.          (116-117)

Then, like a musical change, comes Benvolio's:

> Madam, an hour before the worshipped sun
> Peered forth the golden window of the East ...
>
>                                                             (118-119)

His father, knowing he is sick with black bile or melancholy, sees danger:

> Black and portentous must this humour prove
> Unless good counsel may the cause remove.     (141-142)

Seeking "artificial night" can lead to ignoring the realities of the day.

Romeo appears like Hamlet, brooding and oblivious to the others. Love to him is man's courtly subjection to women's tyranny. He demonstrates all its symptoms, like the equally ridiculous Valentine in *The Two Gentlemen*. For love of Rosaline, Romeo steals into the woods before sunrise to augment the dew with tears and the clouds with sighs. His passion overrules daylight; it is as artificial as his language. Rosaline is also a Capulet and Juliet's cousin.** Love is an illness and a cult:

> Bid a sick man in sadness make his will.
> Ah, word ill urged to one that is so ill!       (202-203)

Romeo combines his role as a devoted slave to his mistress with that of an attack on her chastity — passion is ambivalent. The

---

* Romeo is not mentioned by any of the characters until line 116 and does not appear until line 155. Juliet does not appear until the third scene.

** She is described as "My fair niece Rosaline" in Capulet's letter of invitation to the party (I.ii.68) and as "the fair Rosaline whom thou [Romeo] so loves" (82). She "hath Dian's wit" (209) and "hath forsworn to love." It is to have a chance of rejoicing in the "splendour" of his Rosaline that Romeo consents to go as an uninvited guest to the "ancient feast of Capulet's" (I.ii.81).

Petrarchan conventions are all given to us: love as malady, worship, war and conquest, so exaggerated that Romeo is probably aware that he is "playing at playing."

> *Paris tells Old Capulet he wishes to marry Juliet. Benvolio dares Romeo: his love will vanish if he will look at other girls by crashing the Capulet party (I.ii).*

Lord Capulet bustles about with tireless activity: extravagance, conceit and hurly-burly are dramatized in his language. He and Paris are matchmaking. Paris wants to marry Juliet, but Capulet explains:

> My child is yet a stranger in the world;
> She hath not seen the change of fourteen years. (8-9)

Old Capulet seems to give Juliet partial freedom to choose her mate:

> But woo her, gentle Paris, get her heart.
> My will to her consent is but a part ...          (16-17)

This is an excuse, like Baptista's about Bianca in *The Shrew*: marriage is a business arrangement.

Capulet hands a guest list to a servant. But the servant cannot read. Benvolio advises Romeo of Elizabethan medical views on how to cure melancholy: "one fire burns out another's burning."* If Romeo could be infected by a new love he would purge the old. At this point, the servant comically gives Romeo the list on which is Rosaline's name. Benvolio wagers that at the feast he will show Romeo women who will purge his melancholy:

> Compare her face with some that I shall show,
> And I will make thee think thy swan a crow.      (85-86)

---

* Proteus in *Two Gentlemen* also announces the transfer of his affections from Julia to Silvia with the words

> Even as one heat another heat expels,
> Or as one nail by strength drives out another,
> So the remembrance of my former love
> Is by a newer object quite forgotten.          (II.iv.190-193)

"One fire drives out another" and "One nail by strength drives out another" were well-known proverbs in the Renaissance.

Romeo is horrified, comparing his love to the holiness of faith:
> The all-seeing sun
> Ne'er saw her match since first the world begun.
>
> (91-92)

Believing such artificiality, Romeo is ready to fall in love at first sight.

> *In a humorous scene, Lady Capulet, the old Nurse and*
> *Juliet discuss love and marriage (I.iii).*
> Now, by my maidenhead at twelve year old,
> I bade her come. What, lamb! What, ladybird! –
> God forbid! — Where's this girl? What, Juliet!     (2-4)

It is the Nurse's unique voice that calls. With Lady Capulet, she has trained the young Juliet with deep affection, even suckling her as a baby. Hers is a living voice, as real as those of Falstaff and Hamlet. In her rambling way she talks bawdy low comedy with a strong sense of time. This garrulous old woman, unlike Mercutio who hides his feelings behind his mask of wit, happily reveals herself whenever she opens her mouth. Old Angelica — a name full of irony — is vital to the tragedy: her worldly morality and realistic language heighten the lyricism of the lovers by contrast. Her bawdy and that of Mercutio complement the lovers' idealism. She eventually is a go-between for the lovers — an ancient theatrical figure — yet she is also completely in the English comic tradition. Her long speech marks the maturation of the young Shakespeare's style: now he gives blank verse the flexibility and rhythms of prose, the shifts in tone and breaks in phrase to reveal character, and the parentheses and repetitions of the gossip.

> LADY C:   Thou knowest my daughter's of a pretty age.
> NURSE:    Faith, I can tell her age unto an hour
> LADY C:   She's not fourteen.
> NURSE:    ... Come Lammas Eve at night shall she be
> fourteen.
> Susan and she — God rest all Christian souls! –
> Were of an age. Well, Susan is with God.
> She was too good for me. But, as I said,
> On Lammas Eve at night shall she be fourteen.
> That shall she, marry! I remember it well.
> 'Tis since the earthquake now eleven years;

And she was weaned — I never shall forget it —
Of all the days of the year, upon that day ....
For even the day before she broke her brow.
And then my husband — God be with his soul!
'A was a merry man — took up the child.
'Yea,' quoth he, 'dost thou fall upon thy face?
Thou wilt fall backward when thou hast more wit.
Wilt thou not, Jule?' And, by my holidam,
The pretty wretch left crying and said 'Ay.'
To see now how a jest shall come about!
I warrant, an I should live a thousand years,
I never should forget it. 'Wilt thou not, Jule?' quoth he,
And, pretty fool, it stinted [stopped] and said 'Ay.'
(11-13, 18-26, 39-49)

In this huge digression the verse appears to flow spontaneously from her lips, her character unfolding as it goes. She is a glory to act: she needs no expansion by the player because she expounds herself at every opportunity.

Juliet's attitude to love is different from Romeo's. She lacks comprehension of marriage: "It is an honour that I dream not of" (67). Lady Capulet's praise of Paris is contrasted with the Nurse's:

LADY C:   The valiant Paris seeks you for his love.
NURSE:   A man, young lady! Lady, such a man
         As all the world — why, he's a man of wax.
LADY C:   Verona's summer hath not such a flower.
(75-78)

To Lady Capulet marriage is a business, with Juliet an economic commodity:

LADY C:   So shall you share all that he doth possess,
         By having him making yourself no less.
NURSE:   No less? Nay, bigger! Women grow by men.
(94-96)

The Nurse gives her words a double meaning. Juliet is obedient but careful: "I'll look to like, if looking liking move" (98). So the lovers are going to the ball: he to see the woman he thinks he loves; she to see the man her parents want her to love.

*Maskers are on their way to the ball. Romeo has a battle of wits with Mercutio (I.iv).*

It is a festive night scene: among the maskers, torch-bearers, and others, the lively and witty young bachelors, Romeo, Mercutio, and Benvolio, are about to enter the Capulet feast in masks. As the maskers are uninvited they must make a speech of apology for their visit and then do a figure dance (a "measure"); later they can mingle with the invited guests.

Mercutio is entirely Shakespeare's creation with no resemblance to his namesake in Brooke's poem. The most likeable person in Verona, his cynical and aggressive wit and full-blooded sensuality belong to high comedy and must be played with energy. Mercutio's name means the wild, impulsive, fiery and harsh — a good foil to Romeo, whose dull puns are those of courtly love. Romeo has had a disturbing dream. Mercutio, trying to correct Romeo's melancholy love, gives a description of Queen Mab. She is the fairies' midwife; during sleep, when reason is relaxed, she gallops through sleeping imaginations, filling our dreams with secret fantasies:

> And in this state she gallops night by night
> Through lovers' brains, and then they dream of love;
> O'er courtiers' knees, that dream on curtsies straight;
> O'er lawyers' fingers, who straight dream on fees;
> O'er ladies' lips, who straight on kisses dream,
> Which oft the angry Mab with blisters plagues,
> Because their breaths with sweetmeats tainted are.
> Sometime she gallops o'er a courtier's nose,
> And then dreams he of smelling out a suit.
> And sometime comes she with a tithe-pig's tail
> Tickling a parson's nose as 'a lies asleep;
> Then he dreams of another benefice.          (70-81)

Queen Mab brings the deceptions of dream, like Romeo's love melancholy. But Romeo misses the point: "Thou talkest of nothing" (96). He suddenly has a terrible premonition that disaster awaits him:

> my mind misgives
> Some consequence, yet hanging in the stars,
> Shall bitterly begin his fearful date
> With this night's revels and expire the term
> Of a despisèd life, closed in my breast,
> By some vile forfeit of untimely death.          (106-111)

*At the Capulet ball, Romeo forgets Rosaline when he and
Juliet fall in love at first sight. Tybalt wants to fight
Romeo, but Capulet prevents it. The lovers discover that
each is of the enemy family (I.v).*

This scene runs on from the last as the maskers move into
the noisy Capulet ballroom; the servants take away the remains
of the dinner, and the musicians tune up. Capulet is delighted
with the maskers; in his youth he was quite a gallant:

I have seen the day
That I have worn a visor and could tell
A whispering tale in a fair lady's ear,
Such as would please. 'Tis gone, 'tis gone, 'tis gone!

(22-25)

Capulet's sense of time frames the lovers' few days — age
frames youth.

The dance begins. Old Capulet and his cousin (sketch-
es for Silence and Shallow) reminisce about the old days. Our
attention is divided between them, the dancers, and Romeo
who is watching Juliet. He falls instantly in love, ridding himself
of the past:

Did my heart love till now? Forswear it, sight!
For I ne'er saw true beauty till this night.          (52-53)

Ironically he uses the same language he used for Rosaline. He
is also doing just what Benvolio wanted him to do — purge his
love melancholy by falling in love with another. Romeo's new
intensity is given by the images that begin artificially but end in
sincerity.

O, she doth teach the torches to burn bright!
It seems she hangs upon the cheek of night
As a rich jewel in an Ethiop's ear ...*          (44-46)

Tybalt menaces the masked Romeo: "This, by his voice, should
be a Montague" (54). Tybalt, a violent cousin of the Capulets,
recognizes Romeo and sees his presence at the Capulet feast as

---

* Romeo's first judgment of Juliet's beauty is rich in its unforgettable images
and in the subtlety of its wordplay. Hers is a "Beauty too rich for use, for earth
too dear!" (47). "Use" means "employment," "interest," and "wear and tear."
"Earth" means "mortal life" and "the grave." "Dear" means "cherished" or
"costly." There is possibly a play upon "beauty" and "booty" [as in *1 Henry IV*,
I.ii.28]. Clearly the range of meanings in these lines becomes very wide
indeed.

an insult to family honour. Tybalt is a static character: he believes in his social role.* Tybalt symbolizes death: he embodies the hatred of the feud, and his excess of yellow bile (choler) makes him angry and aggressive — like the disease gnawing at Verona. Old Capulet says Romeo is "a virtuous and well-governed youth" (68). Also, the code of hospitality demands that a host never insult a guest in his home. When Tybalt refuses to be quiet, old Capulet is furious. In a brilliant Shakespearean touch, his tirade against Tybalt is interspersed with pleasant remarks to dancers as they glide past the two men:

> *(to dancers)* Well said, my hearts! —
> > *(to Tybalt)* You are a princox, go!
> Be quiet, or — *(to dancers)* More light, more light!
> > *(to Tybalt)* — For shame!
> I'll make you quiet, what ! —
> > *(to dancers)* Cheerly, my hearts!          (86-88)

Capulet is the complete gentleman, the genial host, if no one crosses him. Tybalt rushes off vowing revenge.

Then, in one of Shakespeare's great love scenes, Romeo and Juliet meet for the first time. The dance is over, and as the chattering guests begin to leave, the two find themselves alone. Romeo, his mask off, says:

> If I profane with my unworthiest hand
> This holy shrine, the gentle sin is this.
> My lips, two blushing pilgrims, ready stand
> > To smooth that rough touch with a tender kiss.     (93-96)

The lines they speak have the form of an Elizabethan sonnet, ironically with the same images Romeo used when he told Benvolio he would only look at Rosaline. The lovers talk "the religion of love" with conceits and quibbles — "palm to palm is holy palmers' kiss," and "grant thou, lest faith turn to despair"

---

* Often these static characters are called thematic characters because, in a quasi-allegorical manner, they tend to carry one theme at a time. Tybalt is a clear example of such a character. Benvolio is another example. His function is to be the backing for the bachelor life of Romeo — a specific social context for the young lover. He often serves as a foil for Mercutio's and Romeo's jokes or declamations. Paris is another; he is a complement to Romeo. He is neither Capulet nor Montague but Mercutio's kinsman, part of the Prince's family.

(100, 104). The comparison of romantic love and sacred devotion, basic to medieval and Renaissance courtly love poetry, gives their action on stage a sacramental effect — something shy and sweet. Romeo gently woos her in true Renaissance style: a word duel in which the weapons are sharp intelligence and puns, the movement is of the words, and the expectancy is of the rhymes. The final couplet of the sonnet merges into their kiss:

> JUL:   Saints do not move, though grant for prayers' sake.
> ROM:   Then move not while my prayer's effect I take.
>                                                   (105-106)

Juliet says: "You kiss by th'book" (110) — an insight into Romeo's previous love life.

The lovers speak the first quatrain of another sonnet (107-110) but are interrupted. Her mother calls Juliet, as Benvolio urges Romeo out of danger. Juliet sends the Nurse for Romeo's name, foreshadowing her own death:

> If he be marrièd,
> My grave is like to be my wedding bed.         (134-135)

Romeo learns the fatal truth — Juliet is a Capulet. She also learns Romeo's identity and cries out in paradoxes that her love is a monster,

> My only love, sprung from my only hate!
> Too early seen unknown, and known too late!
> Prodigious birth of love it is to me
> That I must love a loathèd enemy. (138-141)

Love and hate are abruptly juxtaposed. The scene ends with exquisite irony. The Nurse speaks to Juliet as to a tired child after a party: "Come, let's away. The strangers all are gone" (144). But Romeo is no longer a stranger and Juliet no longer a child. The end of the scene is rightfully the first major climax of the tragedy.

## Second Movement: The Conflict

*The Chorus comments on the action and future possibilities. He speaks again in a formal sonnet (II. Pro.).*

This chorus is usually cut, as it likely was in Shakespeare's day. It does not appear in Q1.

> *Benvolio and Mercutio try to rouse Romeo, who hides*
> *(II.i).*

Romeo walks near the Capulet house. Hearing Benvolio calling, Romeo hides (leaping over the wall into Juliet's garden is a much later addition). Mercutio calls him: "Romeo! Humours! Madman! Passion! Lover!" (7). Receiving no answer, he playfully tries to "conjure" him (in one of the bawdiest passages in Shakespeare) in the name of specific parts of Rosaline's anatomy. Romeo's friends then leave.

The effect of this scene is carefully contrived. Romeo hears all the indecencies; as they refer to the chaste Rosaline, they are doubly effective. Then Juliet appears on her balcony in the moonlight ...

> *Juliet on her balcony and Romeo below speak their love to*
> *one another. Juliet desires marriage. Romeo goes to arrange*
> *it with his confessor, Friar Laurence (II.ii).*

Mercutio's ribaldry has hardly died away when Juliet is at her window. Audiences for four hundred years have been swept away in the romance of the love duet of Romeo and Juliet. Oxford students had read this scene so often that the Bodleian First Folio was worn to tatters by 1664. The scene is like the singing of a duet; and it sustains its great length with little plot beyond the simple joy of two people.

Looking up into the moonlight night, Romeo sees Juliet:

> But soft! What light through yonder window breaks?
> It is the East, and Juliet is the sun! (2-3)

Knowing she cannot hear him, he praises her with great feeling; the prime image is the light Juliet brings into the dark night. The night has its own magic: their love can release itself in the quiet night-world as it cannot in the daylight world of Verona. Alongside other images of sparks, torches and lightning are those which associate the lovers with the unquenchable heavenly lights:

> Two of the fairest stars in all the heaven,
> Having some business, do entreat her eyes
> To twinkle in their spheres till they return. (15-17)

Juliet sighs, and for Romeo, she becomes a creature of those heavens that he sees moving behind her. She becomes at once Mercury and an angel:

O, speak again, bright angel! — for thou art
As glorious to this night, being o'er my head,
As is a wingèd messenger of heaven
Unto the white-upturnèd wondering eyes
Of mortals that fall back to gaze on him
When he bestrides the lazy, puffing clouds
And sails upon the bosom of the air.          (26-32)

At first Romeo still speaks the melancholy language, but the "winged messenger of heaven" belongs to a different order of imagination. Juliet does not know that Romeo is below, and speaks without guile:

O Romeo, Romeo! — wherefore art thou Romeo?
Deny thy father and refuse thy name.
Or, if thou wilt not, be but sworn my love,
And I'll no longer be a Capulet.          (33-36)

It is the names, their social roles, that isolate the lovers and stop them from fulfilling their love. Only Romeo's name, "Montague," is her enemy:

O, be some other name!
What's in a name? That which we call a rose
By any other word would smell as sweet.
So Romeo would, were he not Romeo called,
Retain that dear perfection which he owes [possesses]
Without that title. Romeo, doff thy name;
And for thy name, which is no part of thee,
Take all myself.          (42-49)

Juliet speaks with a simplicity absent from the earlier rhetoric. Her youth gives her an artless candour. There is nothing senti-mental about her, so nothing is asked of the boy-actress that is beyond his skill.

Romeo steps forward. He will surrender his name: "new baptized," he will take the name of "love" (50). The practical Juliet asks:

JUL:   Art thou not Romeo, and a Montague?
ROM:   Neither, fair maid, if either thee dislike.
JUL:   How camest thou hither, tell me, and where-
       fore?
       The orchard walls are high and hard to climb,
       And the place death, considering who thou art,
       If any of my kinsmen find thee here.

> ROM: With love's light wings did I o'erperch these
>         walls.
>         For stony limits cannot hold love out,
>         And what love can do, that dares love attempt.
>         Therefore thy kinsmen are no stop to me.    (60-69)

Realizing that he has overheard her declaration of love, Juliet says:

> Thou knowest the mask of night is on my face,
> Else would a maiden blush bepaint my cheek
> For that which thou hast heard me speak tonight.
> Fain would I dwell on form — fain, fain deny
> What I have spoke. But farewell compliment! ...
>                         O gentle Romeo,
> If thou dost love, pronounce it faithfully.
> Or if thou thinkest I am too quickly won,
> I'll frown, and be perverse, and say thee nay,
> So thou wilt woo. But else, not for the world.
> In truth, fair Montague, I am too fond,
> And therefore thou mayst think my 'haviour light ...
> I should have been more strange, I must confess,
> But that thou overheardest, ere I was ware,
> My true-love passion. Therefore pardon me,
> And not impute this yielding to light love,
> Which the dark night hath so discoverèd.        (85-106)

Romeo begins to swear by the moon, a Petrarchan image. Juliet objects. The moon is too inconstant. If he must swear he should swear by himself:

> Which is the god of my idolatry,
> And I'll believe thee.                            (114-115)

She has a moment of premonition:

> I have no joy of this contract tonight.
> It is too rash, too unadvised, too sudden;
> Too like the lightning, which doth cease to be
> Ere one can say 'It lightens.' Sweet, good night!
>                                                   (117-120)

Juliet's frankness leads to her boldest and most beautiful avowal of her feelings:

> ROM: O, wilt thou leave me so unsatisfied?
> JUL: What satisfaction canst thou have tonight?
> ROM: Th'exchange of thy love's faithful vow for mine.

> JUL: I gave thee mine before thou didst request it.
> And yet I would it were to give again.
> ROM: Wouldst thou withdraw it? For what purpose,
> love?
> JUL: But to be frank and give it thee again.
> And yet I wish but for the thing I have.
> My bounty is as boundless as the sea,
> My love as deep. The more I give to thee,
> The more I have, for both are infinite.
>
> (125-135)

Moral perspectives on love are delightfully given by poetical methods.

The Nurse calls Juliet. As she goes in she tells Romeo to wait a moment. Alone, Romeo cannot believe his happiness:

> O blessèd, blessèd night! I am afeard,
> Being in night, all this is but a dream,
> Too flattering-sweet to be substantial.          (139-141)

Juliet returns, and her language is unambiguous:

> If that thy bent of love be honourable,
> Thy purpose marriage, send me word tomorrow,
> By one that I'll procure to come to thee,
> Where and what time thou wilt perform the rite ...
>
> (143-146)

The Nurse calls again, and Juliet goes. She returns and fervently repeats his name. Then, in a delicate passage, they talk of nothing —

> JUL: Romeo!
> ROM:      My nyas? [My dear?]
> JUL:                  What o'clock tomorrow
> Shall I send to thee?
> ROM:                      By the hour of nine.
> JUL: I will not fail. 'Tis twenty year till then.
> I have forgot why I did call thee back.
> ROM: Let me stand here till thou remember it.
> JUL: I shall forget, to have thee still stand there,
> Remembering how I love thy company.
> ROM: And I'll still stay, to have thee still forget,
> Forgetting any other home but this.   (167-175)

As Granville-Barker said,* this is the commonplace made marvellous. Finally, she leaves abruptly, as though a violent departure were the only way:

> Good night, good night! Parting is such sweet sorrow
> That I shall say goodnight till it be morrow.     (184-185)

Romeo lingers after her departure, calling to her:

> Sleep dwell upon thine eyes, peace in thy breast!
> Would I were sleep and peace, so sweet to rest!
>
> (186-187)

Then he goes to the Friar for his help.

### *Romeo asks the Friar to marry him to Juliet that day (II.iii).*

At dawn, as Romeo is leaving Juliet, his confessor Friar Laurence is gathering herbs. He functions as both spiritual guide and scientist (or alchemist), a traditional combination. He looks after the spiritual life of Verona while the Prince dispenses justice. Both men are ineffectual.

Romeo tells the Friar that he has not been to bed that night. "Wast thou with Rosaline?" asks the Friar. And Romeo replies as if amazed:

> With Rosaline, my ghostly father? No.
> I have forgot that name and that name's woe.     (41-42)

To the Friar, he is the "young waverer":

> Holy Saint Francis! What a change is here!
> Is Rosaline, that thou didst love so dear,
> So soon forsaken? Young men's love then lies
> Not truly in their hearts, but in their eyes.     (61-64)

Romeo explains what has happened and that he wants to marry Juliet this day. The Friar sees this as a way to end the feud and prophesies: "Wisely and slow. They stumble that run fast" (90).

### *Benvolio tells Mercutio that Tybalt has challenged the Montagues. Romeo makes arrangements with the Nurse (II.iv).*

This is a highly successful comic scene, with Mercutio dominating the first half, and the Nurse the last half.

---

* Granville-Barker (1963).

Benvolio and Mercutio are looking for Romeo on the streets. Mercutio springs to life with "Where the devil should this Romeo be? Came he not home tonight?" (1-2). A note of warning is struck:

Tybalt, the kinsman of old Capulet,

Hath sent a letter to his father's house.        (6-7)

Although Romeo will answer the challenge, Mercutio laments that Romeo cannot fight, and Tybalt is "More than Prince of Cats" (19); this refers to the Beast Epic of *Reynard the Fox* in which the cat's name was Tybert or Tybalt. Mercutio mocks Tybalt's manner of duelling (23-26). Romeo arrives, and Mercutio jests: "Now is he for the numbers that Petrarch flowed in. Laura, to his lady, was a kitchen wench — marry, she had a better love to berhyme her" (38-40). The joke is that it is a new Romeo. Mercutio is affectionate:

Why, is not this better now than groaning for love? Now

art thou sociable. Now art thou Romeo. Now art thou

what thou art, by art as well as by nature.        (86-88)

The actor finds the key to Mercutio in this speech: be who you are, and accept life (and death) as it is.

Then in sweeps the Nurse in her finery, accompanied by the Capulet servant, Peter, who is carrying her fan. Mercutio senses a new target — "A sail, a sail!" (99) — but cannot even say that it is twelve o'clock without an obscene jest (109-110). The Nurse can be acted broadly with a variety of roles, from her "My fan, Peter" (103) when she tries to play the discreet lady with the young sparks, to playing the bawd with Romeo. He arranges the marriage for that afternoon at the Friar's cell and for a rope ladder so that he and Juliet can consummate the marriage that night.

*Juliet awaits word from Romeo. The Nurse teases her, then announces the appointment at the Friar's cell (II.v).*

Juliet has waited "three long hours" for the Nurse to return. In her reckless delight and quick imagery, staccato rhythm and shifts in speech pattern, her eagerness rivals Romeo's. The Nurse arrives, but her body aches, she moans, and she will not give her message immediately. The delaying trick is one of the oldest gags in farce, deriving from the Latin comedy and the *commedia dell'arte*. Like the lascivious old Latin bawds, the Nurse delights in forecasting the sexual pleasures of the bridal night:

> I am the drudge, and toil in your delight.
> But you shall bear the burden soon at night.     (75-76)

She relents: Juliet must go to Friar Laurence's cell this afternoon.

> *Friar Laurence's cell; Juliet meets Romeo there, and they*
> *are married (off-stage) (II.vi).*

Romeo and the Friar await Juliet. The paradox of love's strength and fragility is expressed in Romeo's triumphant boast:

> Do thou but close our hands with holy words,
> Then love-devouring death do what he dare —
> It is enough I may but call her mine.     (6-8)

The Friar is horrified at such a declaration of absolute love and reproves him in a little homily or sermon. Before he can get his lesson home, Juliet enters.

> Here comes the lady. O, so light a foot
> Will ne'er wear out the everlasting flint.     (16-17)

The Friar declares he will marry them.

> *Tybalt challenges Romeo for crashing the ball. Romeo*
> *refuses to duel. Mercutio takes his place and is killed.*
> *Romeo then slays Tybalt and is banished (III.i).*

In striking contrast to the quiet end of the previous scene, Mercutio and Benvolio stride in, swords on hips, with armed servants. Mercutio is touchy, and the prudent Benvolio begs him:

> I pray thee, good Mercutio, let's retire.
> The day is hot, the Capels are abroad.
> And if we meet we shall not 'scape a brawl,
> For now, these hot days, is the mad blood stirring.     (1-4)

The heat is oppressive, and violence is in the air. The two men are bored and quarrel irritably. Then the most theatrically striking events in the play happen quickly: two men are killed and another banished for life. Romeo encounters Tybalt face to face. Tybalt taunts him:

> Romeo, the love I bear thee can afford
> No better term than this: thou art a villain.     (59-60)

There is an eloquent silence which amazes Benvolio, Mercutio and Tybalt, but we know Romeo has goodwill toward the Capulets — he has just married one. He is full of emotions which the player may interpret in several ways and so affect the later action: is he so rapt in love that he misses the insult? Does he flash into passion and check it? Does he count as nothing his pride and the scorn of his friends? What he says is:

> Tybalt, the reason that I have to love thee
> Does much excuse the appertaining rage
> To such a greeting. Villain am I none.
> Therefore farewell, I see thou knowest me not.  (61-64)

The rest are aghast as he says:

> good Capulet, which name I tender
> As dearly as mine own, be satisfied.  (70-71)

The riddle is clear only to the audience. It affects each man differently.* How can the peaceable Benvolio defend Romeo's inaction? For Tybalt it is a let-down; he looks ridiculous and grows angrier. Mercutio adds the most important element to the situation, the unforeseen: Romeo's behaviour is "calm, dishonourable, vile submission" (72), and Mercutio, itching to teach Tybalt a lesson, draws his sword on him. Romeo tries to separate them, but Mercutio is fatally wounded. He is brutally honest with Romeo: "Why the devil came you between us? I was hurt under your arm." Then he ignores Romeo's futile, "I thought all for the best" (102-104). The catastrophe is arbitrary. Mercutio is hit in a feud of which he is not a part. With no regrets, he is angry that he has been beaten by Tybalt. "The hurt cannot be much," Romeo reassures him. Mercutio offers grim humour:

> No, 'tis not so deep as a well, nor so wide as a church door. But 'tis enough. 'Twill serve. Ask for me tomorrow, you shall find me a grave man. I am peppered, I warrant, for this world. A plague a'both your houses! Zounds, a dog, a rat, a mouse, a cat, to scratch a man to death! A braggart, a rogue, a villain, that fights by the book of arithmetic!  (96-102)

Romeo has been so inept that Mercutio ignores him and asks

---

* Shakespeare also learns how successful the method is. Later he uses this relativity of perspective in *Julius Caesar*, where he experiments with it, and then in *Hamlet* in a much expanded form.

Benvolio and not Romeo to help him into a house as he gives a dying man's curse. For the Elizabethans this was ominous; they would see in later events the working out of Mercutio's cynicism that love is inseparably mixed with hate.

Romeo, left alone, sees the disgrace of his situation. Shakespeare uses the unexpected to force a change in Romeo. A simpler and graver feeling now begins to throb in his measured verse:

> This gentleman, the Prince's near ally,
> My very friend, hath got this mortal hurt
> In my behalf — my reputation stained
> With Tybalt's slander — Tybalt, that an hour
> Hath been my cousin. O sweet Juliet,
> Thy beauty hath made me effeminate
> And in my temper softened valour's steel!      (109-115)

There is a sudden change of feeling when Benvolio enters and says that "brave Mercutio is dead!" (116). The mood darkens. Romeo conveys the turn of fortune's wheel in a clear premonition:

> This day's black fate on more days doth depend.
> This but begins the woe others must end.      (119-120)

With Mercutio slain, the revenge code exacts obedience. Now Romeo must kill Tybalt. But the player must not miss Romeo's desperation:

> Alive in triumph, and Mercutio slain!
> Away to heaven respective lenity,
> And fire-eyed fury be my conduct now!      (122-125)

This is the language of an avenger. Romeo requites the insult to him and Mercutio's death: he kills Tybalt.

Benvolio cries out that "the citizens are up" and that the Prince will condemn Romeo to death if he does not flee. Romeo recognizes the power of fate: "O, I am fortune's fool!" (136). He flees. The Montagues and Capulets gather. The Prince exiles Romeo.

Here is the turning point of the play. Mercutio's death only allows for tragedy. By using the code of honour, Romeo is a murderer and so "death-marked": he suffers because of his own choice. Yet like all human actions, Romeo's are ambiguous. He is both right and wrong, and for that ambiguity he will suffer tragically.

> *Juliet awaits news from the Nurse, who enters and leads*
> *her to believe that Romeo is dead. When she reveals it is*
> *Tybalt who is slain, Juliet reasons that Romeo must have*
> *killed him in self defence (III.ii).*

The scene opens with one of the loveliest speeches of the play:
an "epithalamium," one of several verse forms in this extremely
lyric drama. Parts are almost identical to Spenser's great poem,
*Epithalamium*, in which the young husband longs for the delights
of the marriage bed. Here the roles are reversed as Juliet waits
breathlessly for night to bring her husband to her arms:

> Gallop apace, you fiery-footed steeds,
> Towards Phoebus' lodging! Such a waggoner
> As Phaëton would whip you to the West
> And bring in cloudy night immediately.                    (1-4)

There is intense purity in Juliet's anticipation of the "amorous
rites" that are to be "Played for a pair of stainless maiden-
hoods" (13). What she says is not crude; beyond it lies a genuine and ideal love for Romeo. She even suggests Romeo's sexual posture in the night:

> For thou wilt lie upon the wings of night
> Whiter than new snow upon a raven's back.         (18-19)

Elaborately she relates Romeo to the star imagery that dominates the play:

> Give me my Romeo. And when I shall die,
> Take him and cut him out in little stars,
> And he will make the face of heaven so fine
> That all the world will be in love with night
> And pay no worship to the garish sun.                    (21-25)

Their love is as permanent as the sun and stars when it is
placed out of the range of time. "Cut" into little stars (the old
idea of apotheosis: a hero became a star), Romeo will make
dark better than day; exhausted from love ("dead") he will be a
brighter, truer light than the sun. She cries:

> O I have bought the mansion of a love,
> But not possessed it; and though I am sold,
> Not yet enjoyed. So tedious is this day
> As is the night before some festival
> To an impatient child that hath new robes
> And may not wear them.                              (26-31)

Although she is about to become a woman, she is still a child of fourteen, and her deepest experiences so far are those of her childhood.

We speed on. The Nurse, ironically carrying the ladder of cords — the highway to the marriage bed (34) — cries, "He's dead, he's dead, he's dead!" (37). Thinking she means Romeo and near to collapse, Juliet expresses dread in a plethora of puns, usually cut today (and we can hardly blame the player). But to the Elizabethans puns were not necessarily comic:

> Hath Romeo slain himself? Say thou but 'Ay,'
> And that bare vowel 'I' shall poison more
> Than the death-darting eye of cockatrice.
> I am not I, if there be such an 'I'
> Or those eyes shut that makes thee answer 'Ay'.
> If he be slain, say 'Ay'; or if not, 'No.'
> Brief sounds determine of my weal or woe.          (45-51)

The boy-Juliet displayed vocal virtuosity. Today the verse is absurd, like many out-of-date fashions, but the word-music vividly tells her agony and confusion. Then Juliet hears the truth: Romeo has killed Tybalt. In horror, she plays on phrase, paradox, and antithesis:

> Dove-feathered raven! Wolvish-ravening lamb!
> Despisèd substance of divinest show!
> Just opposite to what thou justly seemest —
> A damnèd saint, an honourable villain!          (76-79)

But the emotion is false and temporary. So is the rhetoric, for Shakespeare returns to pure drama with the Nurse's "Will you speak well of him that killed your cousin?" and Juliet's sharp reply, "Shall I speak ill of him that is my husband?" (96-97). To the sound of "banishèd," Juliet says:

> There is no end, no limit, measure, bound,
> In that word's death. No words can that woe sound.
>                                    (125-126)

But the Nurse will bring Romeo to her, and Juliet is in ecstasy again.

> *Romeo cannot bear to leave Juliet; he threatens suicide.*
> *The Friar dissuades him. He and the Nurse arrange for*
> *the pair to spend their wedding night together (III.iii).*

After the desperate Juliet we meet a desperate Romeo. Like Juliet, Romeo's reaction (in a stream of rhetoric) to the Prince's command is that death is preferable to banishment.

The Friar advises the comfort of "adversity's sweet milk, philosophy" (56). Romeo is exasperated:

> Hang up philosophy!
> Unless philosophy can make a Juliet,
> Displant a town, reverse a prince's doom,
> It helps not, it prevails not. Talk no more.      (58-61)

He hysterically throws himself on the floor in despair, a scene taken almost intact from Brooke. The Nurse enters: Juliet too lies "Blubbering and weeping, weeping and blubbering" (88). Romeo's violent emotion must be acted with rhetorical abandon, poetically, not with realism; and on no account should he sob like a big baby, as so often happens. Romeo threatens to take his own life. The Friar restrains him:

> Hold thy desperate hand ...
>                 Thy wild acts denote
> The unreasonable fury of a beast ...
> Hast thou slain Tybalt? Wilt thou slay thyself?
> And slay thy lady that in thy life lives,
> By doing damnèd hate upon thyself?      (108-118)

Romeo forgets the Friar's teaching: he puts passion before reason, abuses his wit (intelligence) and misuses his abilities:

> Thy wit, that ornament to shape and love,
> Misshapen in the conduct of them both,
> Like powder in a skilless soldier's flask
> Is set afire by thine own ignorance,
> And thou dismembered with thine own defence.
>                                         (130-134)

Romeo is to go to Juliet's chamber that night and then flee to Mantua. There he can stay until the marriage is revealed, Romeo forgiven and returned to Verona "With twenty hundred thousand times more joy" (153).

*Paris now presses his suit, and Capulet agrees to marry his daughter to Paris the following Thursday (III.iv).*

On the Elizabethan stage, Juliet is aloft behind curtains; supposedly weeping for Tybalt, she is enjoying her wedding night. Below on the stage Paris urges his suit with her parents. Capulet wants Juliet to marry the Prince's kinsman:

> 'Tis very late. She'll not come down tonight.
> I promise you, but for your company,

I would have been abed an hour ago. (5-7)

Paris, leaving, asks Lady Capulet to commend him to her daughter. She says:

I will, and know her mind early tomorrow.
Tonight she's mewed up to her heaviness. (10-11)

But we know she is not. With a sudden impulse, Capulet recalls Paris:

Sir Paris, I will make a desperate tender
Of my child's love. I think she will be ruled
In all respects by me. Nay more, I doubt it not.
Wife, go you to her ere you go to bed.
Acquaint her here of my son Paris' love,
And bid her — mark you me? — on Wednesday next ...
(12-17)

With that sudden impulse the tragedy is precipitated.

Well, Wednesday is too soon.
A'Thursday let it be. (19-20)

He has dropped his mourning uncle role and is a jovial father-in-law. Will Lady Capulet go to Juliet's room now? Or leave it until morning?

> *After their wedding night, the lovers say farewell before
> Romeo flees to Mantua. Juliet refuses to marry Paris and
> quarrels with her parents (III.v).*

Now comes an effect well-prepared by Shakespeare. Hardly have the three vanished from the stage below, when the upper curtains open.

> *Enter Romeo and Juliet aloft, at the window.**

JUL: Wilt thou be gone? It is not yet near day.
It was the nightingale, and not the lark,
That pierced the fearful hollow of thine ear.
Nightly she sings on yond pomegranate tree.
Believe me, love, it was the nightingale. (1-5)

In the dawn of Tuesday morning, Juliet and Romeo wake in her bedroom. The nuptial night is over, and he must flee to Mantua. Juliet seeks to keep the illusion that it is still night. A bird has sounded:

---

* This stage direction derives from Q1.

> ROM:  It was the lark, the herald of the morn;
>       No nightingale. Look, love, what envious streaks
>       Do lace the severing clouds in yonder East.
>       Night's candles are burnt out, and jocund day
>       Stands tiptoe on the misty mountain tops. (6-10)

Here is another form of lyric, the "aubade," a song sung at
dawn. Its serene liquid sound is one of the poetic heights of the
tragedy. Romeo has reached the deepest intensity of his passion; the peace he feels is almost religious, and his rhetoric has
the ring of truth:

> Let me be ta'en, let me be put to death.
> I am content, so thou wilt have it so.
> I'll say yon grey is not the morning's eye;
> 'Tis but the pale reflex of Cynthia's [the moon's] brow.
> Nor that is not the lark whose notes do beat
> The vaulty heaven so high above our heads.
> I have more care to stay than will to go.
> Come, death, and welcome! Juliet wills it so.
> How is't, my soul? Let's talk. It is not day.          (17-25)

"It is, it is!" Juliet finally insists — reality cannot be wished away
— "It is the lark that sings so out of tune" (26-27). Shakespeare
has altered Brooke's time: despite their marriage in Holy
Church, their love seems illicit; the morning brings separation;
time that had moved too slowly is now too quick. Dawn's light
brings darkness to their private world: "More light and light:
more dark and dark our woes." (36)

The day world enters with the Nurse who gasps that Lady
Capulet is on her way. Juliet replies: "Then, window, let day in,
and let life out" (41). Romeo kisses Juliet and descends from
the balcony on the rope ladder: *He goes down* (42). Juliet's
expresses the timelessness of their passion:

> Art thou gone so, love-lord, aye husband-friend?
> I must hear from thee every day in the hour,
> For in a minute there are many days.
> O by this count I shall be much in years
> Ere I again behold my Romeo.                    (43-47)

She looks over the balcony, after her lover has climbed down to
the stage, and exclaims: "O, thinkest thou we shall ever meet
again?" (51). Romeo tries to reassure her, but fate enters again.
Juliet has a premonition:

O God, I have an ill-divining soul!
Methinks I see thee, now thou art so low,
As one dead in the bottom of a tomb.
Either my eyesight fails, or thou lookest pale.     (54-57)

Indeed, the next time Juliet sees him he will be lying dead at her side.

Lady Capulet tells Juliet she is to marry the County Paris next Thursday morning. Juliet weeps and vows she will not. Old Capulet arrives on his wife's heels. He assumes Juliet's tears are for Tybalt and warns her about excessive grief:

In one little body
Thou counterfeitest a bark, a sea, a wind.
For still thy eyes, which I may call the sea,
Do ebb and flow with tears. The bark thy body is,
Sailing in this salt flood. The winds, thy sighs,
Who, raging with thy tears and they with them,
Without a sudden calm will overset
Thy tempest-tossèd body.                     (130-137)

When he hears of Juliet's refusal, he rages against the obstinate girl:

How, how, how, how, chopped logic? What is this?
'Proud' — and 'I thank you' — and 'I thank you not' —
And yet 'not proud'? Mistress minion you,
Thank me no thankings, nor proud me no prouds,
But fettle your fine joints 'gainst Thursday next
To go with Paris to Saint Peter's Church,
Or I will drag thee on a hurdle thither.
Out, you green-sickness carrion! Out, you baggage!
You tallow-face!                     (149-157)

This moves even Lady Capulet to protest. His fingers itch to give his young daughter a thrashing. Going, he says:

An you be mine, I'll give you to my friend.
An you be not, hang, beg, starve, die in the streets ...
                     (192-193)

Juliet, in abject misery, appeals to her mother. All that Lady Capulet can reply as she exits is, "Do as thou wilt, for I have done with thee" (204).

In her agony Juliet turns to her Nurse:

What sayest thou? Hast thou not a word of joy?
Some comfort, Nurse.                     (212-213)

But the easy-going indulgence with which the Nurse encouraged the affair with Romeo now prompts her to recommend
the easy way out — to marry Paris:

> Romeo is banished; and all the world to nothing
> That he dares ne'er come back to challenge you.
> Or if he do, it needs must be by stealth.
> Then, since the case so stands as now it doth,
> I think it best you married with the County.    (214-218)

This is horrifying and unexpected to Juliet. It is all said casually,
but it is the stroke that completes the Nurse's character. We
were amused by her, but everything about her falls into perspective as she gushes:

> NUR:  O, he's a lovely gentleman!
> Romeo's a dishclout to him. An eagle, madam,
> Hath not so green, so quick, so fair an eye
> As Paris hath. Beshrew my very heart,
> I think you are happy in this second match,
> For it excels your first; or if it did not,
> Your first is dead — or 'twere as good he were
> As living here and you no use of him.  (219-227)

The Nurse is morally repelling; unconscious of saying anything
unsavory, hers like Tybalt's is a spiritual evil. Juliet says ironically, "Well, thou hast comforted me marvellous much" (231).
Alone, Juliet explodes in one of the great moments of the play:

> Ancient damnation! O most wicked fiend!
> Is it more sin to wish me thus forsworn,
> Or to dispraise my lord with that same tongue
> Which she hath praised him with above compare
> So many thousand times?                    (236-240)

The audience should feel a change take place in Juliet. She is
now a married woman who stands alone, caught up in a train
of passionate events.

> *The Friar offers Juliet a desperate plan: to take a sleeping
> potion that will imitate death; when she is in the tomb,
> Romeo can rescue her (IV.i).*

Juliet flies to the Friar. There is Paris, but she does not show
her surprise. For appearance's sake she responds as Paris
claims her as his wife; she must let him kiss her, even! It is a passionate Juliet who turns from Paris to the Friar with:

Oh shut the door! and when thou hast done so,
Come weep with me. Past hope, past cure, past help!
(44-45)

The Friar gives her a vial (a small bottle). She is to drink the
contents the following night: she will appear dead for forty-two
hours; then she will awake as if from a pleasant sleep. Paris on
the nuptial morning will find her dead. The Friar will send a
message to Romeo, and both of them will be there when she
wakes to take her to Mantua.

> *As old Capulet is preparing for the wedding feast, Juliet
> begs his forgiveness. He sends for Paris and speeds up the
> wedding date (IV.ii).*

Juliet flies back to her father, entering with a "merry look"
(14). She plays the hypocrite as she must, even overplaying the
role; she falls before him, begging his pardon for the sin "Of
disobedient opposition" (18). Capulet is overjoyed and sends
for Paris. He will advance the wedding date and have the wedding "tomorrow" (Wednesday). The speeding up of the wedding date is his own decision, and he cannot know he is the
pawn of fate. This is one more act of meaningless chance that
the audience should feel could have been avoided.

> *Juliet takes the potion (IV.iii). [IV.iii, IV.iv and IV.v are
> continuous; they run as one scene.]*

Juliet easily hoodwinks her mother and her Nurse who
leave. The rest of the scene is the long soliloquy, "Farewell!
God knows when we shall meet again ..." (14-59) in which she
determines to fight her fears of the mock death. When she
says, "My dismal scene I needs must act alone" (19), she deeply
embeds the dramatic metaphor in its context of death and
night. She will brave any terror for her love. She drinks to
Romeo:

O, look! Methinks I see my cousin's ghost
Seeking out Romeo, that did spit his body
Upon a rapier's point. Stay, Tybalt, stay!
Romeo, Romeo, Romeo.
Here's drink. I drink to thee. (55-59)

Juliet's soliloquy is one of Shakespeare's great linguistic
achievements in the play: he uses blank verse so flexibly that it

seems to reveal Juliet's emotional turbulence with no hindrance by the form.

This and the following scene include a vital effect that depends on the theatre for which it was designed [see *End Notes*]. The curtains of the inner stage are drawn back to show us Juliet's bed. Her Nurse and her mother leave her; she drinks the potion, and *She falls upon her bed within the curtains:* that is, the curtains of the inner stage close on her.

*Preparations on the morning of the wedding day. Juliet is found dead (IV.iv).*

This scene opens in front of the curtains with great rush and bustle as the Capulet household is all astir with preparations. It is the dawn of the wedding day of Juliet and Paris.

Shakespeare emphasizes a sharp conflict between youth and age. He also keeps us conscious of the bed and Juliet hidden by the curtain. Capulet and the servants, Lady Capulet and the Nurse pass back and forth, laughing and joking over the wedding preparations. Then the music of the County Paris' retinue is heard. Juliet is to be awakened. The bridegroom has come, and the Nurse bustles up to draw back the curtains ...

*Juliet's body is found by the Nurse. Her parents must now change the wedding into a funeral (IV.v).*

The Nurse, as she tries to rouse Juliet from her deathlike sleep in order to marry Paris, uses the same kind of lewd jokes as before:

> Mistress! What, mistress! Juliet! Fast, I warrant her, she.
> Why, lamb! Why, lady! Fie, you slug-abed!
> Why, love, I say! Madam! Sweetheart! Why, bride!
> What, not a word? You take your pennyworths now.
> Sleep for a week. For the next night, I warrant,
> The County Paris hath set up his rest
> That you shall rest but little. God forgive me!
> Marry, and amen! How sound is she asleep!
> I needs must wake her. Madam, madam, madam!
> Ay, let the County take you in your bed.
> He'll fright you up, i'faith. Will it not be?
> What, dressed, and in your clothes, and down again?

I must needs wake you. Lady! lady! lady!
Alas, alas! Help, help! My lady's dead!
O weraday that ever I was born!
Some aqua vitae, ho! My lord! My lady!           (1-16)

This is one of the young Shakespeare's most extraordinary achievements: there are no adjectives and no figures; the whole speech is made up of questions, exclamations and small talk. Yet it is superb dramatic poetry. It could be no one but the Nurse.

The personification of death as the lover and bridegroom occurs from the start of the play but, for Capulet, death lies on Juliet

like an untimely frost
Upon the sweetest flower of all the field.           (28-29)

This early frost forestalls the heat of the sun in Italy, as well as the blight in the bud. To Paris he says:

O son, the night before thy wedding day
Hath death lain with thy wife. There she lies,
Flower as she was, deflowerèd by him.
Death is my son-in-law. Death is my heir.
My daughter he hath wedded. I will die
And leave him all. Life, living, all is death's.           (35-40)

The Friar halts the laments: the body should be borne in wedding attire to the vault of the Capulets. Old Capulet then reverses all the festivities of the day, turning "Our wedding cheer to a sad burial feast" (87).

There is then a comic interlude, probably created for Will Kempe who played the role of Peter, but in a form that quickly went out of date. It is ironic that this scene, given almost totally to lament, should be for someone who is not dead at all, while the suicides at the play's end should have little or no formal mourning.

### Third Movement: The Catastrophe

*In Mantua, Balthasar, Romeo's servant, arrives: he has seen Juliet dead in Verona; he brings no letter from the Friar. Romeo vows to lie in the tomb with Juliet, buys poison from an apothecary, and hastens to the graveyard (V.i).*

Romeo awaits news from Verona. He shows a new maturity and manly dignity: a cloak and top-boots — a small but effective touch — can strike the right note. He relates his dream with a sense of foreboding:

>      I dreamt my lady came and found me dead —
>      Strange dream that gives a dead man leave to think! —
>      And breathed such life with kisses in my lips
>      That I revived and was an emperor.                    (6-9)

Balthasar enters and says Juliet is dead. When Romeo hears this news, with wonderfully simple words he rises to the dignity of despair:

> ROM:  Is it e'en so? Then I defy you, stars!*
>        Thou knowest my lodging. Get me ink and
>        paper,
>        And hire posthorses. I will hence tonight ...
>        Hast thou no letters to me from the Friar?
> BAL:  No, my good lord.
> ROM:           No matter. Get thee gone
>        And hire those horses. I'll be with thee straight.
>        [Exit Balthasar] Well, Juliet, I will lie with thee to-
>        night.                                        (24-34)

When we hear there are no letters from the Friar, we recognize chance once more. The dialogue has become plain through dynamic phrases that can sum up simply a ferment of emotion and thought. This demands sheer acting, the expression of emotion without the aid of rhetoric — comparatively new when the play was written.

Seeking the means for his suicide, Romeo remembers an apothecary nearby. Romeo and Juliet are now reduced, as outcasts from society, to this kind of underworld. Romeo's deeply tragic experience opens his eyes to suffering humanity for the first time. He continues to grow: he scornfully contemplates what men come to — those who will not dare to gamble with fate for happiness, and who are content to lose rather than be

---

* The stars have functioned in two ways in the play: to represent the lovers to each other in their light-darkness imagery as a kind of free will for each other; and to symbolize the forces of Fate working on the lovers. Here Romeo refers to this second function.

denied. We realize Romeo's impetuosity ("I stand on sudden haste") by the way he talks to the apothecary:

> A dram of poison, such soon-speeding gear
> As will disperse itself through all the veins,
> That the life-weary taker may fall dead
> And that the trunk may be discharged of breath
> As violently as hasty powder fired
> Doth hurry from the fatal cannon's womb.      (60-65)

And the buying of the poison shows us a grown-up Romeo:

> There is thy gold — worse poison to men's souls,
> Doing more murder in this loathsome world,
> Than these poor compounds that thou mayst not sell.
> I sell thee poison. Thou hast sold me none.      (80-83)

Romeo's values are reversed: the world's gold becomes poison, life a sickness. To the apothecary he says: "Farewell. Buy food and get thyself in flesh" (84). This is his first purely selfless thought. "Juliet's death has made a Christian of him."*

> *Friar John tells Friar Laurence that he could not take the letter to Romeo (V.ii).*

Friar Laurence welcomes a brother friar, Friar John, who had taken a letter (telling of Juliet's potion) to Romeo in Mantua. The short scene is all plot, and John's story is one of accident. Before he left Verona for Mantua, he stopped at a house with the plague, and was sealed up there until today. No one would deliver the letter for fear of infection. Friar Laurence immediately demands a crowbar to force the vault open. Juliet will wake in three hours. Romeo, not having received the letter, will not be there. Friar Laurence will keep her in his cell until Romeo arrives, and he ends the scene by setting the mood for the next: "Poor living corse, closed in a dead man's tomb" (29).

> *Paris accosts Romeo, who he thinks is desecrating the vault, and is slain. Romeo enters the tomb, finds Juliet supposedly dead, drinks poison, and dies. The Friar arrives as Juliet wakes; when Juliet will not leave, he runs*

---

* Knight (1967).

> *away. She kills herself with a dagger. Capulet, Montague*
> *and the Prince seek explanations. Capulet and Montague*
> *agree to end the feud and will erect monuments to the*
> *lovers (V.iii).*

Stage directors are inclined to cut *Romeo and Juliet* in many places, but nowhere more flagrantly than in this final scene. Often they leave nothing but the deaths of Paris, Romeo and Juliet, and a symbolic tableau of Montagues and Capulets reconciled at the end. Shakespeare did not envisage the scene this way. His original staging again helps us to understand his aims. The outer stage is now the churchyard, so the action on it is prominent. The inner stage is the Capulet vault, closed in by gates — Paris casts his flowers through their bars, and Romeo breaks them open. In the vault, Juliet lies upon a tomb like an effigy (a block of stone low and wide enough for Romeo to lie beside her) and around her may be other such monuments, Tybalt's among them, which are uneffigied.

It is late at night in the churchyard. Paris appears with his page and instructs him to whistle if anyone approaches. He then strews flowers outside Juliet's vault as he delivers an elegy:

> Sweet flower, with flowers thy bridal bed I strew —
>     O woe! thy canopy is dust and stones —
> Which with sweet water nightly I will dew;
>     Or, wanting that, with tears distilled by moans.
> The obsequies that I for thee will keep
> Nightly shall be to strew thy grave and weep.     (12-17)

Suddenly the boy whistles. Paris hides.

Romeo and Balthasar come with a torch and tools to open the vault. The player of Romeo, with his heavy step and set looks, must express his deadly and rigid intent. He gives his servant a letter to his parents, telling them of the reasons for his death, and orders Balthasar not to follow him into the vault. If he should try to do so:

> By heaven, I will tear thee joint by joint
> And strew this hungry churchyard with thy limbs.
>
>                                             (35-36)

Romeo hands him a purse of gold and bids him farewell: "Live, and be prosperous" (42). His feeling for his servant, like his later feeling for Paris (59-67, 74-87), reveals his new-found sympathy for all creatures. Balthasar hides in the churchyard.

Romeo violently tears the vault open with his tools. His extraordinary metaphor emphasizes the violence of his defiance of death:

> Thou detestable maw, thou womb of death,
> Gorged with the dearest morsel of the earth,
> Thus I enforce thy rotten jaws to open,
> And in despite I'll cram thee with more food.     (45-48)

He rapes death: the suicides of the lovers will be the death-marriage about to be consummated in the tomb. Romeo for the last time will enter the "womb of death" and climax his love by "dying."

Paris assumes Romeo aims to damage the Capulet vault where Tybalt lies. He steps forward and tells Romeo to stop "thy unhallowed toil" (54). Romeo, strained beyond endurance, is provoked, but Paris will not leave. They fight, and the page runs out to call the Watch. Paris is slain. His last wish is to be placed beside Juliet. Romeo agrees. Only when he looks at his face does he recognize him and is sobered by seeing what he has done. Love has matured Romeo more than Paris and has given him universal sympathies and the feeling of wisdom and age.* One of the repeating ironies in the tragedy is that men die without knowing the full consequence of their acts: Paris cannot know that Romeo is married to Juliet. Paris genuinely loves her: his touching elegy and his desire to cleanse and keep watch over her tomb show the depth of his emotion. Romeo is right when he calls him brother.** As he opens the vault, in another gesture of universal sympathy, Romeo takes Paris' body inside:

> How oft when men are at the point of death
> Have they been merry! which their keepers call
> A lightning before death. O how may I
> Call this a lightning?                              (88-91)

---

* We should note the aging of Romeo. To the contemptuous Tybalt he was a boy; Paris to him, when they meet, is a "Good gentle youth" (59).

** The County Paris is often treated unfairly on the stage. Shakespeare refused to make him a villain, as a lesser dramatist might have done. As the Nurse praised him as "a man of wax," Paris is often played as a weakling and something of a fop; that he is valiant withers before stage tradition — Romeo appears manlier if Paris is effeminate!

In a terrible sense Romeo and Juliet's love is "A lightning before death."

Romeo moves to where Juliet lies in her wedding dress. He can barely speak: "O my love! My wife!" The dramatic effect lies in the chance that at any minute Juliet may wake or Friar Laurence arrive; but Romeo's haste precipitates the final tragedy. Climaxing death as the lover, he says:

> Shall I believe
> That unsubstantial death is amorous,
> And that the lean abhorrèd monster keeps
> Thee here in dark to be his paramour?          (102-105)

To prevent the love-death, Romeo says he will never leave "this palace of dim night":

> here will I remain
> With worms that are thy chambermaids. O here
> Will I set up my everlasting rest
> And shake the yoke of inauspicious stars
> From this world-wearied flesh.          (108-112)

In the reference to stars, the audience recognizes that the force of fate has come full circle. Romeo prepares to kill himself. "Lips" that are "the doors of breath" are to kiss Juliet, to:

> seal with a righteous kiss
> A dateless bargain to engrossing death!
> *[To the vial]* Come, bitter conduct, come, unsavoury
>       guide!
> Thou desperate pilot, now at once run on
> The dashing rocks thy seasick weary bark!          (114-118)

At the height of despair, he drains the vial and dies kissing Juliet, never ceasing for one moment to believe in the eternity of his passion. Ironically, he performs the wedding rite with death as lover, as does Juliet: the ritual of suicide.

The Friar enters the churchyard whispering

> Saint Francis be my speed! How oft tonight
> Have my old feet stumbled at graves!          (121-122)

He moves on and, when he sees the body of Paris, he cries out:

> Ah, what an unkind hour
> Is guilty of this lamentable chance!          (145-146)

The Friar finally acknowledges that fate has overcome his good intentions.

At this moment Juliet begins to stir from her drugged

sleep. She wakes in the vault, hopefully, happily. She asks the Friar for Romeo:

> O comfortable Friar! Where is my lord?
> I do remember well where I should be,
> And there I am. Where is my Romeo? (148-150)

The sound of approaching townspeople is heard. He quickly says:

> A greater power than we can contradict
> Hath thwarted our intents. Come, come away.
> Thy husband in thy bosom there lies dead;
> And Paris too. Come, I'll dispose of thee
> Among a sisterhood of holy nuns.
> Stay not to question, for the Watch is coming.
> Come, go, good Juliet. I dare no longer stay. (153-159)

But she delays: in these brief moments the impact of the tragedy strikes her. The sudden brutal blow by which her childish faith in the Friar is shattered precipitates her rush to escape from a life that, without Romeo, is no life. There is scorn in her "Go, get thee hence, for I will not away" (160). So he flees, not so much in weakness as simple confusion.

Juliet will follow Romeo. In her unreflecting haste lies her peculiar tragedy. She opens Romeo's hand, finds the vial, and chides him for having

> drunk all, and left no friendly drop
> To help me after? (163-164)

She kisses him, hoping some poison still remains on his lips. She finds them still warm. The Watch is heard approaching, and Romeo's dagger is all she has left. She thrusts it into her body:

> O happy dagger!
> This is thy sheath; there rust, and let me die. (169-170)

Death has long been Romeo's rival and enjoys Juliet at the last.

The page leads the Watchmen through the churchyard into the vault:

> PAGE: This is the place. There, where the torch doth
> burn.
> 1 W: The ground is bloody. Search about the
> churchyard. (171-172)

The stage is full of cries, confusion and bustle. Some of the Watch bring back Balthasar, others the Friar. The Prince arrives with his train. The Capulets surge in. Then the Montagues arrive. Quietly Montague announces that his wife has died the previous night from grief over Romeo's banishment. The whole front stage is filled with comings and goings. Behind, in ghastly contrast with the torchlight flickering on them, Romeo and Juliet lie still.

The Prince's authoritative voice silences everyone:

> Seal up the mouth of outrage for a while,
> Till we can clear these ambiguities
> And know their spring, their head, their true descent.
>
> (216-219)

Friar Laurence comes forward and proceeds to tell the story of the lovers. His long explanatory account has often been felt to be theatrically unnecessary and is cut in performance: it tells nothing that the audience does not already know. But to Elizabethans, the love of Romeo and Juliet is now a public event. The Prince, moreover, must learn the facts before making a judgment. The Friar does not forget to blame himself (266-269).

The Prince, forgiving the Friar, decides that the real villains are those who have kept up the feud which has finally destroyed the heirs of both warring families:

> Where be these enemies? Capulet, Montague,
> See what a scourge is laid upon your hate,
> That heaven finds means to kill your joys with love.
> And I, for winking at your discords too,
> Have lost a brace of kinsmen. All are punished.
>
> (291-295)

The solution comes with Capulet's "O brother Montague, give me thy hand" (296). Like saints or heroes, Romeo and Juliet will be given statues of pure gold that will remind all Verona of the merit of two martyrs. Their love finally serves a moral and religious purpose, healing the society of Verona. The conclusion of *Romeo and Juliet* should be stately and ceremonious, with no hurry. Looking on the dead lovers, who die that Verona may learn to live in peace, Capulet knows they are "Poor sacrifices to our enmity" (304). The Prince sums up: "A glooming peace this morning with it brings" (305).

## THE LOVERS AND THE PARTS

The two lovers are the core of the play, and they in particular must be well performed, or the play is unsuccessful on stage.

It has been said that Romeo is Hamlet in love. Both heroes are young, gifted, sensitive, melancholic, and unequal to a situation they cannot change. Romeo is an older teenager (maybe almost twenty) who is the scion of his family. He changes at significant moments in the play; it feels as though he grows in spurts. The actor's first task is to separate the segments that are significant in his growth from those that are not.

At first he is melancholic, full of the manners of courtly love and more in love with love than with Rosaline. He is immature, and the verse he speaks often uses a decorative method that gives him a unique voice:

> Why then, O brawling love, O loving hate,
> O anything, of nothing first create!
> O heavy lightness, serious vanity,
> Misshapen chaos of well-seeming forms ...   (I.i.176-179)

This highly coloured language can at times be accompanied by trite expressions, like:

> Show me a mistress that is passing fair,
> What doth her beauty serve but as a note
> Where I may read who passed that passing fair?
>
> (I.i.234-236)

This is boyish cynicism and shows he is posing to himself, posing to his family and friends, and he likes their concern on his behalf. But as he goes with the maskers to Capulet's feast, his mind:

> misgives
> Some consequence, yet hanging in the stars ...
>
> (I.iv.106-107)

which gives us the particular quality of Romeo. The actor must discover his unique melody of speech along with his significant moments of growth.

His love for Juliet transforms him into a man of action who expresses his love in rich and extravagant verse, full of conceits:

> more courtship lives
> In carrion flies than Romeo. They may seize

On the white wonder of the dear Juliet's hand ...
This may flies do, when I from this must fly.

(III.iii.34-40)

His language deepens as his dramatic situation deepens; what at first seems artificial becomes overwhelmingly real at the end where he outsoars everything else in the play.

Romeo and Juliet are youthful aristocrats. They are products of their families and their education, so they speak well and with assurance. They should not be, as Tyrone Guthrie said of Zeffirelli's lovers, charming young people who have never travelled further than Wimbledon. Juliet is a girl of fourteen. The player must focus on Juliet as a child — the whole play depends on it. Nor is such a youthful heroine unusual for Shakespeare: Miranda is fifteen, Perdita sixteen.

The player must see Juliet's story as a child's tragedy; this gives the part its poignancy. Many of her acts are those of a child: her bold innocence with her lover, her simple trust in her Nurse, her raging temper at Tybalt's death, and her ability to deceive her parents about matters of love. Her fears as she takes the potion become dreadful when the player performs them as childish terrors.

The performer should centre Juliet's conflict between love for her family and love for Romeo. This is the first major obstacle to her marriage to Romeo, as her response to the news of Tybalt's death reveals. But Juliet has a strong and intelligent will. She is sensitive to practical possibilities and the threat of violence; the intensity of her love for Romeo is seen in her willingness to undertake violent acts, like taking the potion and her final suicide.

She is passionately in love with Romeo, but she is no sensualist. Her love for Romeo is as she imagines him to be. In no other way could a boy-actress realize the part. As Granville-Barker pointed out, her passions have imagination for their fount.* The height of her ecstasy comes in the imaginative "Gallop apace, you fiery-footed steeds" which, although anticipated, is never quite realized sexually.

---

* Granville-Barker (1963).

## LANGUAGE

If any Shakespearean play depends on its poetry, it is *Romeo and Juliet*. The way the lovers cope with death, reconciling it with the longing they feel for each other, is through the richly complex language of their final speeches. Their artificiality has gone, replaced by closely packed figures that fuse opposite ideas rather than keep them apart in frozen verbal patterns: the lovers discover a medium wherein they experience the depth of feeling for which they have been striving.

The director and players must pay particular attention to the language. The play is full of quibbles and plays upon words. Elizabethans greatly admired such cleverness in serious as well as in comic situations, and *Romeo and Juliet* sparkles with such linguistic techniques. Today we are not so happy with this frequent verbal quibbling, particularly at moments of deep feeling, and audiences can resist it unless the director takes the greatest care. Indeed, some of the banter between the young men almost defies paraphrase, and the meaning can be entirely missed in the theatre. People incessantly use puns which, by embracing contradiction, can result in an intense compression of language, as when Juliet plays passionately upon "eye," "I" and "ay" (III.ii.45-51). Her feeling is paralleled by Romeo's anguish as he plays on the word "flies" (III.iii.40-43). Shakespeare also tries to reveal a profound disturbance of mind by such word games. He demonstrates the inadequacy of an ordered language* to deal with the emotions of Romeo and Juliet, a psychological discovery he puts to masterly use in later works. There are, in his greatest plays, many times when he allows words to acquire a great ambiguity at moments of intense emotion.

The fewer quibbles in the final scenes have great power. When Romeo has drunk the poison he reaffirms the central paradox of the play:

> O true Apothecary!
> Thy drugs are quick. Thus with a kiss I die.
>
> (V.iii.119-120)

---

* For example, Friar Laurence's confidence in "armour to keep off [the] word" (III.iii.55) is unsubstantiated.

The apothecary's poison (like the Friar's herbs) both heals and destroys: "His drugs are not only speedy, but also quick in the sense of 'life-giving.' Romeo and Juliet 'cease to die, by dying'."* At the most emotional moments Shakespeare uses the ambiguities of words to stress the sublimity and pathos of the situation; they keep the play's imagery in a rich design and provide an outlet for the tumultuous feelings of the central characters.

As always, it is Shakespeare's imagery that remains in the mind. Caroline Spurgeon discovered a repeating, or iterative, imagery in individual plays: disease in *Hamlet,* gardens in *Richard II,* animals in action in *Othello,* and so on.** In *Romeo and Juliet,* as we have seen, there are two predominant image-clusters: love-death, with death the Bridegroom, and light-dark being good and evil.

*Romeo and Juliet* is poetic drama. It is written in such a way that the audience can consciously appreciate the beauty or vivacity of the language. Eventually in his career Shakespeare united this stylization with natural human expression. But here the imagery and language work within specific conventions. The major mode is blank verse, unrhymed iambic pentameter, with variations. The verse at the beginning is smooth and swift while its music is descriptive, so much so that character can be forgotten. Thus the Prince's speech is stern and authoritative, yet he himself has virtually no character. But then:

> *Enter Lady Capulet and Nurse.*
> LADY C:   Nurse, where's my daughter? Call her forth
>                   to me.
> NURSE:   Now, by my maidenhead at twelve year old,
>                   I bade her come. What, lamb! What, lady-
>                   bird! — God forbid! — Where's this girl?
>                   What, Juliet!                                   (I.iii.1-4)

Suddenly the artifice has gone, and the action has such a reality that the theatre seems unreal. The superb character of the Nurse brings the dramatic medium alive; Shakespeare moulds the blank verse convention to the spontaneous expression of her character.

---

* Mahood (1968).

** Spurgeon (1935).

Shakespeare also creates his own linguistic conventions. His diction is dependent on his concept of decorum. Who people *are* determines how they speak: the comic servants and the young bachelors converse in prose with a realistic vocabulary; the lovers speak in heightened blank verse; the Friar and the Prince talk in rhymed blank verse — an impersonal expression suited to their positions — and a lofty but direct choice of words.

*Romeo and Juliet* is Shakespeare's first attempt at tragedy. The *play world* is indeed tragic but not because the ending achieves a tragic equilibrium. It is tragic because it excites and sustains a deep concern with humanity in the ills that befall it. The final victory of time and society over the lovers is counterpoised by the knowledge that it is, in a sense, also their victory. It is a triumph over the most insidious enemy of love, inner hate, and therefore over the world of death.

# JULIUS CAESAR

## THE ROMAN WORLD OF DEATH

T he world of death in *Julius Caesar* has a different feeling from the worlds in the other tragedies discussed in this book. In *Romeo and Juliet*, death the bridegroom is ever-present, while in *Hamlet* the atmosphere is of the graveyard. In both plays the idea of death is ever-present, infused in the very air the people breathe.

In *Julius Caesar*, however, the world of death is the focus of the story. Here death means bloodshed. The assassination of Julius Caesar occurs in the middle of the play; everything leads up to it or away from it. The conspirators kill Caesar because of his egotism: as republicans, they fear he will become a dictator. Brutus keeps the conspirators from killing other Romans by saying the plotters are sacrificers, not butchers. Yet immediately after the murder, Brutus proposes a ritual blood bath over Caesar's body; they stoop and wash their hands in his blood. Are they then sacrificers or butchers? Brutus accepts republicanism as an honourable end that justifies the means: Caesar's murder, but he tries to dignify the act by making it a ceremony. In attempting to make his actions fit the exalted role he thinks he has, he reveals that his own egotism is as bad as Caesar's. Indeed, their tragedies are complementary.

## THE TRAGIC MODE

*Julius Caesar* is tragic in two ways: as the individual tragedies of Caesar, Brutus and Cassius and the public tragedy of those who falsely alter the course of history. It addresses both kinds of tragic issues and raises other questions, universal and particular. Would Caesar have become a dictator? Is the assassination of a *potential* dictator justified? If so, how? In fact, the failure of Brutus and his colleagues results in the death of liberty. The conspirators rely on the idea of *honour*. Cassius has significant things to say about it, and Brutus stakes all on it. He declares that he loves "The name of honour more than I fear death" (I.ii.89). Brutus wants the conspirators to bind themselves by honour only. They are, he tells Antony after the assassination, full of "good regard [purposes]" (III.i.224). Cassius decides that Brutus' "honourable mettle" (I.ii.306) may be changed; there is no one who cannot be "seduced" (I.ii.309), and he successfully brings Brutus into the plot. Is Cassius right? Is no one entirely honest and honourable?

If the director assumes that *Julius Caesar* is a fairly traditional revenge tragedy, then Caesar is the dominant figure, and after his death his spirit relentlessly pursues Brutus to his doom. But the few lines of the Ghost when it appears are not highly significant; nor does Brutus show any sign of the remorse proper to the conventional Elizabethan avenger when visited by a spirit.

The director might interpret the Ghost of Caesar as if it were the spirit of Roman imperialism: the republican principles of Brutus strive in vain against it because the old constitution is doomed by economic and historical changes. However, there is virtually no direct evidence to support this view, and it is very unlikely that Shakespeare believed in historical determinism.

*Julius Caesar* is commonly interpreted as the tragedy of Brutus, the idealist in politics. Idealism and *realpolitik* are certainly contrasted in the play, but they are not its tragic core: the distinction is not sufficiently precise, and Brutus' failures are due more to his bad judgment than to his idealism.

What makes *Julius Caesar* unique among Shakespeare's tragedies is that he does not present one tragic view; Shakespeare sides with neither party. The verdict, if there must be a verdict, he leaves to the audience. His genius shows us many significant and different facets of this tragedy. He deliberately contrasts the private person and the public *persona*, the face and the mask. The tragic illusion wrenches apart the two worlds, personal and public, to give us many perspectives on the events.

The result is a *play world* that is highly complex. Although *Julius Caesar* is the work most often chosen to introduce young students to Shakespeare, this does not mean that the play is lacking in artistic or intellectual subtlety. *Julius Caesar* is the most accessible and deceptive of Shakespeare's plays: the action is swift but complex, the story plain though rich in meaning, the poetry easy yet significant, the characters dignified but uncomplicated. Indeed, the play has a "classic" air of simplicity and clarity.

The play is extremely popular, but it is not metaphysical like *Othello, King Lear* or *Macbeth*; and no character in it is as deeply drawn as Hamlet or Cleopatra. The action in *Julius Caesar* is swift, clear, and superbly organized. The moral and political issues raised by the assassination and its consequences are both significant and timeless. The characters are interesting, diverse as individuals, and splendidly actable. And its tragic perspectives reveal many facets of the human condition.

## HISTORY OF THE PLAY

All the evidence points to 1599 as the date of *Julius Caesar.* This is a time of extraordinary achievement in Shakespeare's working life: he recently completed the great histories, *1 and 2 Henry IV* and *Henry V,* together with *The Merry Wives of Windsor,* it is the period when he writes three masterly comedies, *Much Ado About Nothing, As You Like It* and *Twelfth Night,* and he has probably begun *Hamlet.* Indeed, *Julius Caesar* is the door through which Shakespeare passes to the writing of his great tragedies.

*Julius Caesar* is Shakespeare's first mature attempt to explore the world of ancient Rome; new horizons open to him with mighty themes to develop. He closely examines the contradictions and illusions of political action. The assassination of Caesar in 44 B.C. exerted a profound influence on Medieval and Renaissance men of letters. Informed Elizabethans saw in the Roman civil wars parallels to their own Wars of the Roses. The prevailing opinion was that the principal people in the play were complicated human beings. This ambivalence is reflected in Shakespeare. As always, he is interested more in character than in plot.

While Shakespeare probably knew and was influenced by a variety of works on Caesar, he based his play almost totally on one of the most popular histories of the time: Plutarch's *Lives of the Noble Grecians and Romans,* published in 1579 in the English translation of Sir Thomas North (a volume of 1,175 pages detailing the lives of fifty men); a second edition was released in 1595. This book provides most of the material for *Julius Caesar, Antony and Cleopatra,* and *Coriolanus,* together with the plot of *Timon of Athens.* In *Julius Caesar,* Plutarch gives Shakespeare not only the story he must follow but also the living characters.

A Swiss doctor, Thomas Platter, visited London in 1599, and gives us a brief eye-witness account of an Elizabethan performance of *Julius Caesar:*

> On September 21, 1599: After lunch, at about two
> o'clock, I and my companions rode over the water.
> There, in the house with the thatched roof we saw
> the tragedy of the first Emperor Julius Caesar excel-
> lently performed by about fifteen persons; at the end
> of the play, as is their custom, they danced very skill-
> fully, in groups of four, two in men's clothing and
> two in women's.*

*Julius Caesar* was almost certainly one of the first plays to be performed by the Lord Chamberlain's Men at their new theatre, The Globe, which they had built on the Bankside in the early months of that year [see *End Notes*].

The tragedy was first printed in the Folio edition of Shakespeare's plays of 1623. This excellent version is probably of a transcript rather than Shakespeare's own script. The play has been continuously popular except for the last quarter of the eighteenth century.**

The prompter in Davenant's company, Thomas Downes, recorded various performances of the tragedy until the early eighteenth century, including one by Quinn (badly) and both Robert Wilks and William Milward as Antony. In John Kemble's revival at Covent Garden (1812), which was seen by the German critic Ludwig Tieck, Kemble played Brutus, while

---

* See Nagler (1964) 7.

** For stage history, see Sprague (1944, 1953) and Sprague and Trewin (1970).

Charles Mayne Young was a notable Cassius. Later Macready also played Cassius. In 1881 the Meiningen Court Company performed several Shakespearean plays in London, including *Julius Caesar* which was greatly admired for its ensemble.

The play has remained popular in the twentieth century, with many renowned performances including those of Henry Ainley and Christopher Plummer (Antony), John Gielgud (Cassius) and Brian Bedford (Brutus). In the early years it still endured heavy cutting. The play can also suffer from huge realistic sets, as when Godfrey Tearle's ponderous but majestic Mark Antony (Alhambra, London, 1934) appeared among tons of marble. It was much easier to handle the crowd scenes with two staircases up from the pit, which Harcourt Williams used at Sadler's Wells (1932). The line "But I am constant as the northern star" (III.i.60) prompted the ingenious Glen Byam Shaw to use a single star that remained in the sky from the Forum scene onwards (Stratford-upon-Avon, 1957). A different view was given by the designer Nicholas Georgiadis, who saw Rome as a place of rough and rusty scaffolding with its citizens most shabbily arrayed (Old Vic, 1962).

*Julius Caesar* works very well on an open stage. This was clear from the first modern production on such a stage (Stratford, Ontario, 1955; director Michael Langham), which had a brilliant Canadian cast: Robert Christie (Caesar), Lorne Greene (Brutus), Lloyd Bochner (Cassius), Donald Davis (Antony), Donald Harron (Octavius), Douglas Campbell (Casca), Bruno Gerussi (Marcellus and Pindarus), and William Shatner (Lucius). *Julius Caesar* has also been made into two films. The first (1953: director, Joseph L. Mankiewicz), which was well received, included John Gielgud (Cassius), James Mason (Brutus), Marlon Brando (Antony), Louis Calhern (Caesar) and Edmund O'Brien (Casca). Less well received was the second (1969: director Stuart Burge) with Charlton Heston (Antony) and Gielgud once more, this time as a stately but irritable Caesar.

## PERSPECTIVES AND ILLUSIONS

In *Julius Caesar* a significant act can assume different shapes, as a statue does when seen from different positions. Calpurnia's dream of one:

Which, like a fountain with an hundred spouts,
Did run pure blood ...                                    (II.ii.77-78)

becomes for Decius "a vision fair and fortunate" (II.ii.84).

Likewise the assassination, the central act of the tragedy, is seen in different ways. It is a noble act for liberty and freedom for the conspirators; but it must appear, Brutus says, a necessary deed, and Caesar himself a tyrant rather than legal ruler, "Or else were this a savage spectacle" (III.i.223). The assassination is many things to many people. Antony sees those who did it as "butchers" (III.i.254). "As Caesar loved me," Brutus says, "I weep for him; as he was fortunate, I rejoice at it; as he was valiant, I honour him; but, as he was ambitious, I slew him" (III.ii.24-26). What we know about the event consists of separate observations; all are "true" to the person making them. There is some truth in the view that Caesar seeks power, but a simple judgment cannot be made. Brutus, however, does simplify, concentrating on a selection of the facts in the interest of an abstract view of "the general good":

It must be by his death; and for my part,
I know no personal cause to spurn at him,
But for the general.                                    (II.i.10-12)

In this way Brutus gets caught up in a web of specious argument, and he constructs his own *play world*: a fiction where he sees reality as he *wishes* it to be. This unreal world — the imaginative world where his decisions are formed — does not match reality, the actual world where acts have necessary consequences. Thus his choices and his resulting actions are disastrous. Brutus deceives himself: he tries to make the public world independent of the practical world of living human beings:

O, that we then could come by Caesar's spirit,
And not dismember Caesar! But, alas,
Caesar must bleed for it. And, gentle friends,
Let's kill him boldly, but not wrathfully;
Let's carve him as a dish fit for the gods,
Not hew him as a carcass fit for hounds.    (II.i.169-174)

But this is far from practical reality, as Antony reminds us later:

... when your vile daggers
Hacked one another in the sides of Caesar:
You showed your teeth like apes, and fawned like
hounds ...                                              (V.i.39-41)

The incongruity between the intention and the effect is ironically under-lined in the excited proclamation after the murder:

> And waving our red weapons o'er our heads,
> Let's all cry, 'Peace, freedom, and liberty!'

(III.i.109-110)

In this sense the play is a powerful study of illusion in public life: over-simplification for "reasons of state" is an ineffective illusion.

Illusion is a powerful focus in all of Shakespeare's plays. One way in which it affects *Julius Caesar* is in the theme of the Player King. Casca scornfully describes how Antony offers Caesar a crown before the populace of Rome, and the common people "clap him and hiss him, according as he pleased and displeased them, as they use to do the players in the theatre" (I.ii.256-258). It is common for Shakespeare to use theatrical imagery to express the insecurity of a king — the fatal division between the individual and the crown, the real king and the mock king.

People in *Julius Caesar* often remark that they see themselves in disguise, an image that derives from the Elizabethan theatre. Brutus bids the conspirators model themselves upon the players:

> Let not our looks put on our purposes,
> But bear it as our Roman actors do,
> With untired spirits and formal constancy. (II.i.225-227)

As the conspirators bend down to bathe their hands in Caesar's blood, they reflect on the immortality they have gained:

> CAS:   Stoop then, and wash. How many ages hence
> Shall this our lofty scene be acted over,
> In states unborn, and accents yet unknown!
> BRU:   How many times shall Caesar bleed in sport,
> That now on Pompey's basis lies along,
> No worthier than the dust!
> CAS:         So oft as that shall be,
> So often shall the knot of us be called
> The men that gave their country liberty.

(III.i.111-119)

These three speeches are very significant and catch our attention in the theatre. Shakespeare's play is suddenly defined as a play. Members of the audience become keenly self-conscious about themselves and their responses. There is an ironic discrepancy between the characters' assumptions about their activity and its true nature.

The scene shows that an event in life is potential material for drama. Thus it belongs to a most traditional class of play images (e.g., a Plautine joke with the audience or an excuse for artificiality) but it has a different quality from many of these.

The stage is glorified, because the actors, Shakespeare's own company (his companions and friends), are the chroniclers of great human deeds; in the theatre the noble actions of the world are preserved for future generations.

Cassius glorifies the murder of Caesar and thereby defines himself as better than he is, showing a self superior to reality. Self-glorification is absent from most of the explicit role-playing, but projecting a representation of the self which is superior to reality is the most characteristic act of the people in the play.

As Anne Righter writes about this kind of play-acting,

> Nothing quite like this attitude can be found in the plays of Shakespeare's contemporaries. Their work abounds with topical references, with the sort of comment on the London theatre which now requires an explanatory footnote. It is against the background of such a passage that one must see not only the "Roman actors" of *Julius Caesar* but also the tragedians of the city who arrive so suddenly at Elsinore, "the abstract and brief chronicles of the time" *(Hamlet,* II.ii.518).*

There are many allusions to role-playing in *Julius Caesar,* and all evoke the idea of discrepancy. After Casca describes Caesar's rejection of the crown as fakery, he sees the whole occasion in theatrical terms: "If the tag-rag people did not clap him and hiss him, according as he pleased and displeased them, as they use to do the players in the theatre, I am no true man" (I.ii.256-259). Brutus advises his fellow conspirators to "look fresh and merrily" (II.i.224) on the morning of the assassination; in performance, their fixed smiles become an acted

---

* Righter (1982).

metaphor of discrepant role-playing. Antony later uses the conspirators' own technique against them when he hides his intentions and then makes the speech which rouses the Roman crowd. Notably, Lucilius at Philippi poses as Brutus in order to protect him. In fact, this theme is present from the beginning of the play. When the commoners are milling about the streets of Rome, what first disturbs the Tribunes Flavius and Marullus is that the plebeians are out of costume; they fail to observe the proper decorum, and they misplay their social roles (I.i.1-8). Thomas Van Laan has shown that this idea is so pervasive that it is part of the play's structure.*

Finally, *Julius Caesar* is pervaded by the role of "lover." In none of Shakespeare's other plays do the words "love" and "lover" occur so often. Specifically, the terms indicate the love of deep friendship and not sexual love. Even Portia's role with Brutus is one of gentle companionship rather than of sexual passion. Most people in the play see themselves in the roles of "lovers." There are many major and minor love-themes: love is expressed or suggested between Brutus and Cassius, Brutus and Caesar, and Antony and Caesar; Brutus and Portia, Brutus and Volumnius, Brutus and Lucius; Caesar and Decius, Cassius and Lucius Pella, Cassius and Titinius; Ligarius and Brutus, Artemidorus and Caesar. G. Wilson Knight says that the atmosphere of the play is charged with a general eroticism but not passion: "Love is here the regal, the conquering reality: the murder of Caesar is a gash in the body of Rome, and this gash is healed by love, so that the play's action emphasizes first the disjointing of 'spirit' from 'matter' which is evil, fear, anarchy; and then the remating of these two elements into the close fusion which is love, order, peace."** Though the events may be "Most bloody, fiery, and most terrible" (I.iii.130), and the action is spirited and adventurous with noble blood spilt bravely in the third act, yet the roles people play in their inter-actions are often of gentle sentiment, melting hearts, tears and the soft fire of love.

## STRUCTURE

*Julius Caesar* is the play in which the boundaries of Shakespeare's art begin to widen with a bold and free stage-

---

* Van Laan (1978).
** Knight (1967).

craft. While his play construction was strong from his beginnings, there is a new masterly ease in this play's structure. He is helped by Plutarch's ability to make, with a brief touch, even small characters vividly human, and by the Globe's stage [see *End Notes*], with its freedom to work with people and incidents.

## THE STRUCTURAL UNIT

*Julius Caesar* illustrates very well the details of Shakespeare's methods of construction. He builds his plays with the following elements: an act + a speech = the primary unit; several primary units = dramatic action; a segment of dramatic action = a scene; and several scenes = a play.

An act is what people do, either physically (a motion) or mentally (an idea).* Shakespeare begins I.i with the following acts:

[1] Flavius tells the crowd to go home (1),

[2] on a working day when they are not dressed for work (2-5).

[3] One commoner says he is a carpenter (6).

[4] Marullus asks where his apron and rule are, and why he has his best clothes on (7-8).

Shakespeare then translates this into speech:

FLA:  Hence! home, you idle creatures, get you home:
      Is this a holiday? What, know you not,
      Being mechanical, you ought not walk
      Upon a labouring day without the sign
      Of your profession? Speak, what trade art thou?

CAR:  Why, sir, a carpenter.

MAR:  Where is thy leather apron, and thy rule?
      What dost thou with thy best apparel on?

(I.i.1-8)

Each scene is made up of many such dramatic actions; how they connect depends on the purpose of the scene. For example: I.i shows:

• the confrontation of the commoners by the Tribunes (the plot's action); the crowd's amiable mindlessness is com-

---

* In the history of world theatre, the primary dramatic act is the Vaunt: the "I am" physical and spoken statement that is the basis of all ritual drama (found today, for example, in the English Mummers' Play, the Japanese *Noh* theatre, the South India *Kathakali* theatre).

pared to the stricter attitudes of the Tribunes (an atmospheric contrast which prefigures the contrast of Brutus with the mob);
- the time is the moment of Julius Caesar's arrival in Rome; it is also a religious day, the Lupercal; after the commoners have gone, the Tribunes remove the decorations from Caesar's statues (temporal action);
- the place is a street in Rome;
- the situation, the commoners' illegal roaming in the streets and holiday from work, is condemned by their own representatives, the Tribunes (they guard republicanism and require more intelligence from the commoners).

Each scene is a fully conceived unit carefully designed to contribute to the forward movement of the total play. In *Julius Caesar,* the whole is unified through the particular use of time, space, ritual, illusion-reality, movement and linear structures.

## TIME AND SPACE

The unities of time and place are not observed in *Julius Caesar;* they rarely are by Shakespeare. As always, his plays operate in the "here and now," even though *Julius Caesar* is about historical events. He telescopes actual historical time to fit performance time.

The structure of time in *Julius Caesar* is designed by the way speech relates to sound effects and music. Orally and aurally the play moves in a unique way. In the middle action, for example, it moves as follows:
- the cheerful flourishes and shouts of approval for Caesar;
- the fiercely ominous roar of the thunderstorm, briefly interrupted;
- the flourish that brings Caesar to the Senate House;
- the renewed shouts of the crowd as they move from approval of Brutus to a howling for blood incited by the oratory of Mark Antony;
- the final chaotic hubbub of the killing of Cinna the poet.

This pattern of ceremonial sound, crowd voices, speech and thunder continues to the resolution on the battlefield amid the military marches and alarums; the musical contrast in this clamorous battle sequence comes in the quiet song of Lucius in Brutus' tent. Typically, a Shakespearean play is built around the musical contrast of tempest (chaos) and harmony (order). The director should plan to unify speech with sound so as to accord with Shakespeare's temporal structure.

The space of *Julius Caesar* is designed around various localities in Rome (I.i–III.iii) and at or near Philippi (IV.i–V.v). The action well fits the staging principles of the *house* and the *place* [see *End Notes*], particularly as many scenes are continuous.

I have directed *Julius Caesar* twice using the principles of the *house* and the *place*. In both cases I had to cope with very difficult spaces which had to be adapted to Shakespeare's spatial requirements. In my first production, with an all-male cast (Harehills School, Leeds, 1953), I created an open stage: at the rear of an existing small proscenium stage was a sky-cloth; in front of this stage, three steps led down to a forestage of greater width; from the forestage, it was two steps down to the auditorium floor, with entries on either side. The only decoration was a statue of Pompey on the proscenium stage for Acts I-III, which was replaced with a windswept tree for Acts IV-V. This arrangement worked very well: in Acts I-III, interior scenes were played on the stage, street scenes on the forestage, and the crowds poured out of the side entries onto the auditorium floor and forestage; in Acts IV-V, the battles were fought on the auditorium floor, generals in the field met on the forestage, and interiors (IV.i and IV.iii) were played on the stage.*

The production of *Julius Caesar* I designed for Bradford Civic Hall (1956) faced greater physical obstacles, and the results were less satisfactory. I had to contend with a flight of wall-to-wall steps of enormous width, leading up to an organ of great height. In front of these steps was a narrow wall-to-wall forestage with entries either side; this had bad sight-lines from most of the auditorium, so I used it and the first step for the crowd and the battles. I designed huge grey draperies to cover the organ and its pipes and also to simulate three *houses* halfway up the great flight of steps. When lighting instruments were hidden behind the draperies eight feet above the actors'

---

* This production also demonstrated that Shakespeare's writing for the two female characters (Portia and Calphurnia) is admirably suited to young male actors. Neither teenage boy is asked to express an emotion outside his normal experience.

heads, the great height of the organ and the auditorium ceiling became lost in darkness.

## RITUAL

The structure of *Julius Caesar* is infused with ritual and ceremony. Derived largely but not slavishly from Plutarch, the theme of incantation and ritual is prominent throughout the tragedy. Its high point is the assassination — Brutus' sacrificial rite — followed by Antony's comments upon butchery under the guise of sacrifice that takes its ironical final form in the parley before Philippi (IV.iv).

The play begins by emphasizing "mock-ceremony." In I.i, the Tribunes denounce the ceremony planned for Caesar's entry, send the idolatrous crowd to rites of purification, and then themselves desecrate the devotional images. In I.ii, the many ceremonies conclude with Casca's satire which turns the crown ritual into a lunatic farce. In Act V, both Cassius and Brutus commit suicide with due regard to the proper ritual.

## ILLUSION AND REALITY

*Julius Caesar* dramatizes human failure by stressing the unsatisfactory reality people experience ("history") despite their grandiose dreams. The main characters exemplify a contrast between what they think themselves to be and what they really are, between their false and their true selves, between dream and reality. The whole action of the play is structured around the contrasts between people's aspirations and what really happens to them. The roles people play are merely the outer, explicit dimension of a dramatic design that embraces the entire action of the play. This design is embodied in Cassius' anticipation of future plays.

## RHYTHMS

The larger rhythms of *Julius Caesar* are two: that of Acts I, II and III, and that of IV and V. The first of these, which is framed by crowd scenes, is virtually continuous: it is one of rising tension (despite small falls) to the climax of the assassination, a second climax with Antony's speech in the Forum, and the final chaos of the street murder of Cinna the Poet. It is superbly designed and executed, one of Shakespeare's greatest structural achievements.

The second large rhythm is that of retribution overcoming the conspirators in battle. It begins with a horrifyingly cold scene (IV.i) where Caesar's successors plan the non-republican future of Rome in a slow and methodical rhythm. From IV.i to the end, however, the rhythm is that of war and the cumulative collapse of the republican cause; it steadily gathers speed until Brutus's death, when it relaxes into a final calm.

## LINEAR STRUCTURE

Shakespeare's structure probably had no acts, and in accordance with Elizabethan stage practice, many of the scenes were continuous. However, the acts inserted by later editors make more dramatic sense in *Julius Caesar* than in most of Shakespeare's plays. The rhythm of the play has the following Movements:

*First Movement* (I.i–III.iii)

> Caesar's murder is the theme. The action moves in a barely checked crescendo. The mob is a recurrent chorus of confusion that begins and ends this Movement. It has the following segments:
>
> - Introduction (I.i–I.iii): This begins with the mob harangued by the Tribunes and ends in the height of the storm.
> - The conspirators win Brutus (II.i–II.iv): This begins at night with Brutus reading the letters and ends with Portia and the Soothsayer.
> - The assassination and its immediate effects (III.i–III.iii): This begins with the ominous
>   CAESAR:   The Ides of March are come.
>   SOOTH:   Ay, Caesar, but not gone.   (III.i.1-2)
> It ends with the mob's murder of Cinna the Poet.

*Second Movement* (IV.i–V.v)

> The murder's retribution is the theme. The scenes are martial and, for all the fighting at the end, are consistently pitched in a lower key than the First Movement. This movement has the following segments:
>
> - Preparations for war (IV.i–IV.iii): This begins with Antony's sinister, "These many then shall die; their names are pricked" (IV.i.1), and concludes with the tent scene of Brutus and Cassius.

- The Battle of Philippi (V.i–V.v): This begins with
  Octavius' triumphant "Now, Antony, our hopes
  are answerèd" (V.i.1) and concludes with the
  deaths of Cassius and Brutus.

The play is too long to be acted without at least one pause
today. This naturally occurs at the end of Act III.

## ACTION

### First Movement: The Assassination

*Rome is politically divided as Caesar makes his triumphant
entry in 44 B.C., following his defeat of Pompey's sons,
after Pompey's death. In the street two factions quarrel: the
populace approves of Caesar; the Tribunes, republicans, are
opposed to rule by one man (I.i).*

In a colourful street scene on the Feast of Lupercal
(February 15), the Romans in holiday mood celebrate Caesar's
victory. Flavius shouts:

Hence! home, you idle creatures, get you home:
Is this a holiday?                                    (1-2)

These and other lines operate as stage directions for the commoners.

Roman "triumphs" (city processions) were only made over
foreigners, never over Roman citizens — which Caesar now
does. Flavius and Marullus, two Tribunes (protectors of commoners' rights), are republicans; they support government by
the people and bitterly oppose the Caesar idea of rule by one
man. Marullus rebukes the people for their idolatry of Caesar:

Wherefore rejoice? What conquest brings he home?
What tributaries follow him to Rome,
To grace in captive bonds his chariot wheels?
You blocks, you stones, you worse than senseless things!
O you hard hearts, you cruel men of Rome,
Knew you not Pompey? Many a time and oft
Have you climbed up to walls and battlements,
To towers and windows, yea, to chimney-tops,
Your infants in your arms, and there have sat
The livelong day, with patient expectation,
To see great Pompey pass the streets of Rome ...

And do you now put on your best attire?
And do you now cull out a holiday?
And do you now strew flowers in his way,
That comes in triumph over Pompey's blood?     (32-51)
Marullus prescribes a ritual expiation:
Run to your houses, fall upon your knees,
Pray to the gods to intermit the plague
That needs must light on this ingratitude.     (53-55)
Though the verbal cleverness of the cobbler exasperates Flavius
and Marullus, the people obey and go to conduct these rites of
atonement. The two Tribunes remove the wreaths or garlands
from Caesar's statues.

The director should note that the first full speech of the
play has Pompey for a theme: the player should emphasize the
first sound of his name. The scene anticipates the later civil
strife: we note that the crowd can be swayed, controlled and
silenced; it gives a unity to the First Movement by its presence
at the start and finish.

Flavius and Marullus leave the stage at one side; immediately the object of their fear, Caesar himself, enters at the other
side.

> *Caesar and his train pass across the stage. Cassius plays
> on Brutus' fears of Caesar's ambition. Caesar returns,
> voicing his distrust of Cassius to Antony before he departs.
> Casca tells Brutus and Cassius that Caesar was thrice
> offered the crown but rejected it. Cassius thinks he can get
> Brutus to join the plot to kill Caesar (I.ii).*

After the disorder of the first scene, Julius Caesar's spectacular procession enters with music and a huge crowd of friends
and officials — a great stage effect. We see Caesar briefly, but
his dominance is given simply: over the hubbub we hear his
name sounded seven times in twenty-four lines. On stage, the
very name dominates.

They are going to the Forum to celebrate the festival of
Lupercal: younger public officials, stripped to the waist, are to
run an ancient foot race. Caesar's legendary eminence is
emphasized as everyone's attention hangs on his words, "Peace,
ho! Caesar speaks" (1). He tells his wife, Calphurnia, to stand
near the runners; he orders Antony, one of the runners, to

remember to touch her since this ritual is supposed to cure a woman of barrenness. Finally Caesar commands: "Set on, and leave no ceremony out" (11). Shakespeare's emphasis on ritual and ceremonial is based on Plutarch's description of the Lupercalia.

The procession is about to move on when a Soothsayer calls to Caesar to beware the Ides of March (March 15th). Caesar dismisses him as a dreamer. He disregards any sort of warning (here and later). Caesar's pride contributes to his downfall. Shakespeare often uses predictions to create ominous anticipation. The procession passes.

We reach the first of two great duets between Brutus and Cassius. Cassius leads throughout. The interchange is accompanied by the off-stage noise of a symbolic spectacle. Brutus is withdrawn:

> I am not gamesome: I do lack some part
> Of that quick spirit that is in Antony.
> Let me not hinder, Cassius, your desires;
> I'll leave you.                              (28-31)

The first line is ironic. As Granville-Barker says, it gives us something of Brutus' quality — thoughtful, dispassionate, aloof, and a little cold — which is expanded later.* Cassius' first approach to Brutus is:

> I do observe you now of late:
> I have not from your eyes that gentleness
> And show of love as I was wont to have.       (32-34)

Cassius' passion and swift pace give tone and colour to the long duologue that follows. He is partly an ascetic and partly a fanatic; he is envious and thin-skinned, quick to resent any slight. Brutus says he is "with himself at war" (46) — which is Cassius' opportunity to hint at assassination. Brutus is cautious:

> Into what dangers would you lead me, Cassius,
> That you would have me seek into myself
> For that which is not in me?                  (63-65)

Cassius begins his masterly persuasion. He starts cautiously, but two offstage shouts from the crowd, carefully placed in the development of the argument, bring forth almost involuntary responses from Brutus. He, too, thinks about Caesar and his

---

* Granville-Barker (1963).

ambition. To Brutus' first reaction

> I do fear the people
>
> Choose Caesar for their king.                              (78-79)

Cassius replies with great care: "Then must I think you would not have it so." Cassius wants Brutus, rather than himself, to be the one who first suggests the danger of Caesar. Brutus plays into his hands:

> What is it that you would impart to me?
>
> If it be aught toward the general good,
>
> Set honour in one eye, and death i'th'other,
>
> And I will look on both indifferently;
>
> For let the gods so speed me as I love
>
> The name of honour more than I fear death.     (84-89)

But Cassius is too clever to press the point home immediately. Instead, he takes up Brutus' phrase, "the name of honour," and likens honour to the idea of freedom — specifically with freedom from Caesar. Cassius is totally sincere in his belief that he

> had as lief not be as live to be
>
> In awe of such a thing as I myself                       (95-96)

because he was "born as free as Caesar."

Brutus' ignorance of Cassius' manipulation makes him look naive; he is so wrapped in himself that he hears only the ideas that are connected to his own. Cassius uses Caesar's physical limitations, given in Plutarch, to demonstrate his weakness. The story of Cassius' rescue of Caesar from the Tiber reduces Caesar from godlike superiority to human frailty:

> The torrent roared, and we did buffet it
>
> With lusty sinews, throwing it aside
>
> And stemming it with hearts of controversy.
>
> But ere we would arrive the point proposed,
>
> Caesar cried, 'Help me, Cassius, or I sink!'     (107-111)

He sees Caesar's political success as a personal injustice:

> And this man
>
> Is now become a god, and Cassius is
>
> A wretched creature, and must bend his body
>
> If Caesar carelessly but nod on him.                  (115-118)

About here, the actor finds Cassius' long speech is very demanding; it takes great skill to deliver the many monosyllables in an agreeable and natural rhythm, as when he remarks with disdain:

And when the fit was on him, I did mark
How he did shake; 'tis true, this god did shake ...
                                                    (120-121)

Cassius is now in full flight. Once he knows Brutus will listen,
his appeals to justice and morality increasingly include personal hatred and envy. Cassius' political ability is limited to immediate practice; politics consists of personal interaction at which
he is awkward, although he craves success at it.

Cassius increases the bitterness of his attack until, at
Brutus' reaction to another offstage shout, Cassius' voice rises
to the fury of:

Why, man, he doth bestride the narrow world
Like a Colossus, and we petty men
Walk under his huge legs, and peep about
To find ourselves dishonourable graves.        (134-137)

This great metaphor is stark, vivid, dramatic. It jolts us for it is
double. Caesar is first juxtaposed to the world: he is so mighty
that he "bestrides" it in a stance, compared to the Colossus,
which brings him vividly before our eyes. Secondly, other men
are juxtaposed to Caesar: they are "petty," so small as to "walk
about under his huge legs"; their vision is described with a min-
imizing verb — they "peep about" only to find "dishonourable
graves" because there is nothing else for them. This disgusts
Cassius. To him, we are masters of our own destiny:

Men at some time are masters of their fates;
The fault, dear Brutus, is not in our stars,
But in ourselves, that we are underlings.        (138-140)

Brutus is still noncommittal. At first puzzled ("What is it
that you would impart to me?"), he is not interested in political
intrigue. We are uncertain how far Brutus has understood him,
but it would be unlike Brutus to accept Cassius' plan immediately. Brutus is not a passionless man, though he may both
despise passion and dread it. A minute later he says:

I would not — so with love I might entreat you —
Be any further moved.                            (165-166)

The player must not compete here with Cassius, who dominates this scene. What Brutus says is ambiguous, but we learn
much about him by the way he talks: choppy rhythms, brief
phrases and short sentences suggest the restricted speech of a
man caught in a powerful conflict. It contrasts with the passion-

ate rhythms of Cassius and his long, powerful phrases. Brutus ends with an uneasy and inconclusive assertion:

> Brutus had rather be a villager
> Than to repute himself a son of Rome
> Under these hard conditions as this time
> Is like to lay upon us. (171-174)

He is almost hooked. Cassius must add but a little more bait to his line.

The games over, the procession returns. Caesar looks angry, Calphurnia is pale, and Cicero is raging inwardly. Antony is obsequious, and Caesar enjoys it. Caesar notes Cassius' presence and, suspicious of him, tells Antony that he distrusts thin, discontented-looking men like Cassius:

> CAE: Let me have men about me that are fat,
> Sleek-headed men, and such as sleep a-nights.
> Yond Cassius has a lean and hungry look;
> He thinks too much: such men are dangerous.
>
> ANT: Fear him not, Caesar; he's not dangerous;
> He is a noble Roman, and well given.
>
> CAE: Would he were fatter! But I fear him not;
> Yet if my name were liable to fear,
> I do not know the man I should avoid
> So soon as that spare Cassius. He reads much,
> He is a great observer, and he looks
> Quite through the deeds of men. He loves no plays,
> As thou dost, Antony; he hears no music ...
> (191-203)

It is ironic that it is Caesar himself who indicates the threat of Cassius most clearly, but when he says,

> I rather tell thee what is to be feared
> Than what I fear; for always I am Caesar (210-211)

his arrogance makes it impossible for him to see the danger he is in. Then Caesar tells us of another weakness (not mentioned in any of the sources):

> Come on my right hand, for this ear is deaf,
> And tell me truly what thou think'st of him. (212-213)

We find two Caesars: the ailing and petulant old man and the colossal spirit commanding the future Roman Empire. The procession moves on.

Casca remains behind to tell Brutus and Cassius what has taken place. Mark Antony three times offered Caesar a crown-like coronet. Each time Caesar put it aside, but each time more reluctantly, and each time the crowd shouted their approval more enthusiastically. Shakespeare adds satire to Plutarch: Casca makes a mockery of the rite which seemed so important when it was off-stage:

> and still as he refused it, the rabblement hooted, and clapped their chopped [chapped] hands, and threw up their sweaty night-caps, and uttered such a deal of stinking breath because Caesar refused the crown, that it had, almost, choked Caesar; for he swooned, and fell down at it. And for mine own part, I durst not laugh, for fear of opening my lips and receiving the bad air.                    (241-248)

Shakespeare departs from Plutarch to paint Casca as a fairly common type on the Elizabethan stage: the cynical realist with harsh speech and an irritating manner better suited to prose than to more formal blank verse. In Casca's report, Caesar is a role-player and demagogue (256-259). Offered a crown, Caesar "would fain have had it" until he sensed the people's displeasure; then he made the dramatic gesture of offering his throat for cutting. He did so with such a show of sincerity that, had Casca been an ordinary member of the crowd, "I would I might go to hell" rather than have not believed him. In other words, Caesar regards himself as a heroic actor and plays to his audience. If Caesar is a fake, then the people are gulls (dupes).

The unflattering portrait of this mob prefigures the next which kills Cinna the Poet. Casca adds, offhandedly, something more sinister: "Marullus and Flavius, for pulling scarfs off Caesar's images, are put to silence" (282-283). Having seen Caesar the demagogue, we hear of Caesar the efficiently brutal tyrant. Brutus leaves after promising to consider what Cassius has said and to listen to him again the next day.

Cassius reveals more of himself in the final soliloquy:

> Well, Brutus, thou art noble; yet I see
> Thy honourable mettle may be wrought
> From that it is disposed: therefore it is meet
> That noble minds keep ever with their likes;
> For who so firm that cannot be seduced?        (305-309)

His hatred for Caesar the tyrant is rooted in jealousy of Caesar the man. In his imagination, Cassius plays the role of the true Caesar. He seeks, through the conspiracy, to set the stage so that he can also play it in reality. His discrepant role-playing is less advanced than Caesar's, but he is satisfied that he has influenced Brutus and will be able to win him over. He decides to forge, in various writing styles, messages saying that Brutus is expected by many eminent citizens to take a stand against Caesar's tyranny; the messages will be thrown in Brutus' windows for him to find.

> *In a storm, Casca tells Cicero of unnatural events. Cassius instructs Cinna to put inflammatory letters in Brutus' way (I.iii).*

As the scene begins: *Thunder and lightning* ... Shakespeare vividly pictures Rome under the portentous storm. The imagery has an intense and nightmarish quality; the "tempest dropping fire" (10) is no ordinary lightning storm. But Shakespeare stresses the personal episodes, the

> hundred ghastly women,
> Transformèd with their fear, who swore they saw
> Men, all in fire, walk up and down the streets ... (23-25)

the slave with his burning hand, the marvel of the lion that "glazed upon" Casca and "went surly by," and the owl that hooted at noon in the market place — "the bird of night," a traditional omen of evil for the Elizabethan audience (21-26). For Casca, "they are portentous things" (28-32). These portents are connected with Caesar: the disorder his tyranny creates in the body politic and the unnatural nature of the conspiracy against him.

Storm for Shakespeare carries a significance that is largely lost for us. The Elizabethans thought of the person, the society ("the state") and the natural world as indivisibly connected. So on the stage disorder and violence in nature could represent disorder in the society and the individual. G. Wilson Knight has shown that in Shakespeare's plays two contrasting images are associated: music with goodness and harmony and storm with evil and strife.* We were told in I.ii that Cassius "hears no

---

* Knight (1954).

music," so we are not surprised that he now welcomes the storm as a "very pleasing night to honest men" (43), which reflects his own anger. How one interprets these phenomena is in accordance with one's point of view, as Cicero notes:

men may construe things after their fashion,
Clean from the purpose of the things themselves.

(34-35)

Cassius is eloquent and passionate still. But it is the same story that he tells. He still sees Brutus as a tool. Only in the later quarrel with Brutus is he strikingly reanimated (IV.ii-iii).

The value of the storm is mainly in its effect upon the emotions of people, for the scene takes the plot little further. Cassius sends Cinna to distribute his forged letters where Brutus will find them. Cassius takes Casca with him to Brutus' house.

*Brutus is drawn into the conspiracy that night and leaves in the morning with Caius Ligarius to join in the pre-arranged plan to accompany Caesar to the Capitol (II.i).*

In the contrasting calm, lightning of the storm flashes in the night sky. The gentle Brutus is sleepless and walks in his garden. The dark night has a subtle but vital symbolic import: the darkness and confusion in Brutus' mind. He calls his slave-boy Lucius to light a candle in his study. Lucius finds one of Cassius' anonymous letters.

Brutus ponders the conspiracy. If he joins, it must be for the good of Rome; the absolute power of a king may change Caesar's nature and make him a tyrant — so he must be stopped. The fallacy is that Caesar is to be killed not for what he *has* done but for *what he may do*. Brutus' soliloquy is a model of Shakespeare's brilliance (which he developed later) in revealing ambiguous or confused thinking that is not clearly realized by the speaker himself. Yet Brutus *seems* certain of what he has to do, for he begins with his answer:

It must be by his death; and for my part,
I know no personal cause to spurn at him,
But for the general. — He would be crowned.
How that might change his nature, there's the question.

(10-13)

This is not republican feeling. It is not what a king will do to Rome that he fears, but what kingship will do to Caesar — not monarchy but a specific monarch — and Brutus expresses this in orthodox Elizabethan political thinking. Brutus chooses to take the general proof over the particular instance:

> And, since the quarrel
> Will bear no colour for the thing he is,
> Fashion it thus: that what he is, augmented,
> Would run to these and these extremities;
> And therefore think him as a serpent's egg
> Which, hatched, would, as his kind, grow mischievous,
> And kill him in the shell. (28-34)

Brutus creates a playlet: he dramatizes Caesar as what he is not: "therefore think him as a serpent's egg." He refuses to join the conspiracy without just, public motives; yet he decides to act even though he has no such motives. Whether we sympathize with or blame Brutus, his attempt to solve his conflict is not rational. The letters he reads evoke his first real commitment to the "cause" (56-58).

> In the interim
> Between the acting of a dreadful thing
> And the first motion, all the interim is
> Like a phantasma or a hideous dream:
> ... and the state of man,
> Like to a little kingdom, suffers then
> The nature of an insurrection. (63-69)

His inward turmoil has its outward parallel in the unnatural happenings of the storm. But what he says is not, like soliloquies in the late tragedies, highly individual. He wraps his meaning in conventional rhetoric:

> O conspiracy,
> Sham'st thou to show thy dangerous brow by night,
> When evils are most free? O then, by day
> Where wilt thou find a cavern dark enough
> To mask thy monstrous visage? Seek none, conspiracy;
> Hide it in smiles and affability ... (77-82)

Conspirators are players: smiles must hide their monstrous visages. While he insists (and we believe him) on his integrity and honesty, Brutus must use a mask.

The soliloquy is a masterpiece and the kernel of the play: it reveals Brutus as virtuous but deluded. The honest man is a limited thinker. Despite Cassius' influence, the decision to make the conspiracy a political reality is Brutus' alone. The tension is between his nature and his commitment to an act that violates his nature.

Cassius and five other conspirators (Casca, Decius, Cinna, Metellus and Trebonius) arrive in darkness, muffled in their cloaks. Night, with its associations of secrecy and evil, gives a sinister quality to everything that happens. Brutus is a solitary man, so the scene moves a little stiffly, and Brutus is awkward; while he can command, he cannot stir the others; he is not a born leader. Yet Brutus has already become the leader with the implied consent of Cassius, because the conspirators need Brutus at all costs. He refuses to hear of an oath being sworn. They must not stain

> The even virtue of our enterprise,
> Nor th'insuppressive mettle of our spirits,
> To think that or our cause or our performance
> Did need an oath ...                                   (133-136)

This is Brutus' first mistake: one of this group will betray them to Artemidorus who will try to warn Caesar. Brutus makes his second mistake when he vetoes the suggestion that Cicero be included in the conspiracy: Cicero, he says, will have nothing to do with an enterprise he has not initiated himself. The others quickly agree. So the master orator of the age is excluded, and they later discover that they have no one to offset the influence of Antony's eloquence, which begins their downfall.

Cassius then suggests that Mark Antony should be killed: he may prove a dangerous enemy to them later. Brutus vetoes this suggestion too, because Antony is a useless trifler, incapable of being a threat. Antony's death would introduce a sacrilegious note into what Brutus dramatizes as a religious ceremony in which the body must suffer for the spirit's sake:

> Let us be sacrificers, but not butchers, Caius.
> We all stand up against the spirit of Caesar,
> And in the spirit of men there is no blood.
> O, that we then could come by Caesar's spirit,
> And not dismember Caesar! But, alas,
> Caesar must bleed for it. And, gentle friends,
> Let's kill him boldly, but not wrathfully;

> Let's carve him as a dish fit for the gods,
> Not hew him as a carcass fit for hounds.          (166-174)

Brutus finally accepts his assassin's role only if the conspirators play the roles of sacrificers: the deed must be acted as if it is a religious ritual. Brutus the high-minded becomes the Brutus of symbolic action: the "unwrathful" blood sacrifice is objectified in ceremonial observance. But to transform political killing into ritual is to cloak it with appearances — to dramatize it. Brutus ends his invocation to ritual with a note on practical politics:

> This shall make
> Our purpose necessary, and not envious;
> Which so appearing to the common eyes,
> We shall be called purgers, not murderers.     (177-180)

Brutus amplifies the playlet: the conspirators will "appear" to the citizenry as purgers, not murderers. Not killing Antony is another of Brutus' mistakes, because it is Antony who turns the tide against them.

Cassius is not sure that Caesar will attend the Senate meeting. He notes how superstitions now affect Caesar:

> For he is superstitious grown of late,
> Quite from the main opinion he held once
> Of fantasy, of dreams, and ceremonies.          (195-197)

This is confirmed by Decius Brutus who volunteers to bring Caesar to the Senate

> If he be so resolved,
> I can o'ersway him; for he loves to hear
> That unicorns may be betrayed with trees,
> And bears with glasses, elephants with holes,
> Lions with toils, and men with flatterers.
> But when I tell him he hates flatterers,
> He says he does, being then most flatterèd.     (202-208)

Metellus suggests that Caius Ligarius be included in their number. Brutus promises to persuade him, and Metellus sends for him at once. At three o'clock the conspirators leave to meet later at Caesar's house.

Brutus is left alone with Lucius:

> Boy! Lucius! Fast asleep? It is no matter.
> Enjoy the honey-heavy dew of slumber;
> Thou hast no figures nor no fantasies,

> Which busy care draws in the brains of men;
> Therefore thou sleep'st so sound.               (229-233)

Shakespeare often associates sleep with peace. The stage director must ensure that Brutus' dealings with the boy reflect his
gentleness and humanity, and that the audience sees the distance between Brutus's imagining and the deed he contemplates.

Portia, Brutus' wife, enters so softly that he is unaware of
her until her soft voice says, "Brutus, my lord" (234). Portia and
Lucius indicate all that might have been normal and happy in
Brutus' life if it had not been for the struggles of the conspiracy, his conscience, and the assassination. Through Portia's eyes
we see Brutus in a very different context. She tells us of the cost
of Brutus's decision and how it affects him:

> It will not let you eat, nor talk, nor sleep;
> And could it work so much upon your shape,
> As it hath much prevailed on your condition,
> I should not know you Brutus.               (252-255)

But even from his wife he holds aloof. Portia believes she has
been given the false role of "Brutus' harlot, not his wife" (287).
Even her pride has its modesty:

> I grant I am a woman; but withal
> A woman that Lord Brutus took to wife;
> I grant I am a woman; but withal
> A woman well reputed, Cato's daughter.
> Think you I am no stronger than my sex,
> Being so fathered, and so husbanded? (292-297)

She has given herself a gash in her thigh to convince him of
her loyalty. She appeals to the great vow "Which did incorpo-
rate and make us one" (272-273). Brutus is deeply touched,
and at last he says:

> You are my true and honourable wife,
> As dear to me as are the ruddy drops
> That visit my sad heart.               (288-290)

He promises to be more open with her. Portia is a delightful
person: she talks simply and directly of her "once commended
beauty" (271). She is yielding but strong, with dignity and
courage.

Then Ligarius is shown in with his head bandaged. He has
been ill but rises from his sick-bed at the word of Brutus.

LIG:                                     What's to do?
BRU:   A piece of work that will make sick men whole.
LIG:    But are not some whole that we must make sick?
                                                      (326-328)
A sick man is healthy. He joins the plot, throwing away his head
bandages:

To do I know not what; but it sufficeth
That Brutus leads me on.                          (333-334)

As they go out, Brutus starts to explain the conspiracy to
Ligarius.

*Caesar's wife, Calphurnia, has a bad dream and begs*
*Caesar to remain at home. Decius Brutus convinces*
*Caesar to go (II.ii).*

Caesar has been woken by the storm, with its symbolic associations to human violence. Calphurnia has cried in her sleep,
"They murder Caesar!" Ironically in view of Brutus' recent talk
of sacrificial murder, ritual is stressed: Caesar says, "Go bid the
priests do present sacrifice" (5).

Calphurnia, who has "never stood on ceremonies [omens]"
(13), is now terrified. She tells Caesar not to leave the house,
but he dismisses her fears. There are direct links to the previous scene: Portia intuitively senses that something is wrong,
and Calphurnia has a frightening dream. Both men disregard
their wives and proceed on toward their fatal meeting.

Shakespeare presents Caesar with exceptional skill. He suggests two parts of the man: the self-consciously public figure,
the fearless hero, and the private person who yields to his wife's
fear and may be fearful himself. Caesar in his pride treats the
omens as meaningless:

Cowards die many times before their deaths;
The valiant never taste of death but once.
Of all the wonders that I yet have heard,
It seems to me most strange that men should fear,
Seeing that death, a necessary end,
Will come when it will come.                      (32-37)

He reiterates his fearlessness:

Danger knows full well
That Caesar is more dangerous than he.
We are two lions littered in one day,

> And I the elder and more terrible;
> And Caesar shall go forth. (44-48)

This is only a prelude to the outrageous *hubris* of his speeches just prior to the assassination.

The priests' omens are unfavourable: the sacrificed beast had no heart. Caesar dismisses them too, but Calphurnia, in desperation, kneels to him — just as Portia kneeled to Brutus — and begs that he send Mark Antony to say Caesar is not well. As soon as Calphurnia says "call it my fear" (50), Caesar says, "Mark Antony shall say I am not well" (55). The Colossus is also a man moved by the distress of his wife. But the idea of Caesar as a spiritual power of great force is always far greater than Caesar the man. Caesar thinks so: he has an almost superstitious respect for his own role and is afraid of acting unworthily of it. Decius Brutus arrives:

> CAE: And you are come in very happy time
> To bear my greeting to the senators,
> And tell them that I will not come today:
> Cannot, is false; and that I dare not, falser;
> I will not come today. Tell them so, Decius.
> CAL: Say he is sick.
> CAE: Shall Caesar send a lie?
> Have I in conquest stretched mine arm so far,
> To be afeard to tell greybeards the truth?
> Decius, go tell them Caesar will not come.
> DEC: Most mighty Caesar, let me know some cause,
> Lest I be laughed at when I tell them so.
> CAE: The cause is in my will: I will not come;
> That is enough to satisfy the Senate. (60-72)

Now we know him: a king rules by right and reason but a tyrant by caprice. Decius gives a masterly improvised performance; he interprets the dream as a good sign because the Senate intends to grant Caesar a crown, and feels Caesar runs the risk of being thought afraid. Caesar changes his mind, makes light of Calphurnia's fears, and decides to go to the Senate.

The conspirators enter. The scene is suddenly enlivened with this group of resolute, falsely cheerful men. Have they been found out? Has Decius overreached himself? Caesar is not a fool, and Calphurnia is open to many suspicions. But the smiling masks disperse the last clouds of the ominous night. As

Cassius is not here (why not?), it is the honourable Brutus who leads the moment's events. With tragic irony, Caesar says:

> Good friends, go in, and taste some wine with me;
> And we, like friends, will straightway go together.
>
> (126-127)

This is a subtle touch: we see Caesar now as a man and a host, offering wine to his murderers. The killers — including the "honest" Brutus — drink with their unsuspecting victim. As they leave, Brutus, Caesar's friend, lags back to end the scene:

> That every like is not the same, O Caesar,
> The heart of Brutus earns to think upon.     (128-129)

Only Brutus would use a quibble to express his own grief to his victim.

### *Artemidorus has a list (II.iii).*

In the street Artemidorus, a teacher of rhetoric, stands with his list of all eight conspirators. He also knows the part assigned to each one — information that could only have come from one of the eight. A solitary anonymous figure, he posts himself in a spot from which he will be able to hand Caesar a note as he passes.

### *Portia questions the Soothsayer (II.iv).*

In a brief scene based on a short passage in Plutarch's *Life of Brutus,* we gather that Portia has been told about the plot. In her anxiety for Brutus she sends Lucius to the Capitol but forgets to tell him what to do. Then she tells him to observe what happens, give Brutus her love, say she is merry and bring back his answer. When she questions the Soothsayer for news, she is at first alarmed that the secret may be out. From his reply she realizes that he merely fears a plot but knows nothing.

### *Caesar refuses to listen to warnings and goes to the Capitol. Trebonius diverts Antony while Caesar is killed. When Antony returns he asks permission to speak at Caesar's funeral. Brutus agrees over Cassius' objections (III.i).*

The next three scenes, a superb Shakespearean achievement, run without a break. They are highly theatrical, and the director must visualize the continuous action with the greatest care.

Trumpets sound. Caesar with others passes along the crowded street. We hear a prelude of two voices. Caesar says to the Soothsayer: "The ides of March are come." He receives the reply, "Ay, Caesar, but not gone" (1-2). Artemidorus hands Caesar his list of conspirators. Decius quickly presents Trebonius' petition. Artemidorus shouts to Caesar to read his first: it is vital to him personally. But Caesar will deal with other people's business first.

In the Senate house, the procession arrives; the conspirators edge towards Caesar, their daggers in their togas. Popilius Lena surprises Cassius by wishing him luck (13). The tension increases. If their plot is discovered, Cassius will commit suicide on the spot. Popilius speaks to Caesar ... He smiles ... Popilius has revealed nothing.

The plot starts. Trebonius draws Mark Antony outside where he cannot interfere. Metellus Cimber kneels to present a suit to Caesar who, thinking that it is to repeal his brother's banishment, and disgusted at this un-Roman show of humility, rudely refuses to alter the decree. Caesar's speeches here become most arrogant. He compares the petitioners to flatterers given to "Low-crooked curtsies" and fawning spaniels. As so often, he speaks in monosyllables:

> If thou dost bend and pray and fawn for him,
> I spurn thee like a cur out of my way.          (45-46)

Ben Jonson remarked that Caesar's comment, "Caesar never did wrong, but with just cause" was ridiculous. In F1 it was replaced by the weak,

> Know, Caesar doth not wrong, nor without cause
> Will he be satisfied.          (47-48)

Caesar refuses to show clemency: that would mean that he, like ordinary men, could change his mind. This is self-delusion: we have already seen Caesar cajoled and flattered into changing his mind. Caesar goes on:

> I could be well moved, if I were as you;
> If I could pray to move, prayers would move me;
> But I am constant as the northern star,
> Of whose true-fixed and resting quality
> There is no fellow in the firmament ...
>     I do know but one
> That unassailable holds on his rank,

> Unshaked of motion; and that I am he,
> Let me a little show it, even in this:
> That I was constant Cimber should be banished,
> And constant do remain to keep him so.     (58-73)

The appeals persist, and Caesar is furious: "Hence! Wilt thou lift up Olympus?" (74). Despite his age, infirmity, partial deafness, and epilepsy, Caesar sees himself as a god. He must prove the existence of his identity to the world and to himself; so his egotism becomes compelling and ludicrous. The player projects both Caesars: one physical and weak; the other all but supernatural with a spiritual power blazing in his hyperboles. This Caesar has scarcely any reality apart from his highly ironic attempt to play an unsuitable role.

The conspirators are grouped tightly around him in humble poses. Cassius, after pleading for Caesar's pardon, falls "As low as to thy foot" (56). Cinna and Decius set up a chorus of "O Caesar, Great Caesar"; their fawning is as exaggerated as Caesar's pride. Hypocrisy and betrayal are stressed by Casca's movement as he circles behind Caesar.

Casca strikes the first dagger-blow at the back of Caesar's neck. He bungles his aim in his excitement, but the others repeatedly stab Caesar who, when he sees Brutus among them, ceases to resist. On the stage, Caesar's recognition of his friend as he stabs him — "*Et tu, Brute?*" (77) — and his gesture of hopeless resignation are affecting. For the first time we feel sorry for Caesar; we also recognize the pathos of Brutus as he kills his friend for his principles.

The assassination is the crux of the play:

- *Plot*
  All events lead to it or away from it.
- *Structure*
  Shakespeare puts the assassination only a quarter of the way through the scene — a great structural achievement. The focus of the following action is the emergence of Antony as a dramatic force.
- *Colour*
  When Caesar falls at the base of Pompey's statue it turns red. The world of death in *Romeo and Juliet* is light-dark. In *Hamlet* it is white-black. In *Julius Caesar* it is white-blood red.

- *Ritual*
  The assassination carries out Brutus' ritual prescription in detail: the killing is staged formally with one conspirator after another kneeling until their victim is surrounded. Then they ceremonially bathe their hands in Caesar's blood.
- *Metaphor*
  Caesar's blood is "noble" and "costly" because Caesar was the foremost man in the world. As a political metaphor it is significant when blood pours from Pompey's statue and Caesar's body, and from the skies in the storm.
- *Symbol*
  The Caesar idea ("The spirit of Caesar") controls Caesar while he lives; it survives and avenges him after his death. Whatever our view of Caesar as a man, he is a symbol of something of vast importance, resplendent majesty, and starry purpose.

As Caesar falls there is sudden chaos. In the swirling hubbub on the stage Brutus stands firm. He restrains his followers, comforts an elderly senator, and publicly announces that the conspirators are responsible for what they have done. Trebonius reports Antony has fled to his house. The supernatural disorder of the storm is paralleled in the city where

> Men, wives, and children stare, cry out, and run,
> As it were doomsday.                                    (97-98)

Then a new rhythm appears. The mockery of the counter-ritual slowly begins as a servant of Antony enters and confronts Brutus:

> Thus, Brutus, did my master bid me kneel;
> Thus did Mark Antony bid me fall down;
> And, being prostrate, thus he bade me say:
> Brutus is noble, wise, valiant, and honest;
> Caesar was mighty, bold, royal, and loving:
> Say I love Brutus, and I honour him;
> Say I feared Caesar, honoured him, and loved him.
> If Brutus will vouchsafe that Antony
> May safely come to him, and be resolved
> How Caesar hath deserved to lie in death,
> Mark Anthony shall not love Caesar dead
> So well as Brutus living ...                            (123-134)

The threefold repetition — "kneel," "fall down," and "being prostrate" — almost makes the irony satiric. Brutus sends a verbal safe-conduct. Cassius has grave misgivings, but Brutus is confident of Antony.

We have seen little of Antony so far. Now he arrives in double guise; the message foreshadows him as politician, but he also grieves deeply for his friend's death. This double impression is vital. His arrival changes the direction of the dramatic action. He is a born opportunist with a great opportunity: he is the avenging spirit seeking the conspirators; and he changes the relationship of the characters as the idealistic Brutus and the realistic Cassius now become merely partners in misfortune.

Antony's first words have an extraordinary effect:

> O mighty Caesar! Dost thou lie so low?
> Are all thy conquests, glories, triumphs, spoils
> Shrunk to this little measure? (148-150)

The audience sees the Caesar of history for first time! While he was on the stage we never saw him in this way. Antony then evokes both the holy scene which the conspirators wanted and the savagery which lay below it:

> Now, whilst your purpled hands do reek and smoke,
> Fulfill your pleasure. Live a thousand years,
> I shall not find myself so apt to die;
> No place will please me so, no mean of death,
> As here by Caesar, and by you cut off,
> The choice and master spirits of this age. (158-163)

He is quite sincere; but it is also the way to convince the honourable Brutus not to murder him. It is part of the double role he is for the time being obliged to play. Of Antony's two sides, it is the dark politic aspect that will destroy the conspirators. Brutus, Cassius, and Caesar all have double characers, but Antony's are the most effective. He expresses his genuine affection for Caesar the man, his loyalty to the memory of a dead friend, as he stands before Caesar's blood-stained killers. Brutus says:

> Our hearts you see not; they are pitiful;
> And pity to the general wrong of Rome —
> As fire drives out fire, so pity, pity —
> Hath done this deed on Caesar. (169-172)

Knowing Antony well, Cassius offers material inducements:

> Your voice shall be as strong as any man's
> In the disposing of new dignities.                    (177-178)

Antony responds with a counter-ritual, shaking hands in formal sequence; this makes each conspirator stand alone, unprotected by the rite of blood that had bonded him with the others.

> Let each man render me his bloody hand.
> First, Marcus Brutus, will I shake with you;
> Next, Caius Cassius, do I take your hand;
> Now, Decius Brutus, yours; now yours, Metellus;
> Yours, Cinna; and, my valiant Casca, yours;
> Though last, not least in love, yours, good Trebonius.
> Gentlemen all — alas, what shall I say?          (184-190)

In bitter irony, he caps their ritual with his own: a ritual of friendship — but friendship spilt the blood of Caesar! Suddenly Antony, addressing the body of Caesar, delivers his first profanation of the ritual sacrifice:

> Here wast thou bayed, brave hart;
> Here didst thou fall; and here thy hunters stand,
> Signed in thy spoil, and crimsoned in thy lethe.   (204-206)

His violent outburst indicates the strain he is under. He turns to Cassius:

> Pardon me, Caius Cassius;
> The enemies of Caesar shall say this;
> Then, in a friend, it is cold modesty.              (211-213)

Cassius is shrewdly suspicious of Antony's intentions:

> Will you be pricked in number of our friends,
> Or shall we on, and not depend on you?          (216-217)

Disarmingly, Antony says, "Therefore I took your hands" (218), and requests the reasons why Caesar was dangerous. Brutus promises Antony a full explanation later when the people have been quieted. Antony then requests permission to speak at Caesar's funeral.

As Cassius and Brutus discuss the situation aside, Cassius is still the practical thinker of the conspiracy:

> do not consent
> That Antony speak in his funeral.                    (232-233)

Brutus, the moral leader, can still overrule him but is a very bad judge of people. He has a naïve certainty that his own cause, which is right, need only be put to the people to convince them:

I will myself into the pulpit first,

And show the reason of our Caesar's death      (236-237)

seems to him a sufficient answer to Cassius' doubts. But he makes some conditions: he will speak before Antony does; Antony will not blame the conspirators, and he will speak all the good he can of Caesar; Antony will make the point that he is speaking with the conspirators' permission, and he will speak from the same platform as Brutus does. It is Brutus' greatest mistake. Antony, all docility and humility, accepts. The conspirators leave.

Left alone, Antony turns to Caesar's corpse:

O, pardon me, thou bleeding piece of earth,

That I am meek and gentle with these butchers.

Thou art the ruins of the noblest man

That ever livèd in the tide of times.

Woe to the hand that shed this costly blood!      (254-257)

Antony sees Caesar as a man he loved, a supremely noble man, and a symbol of government and peace. With him slain, disorder will rage unchecked:

Caesar's spirit, ranging for revenge,

With Ate by his side, come hot from hell,

Shall in these confines with a monarch's voice

Cry havoc and let slip the dogs of war,

That this foul deed shall smell above the earth

With carrion men, groaning for burial.          (270-275)

Antony takes the role of avenger for the rest of the play.

A servant of Octavius Caesar arrives: his master is only twenty miles out of Rome. Antony detains the servant to help remove Caesar's body.

> *In the Forum Brutus speaks first to the people. Then*
> *Antony slowly swings the crowd to his side and incites*
> *them into a rioting mob (III.ii).*

This whole scene is two opposing arguments spoken in the Forum before the people of Rome: Brutus' defence of the assassination and Antony's attack on it. Brutus speaks in prose in a calm and factual way, but Antony emotionally uses rhetorical verse.

The Forum is more lively than usual. To the Roman people Julius Caesar was a beloved benefactor and hero, and they

angrily demand an explanation of his death. Brutus splits up
the crowd between himself and Cassius to keep the groups
small. After the people divide, Brutus begins:

> Be patient till the last.
> Romans, countrymen, and lovers, hear me for my
>     cause, and be
> silent, that you may hear.                         (12-14)

He does not begin with a bang or a whimper but soberly, with a
calm intellectual authority. He concedes nothing to their simplicity:

> Censure me in your wisdom, and awake your senses,
>     that you may be the better judge.              (16-17)

Brutus' dry, formal style purposely appeals to reason and
avoids stirring the emotions. Historically, this was Brutus' form
of public speaking, commonly called laconic or Spartan. His
great reputation for uprightness and his dignified presence get
him a hearing from the people. He tells them his love for
Caesar was as great as anyone's:

> not that I loved Caesar less, but that I loved Rome
> more. Had you rather Caesar were living, and die all
> slaves, than that Caesar were dead, to live all free men?
> As Caesar loved me, I weep for him; as he was fortunate,
> I rejoice at it; as he was valiant, I honour him; but, as he
> was ambitious, I slew him ... With this I depart, that, as I
> slew my best lover [friend] for the good of Rome, I
> have the same dagger for myself, when it shall please
> my country to need my death.                        (21-47)

The speech continually uses parallel constructions (e.g., loved-
weep, fortunate-rejoice, valiant-honour, ambitious-slew), which
give the effect of rational and logical development. Brutus' "I
pause for a reply" at the end of each passage has the same
effect and is a mark of his confidence. The citizens are
impressed. "Let him be Caesar," they cry:

> Caesar's better parts
> Shall be crowned in Brutus.                         (52-53)

Brutus wins their sympathies to the cause of the conspirators,
not by what he says but in spite of it — by his personality. They
shout for him as a deliverer, and they want to honour him. He
dampens their enthusiasm by telling them to stay to hear Mark
Antony who speaks with his permission. And he departs.

Brutus in this speech makes two vital errors of judgment that arise from his personality — from who he is. He assumes that, because his cause is just, it needs only to be presented to be believed; and he thinks that others will be persuaded by reason, as he is himself. But they are not. One of Brutus' great defects is to assume the existence of his own virtues in everyone else.

Many editors consider Brutus' speech to be weak and ineffective. When they read it in the study, they have the benefit of hindsight and compare it with Antony's. But this does not happen in the theatre. An audience witnesses Brutus' speech in the "here and now," with no hindsight. It is not ineffective; it attains its end by convincing the crowd. In performance it can stir the audience deeply. It is thoughtful, noble and perfectly reflects Brutus' character.

Mark Antony carries in Caesar's body to face a hostile crowd. His funeral oration is generally considered one of Shakespeare's most effective creations. Granville-Barker comments: "the cheapening of the truth, the appeals to passion, the perfect carillon of flattery, cajoling, mockery and pathos, swinging to a magnificent tune, all serve to make it a model of what popular oratory should be. In a school for demagogues its critical analysis might well be an item on every examination paper."* Yet modern audiences can also be taken in by it. Antony's emotion is genuine; but he subtly manipulates the crowd to his own ends. Antony is not only a highly successful actor, he is also a Machiavellian pseudo-dramatist. Seemingly Antony is apologetic. He appears to obey Brutus' conditions to allow him to speak:

> Friends, Romans, countrymen, lend me your ears;
> I come to bury Caesar, not to praise him. (74-75)

Initially he deals with Brutus' reason for the killing:

> The noble Brutus
> Hath told you Caesar was ambitious.
> If it were so, it was a grievous fault,
> And grievously hath Caesar answered it. (78-81)

---

* Granville-Barker (1963).

He is alert for the crowd's first response. He senses a human appeal with his "He was my friend, faithful and just to me" (86), then draws back:

> But Brutus says he was ambitious,
> And Brutus is an honourable man.                    (87-88)

He stresses both Caesar's lovable personality and his importance as victor and national hero: to Antony, Caesar is Rome's lover. He appeals to the crowd's sentiment and greed: Caesar filled the "general coffers" and "wept" when the poor were unhappy (90-92); and it was at their insistence that Caesar refused the crown offered to him at the feast of Lupercal. "Was this ambition?" (98). But

> I speak not to disprove what Brutus spoke,
> But here I am to speak what I do know           (101-102)

and, with the monosyllables of the last line, he is getting into his stride. His hearers warm to him. He continually repeats "honourable" and "ambitious" until his irony has unconsciously sunk in to them. In refusing to mourn Caesar, Antony says "men have lost their reason" (106).

He allows them to see him apparently overcome with grief for his friend Caesar — an infectious emotion. The citizens' comments show they are sympathetic to him now.

Next Antony uses the rhetorical device of introducing an idea which he wishes his audience to take up, by pretending to deny it. To move the crowd "to mutiny and rage" (123) would be to do wrong to the conspirators, and he would rather "wrong the dead ... and you" (127). It is a subtle touch and suggests to the listeners that they are on Caesar's side, that they have been wronged, and that mutiny and rage may be in order. Thus far Antony has used innuendo and implication. It is time for something solid:

> But here's a parchment with the seal of Caesar;
> I found it in his closet; 'tis his will.                    (129-130)

He displays a document which he says is Caesar's will. A less skillful orator would read it immediately, but Antony holds back. Out of loyalty to the "honourable men" who stabbed Caesar, he will resist the temptation to incite the plebeians against them:

> O masters! If I were disposed to stir
> Your hearts and minds to mutiny and rage,
> I should do Brutus wrong, and Cassius wrong,
> Who, you all know, are honourable men.
> I will not do them wrong; I rather choose
> To wrong the dead, to wrong myself and you,
> Than I will wrong such honourable men.      (122-128)

The crowd want him to read the will, but he works on their suggestibility:

> It is not meet you know how Caesar loved you.
> You are not wood, you are not stones, but men;
> And being men, hearing the will of Caesar,
> It will inflame you, it will make you mad.      (142-145)

Like Caesar, Antony is the master of the monosyllable:

> 'Tis good you know not that you are his heirs;
> For if you should, O, what would come of it?      (146-147)

Antony gives rhetorical questions the force of simple assertion: "You will compel me then to read the will?" (158). They take the bait: "They were villains, murderers! The will! Read the will!" (156-157).

Antony descends to Caesar's body (162). Now he is in complete control, and trick after trick of oratory follows. By showing them the mutilated body of Caesar, Antony re-emphasizes ritual: one intended to show that the original "lofty scene" of assassination was base carnage. Holding Caesar's bloody mantle as a talisman, he reproduces one by one the sacrificial strokes of the individual conspirators, ending with the wound inflicted by "well-belovèd Brutus" (177):

> This was the most unkindest cut of all;
> For when the noble Caesar saw him stab,
> Ingratitude, more strong than traitors' arms,
> Quite vanquished him: then burst his mighty heart;
> And in his mantle muffling up his face,
> Even at the base of Pompey's statue,
> Which all the while ran blood, great Caesar fell.
>
> (184-190)

Antony's re-creation becomes a mockery of the ritual bond:

> O, what a fall was there, my countrymen!
> Then I, and you, and all of us fell down,
> Whilst bloody treason flourished over us.

> O, now you weep, and I perceive you feel
> The dint of pity.                    (191-195)

The crowd is about to riot when Antony stops them:

> Good friends, sweet friends, let me not stir you up
> To such a sudden flood of mutiny.
> They that have done this deed are honourable.
>                                      (211-213)

He is no orator like Brutus; he is just "a plain blunt man" (219) who loves his friend:

> But were I Brutus,
> And Brutus Antony, there were an Antony
> Would ruffle up your spirits, and put a tongue
> In every wound of Caesar that should move
> The stones of Rome to rise and mutiny.    (227-231)

This is enough for the crowd, but as they set off to kill the conspirators, Antony calls them back: "you go to do you know not what" (236). They have forgotten the will. Antony knows that something more is needed to sustain their emotion. So he appeals to their self-interest and greed. He says Caesar has left each man a legacy of seventy-five drachmas (243) and, for their public use, all his famous gardens across the Tiber surrounding his villa (248-249).

Now he lets them go. The crowd becomes a mob. The second great climax in as many scenes occurs as the Romans riot. They seize benches, chairs, anything wooden, and snatch lighted torches as they rush to set fire to the assassins' houses. Antony surveys his act with satisfaction:

> Now let it work. Mischief, thou art afoot,
> Take thou what course thou wilt.         (262-263)

A servant enters to tell him Octavius is in Rome, with Lepidus, at Caesar's house, waiting for him. He goes with the servant.

Actors who play Antony often mistakenly deliver "honourable" too sarcastically at the start; Antony waits until the crowd is ready for such a savage twist — the word "traitors" (198). Many who play Antony are merely good speakers. But it takes a performer of real achievement to give us the complete and complex Antony.

This scene is political in the broadest sense: it deals with the way people seek power and their attempt to justify their actions to others. Until now, much of the play is centered on persuasion: Antony's power works, not through violence but through verbal persuasion. One of Shakespeare's central themes is the inability of the masses to act in a politically responsible way. In this scene, they switch their allegiance back and forth on a purely emotional basis. Their behaviour is an ironic commentary on the republican ideal, and their actions are far from rational. They can be directed by anyone who, like Antony, can manipulate an audience with speech.

### *Death of Cinna the Poet (III.iii).*

This brief scene is one of the most horrifying in Shakespeare. The rampaging Roman mob plunders and burns. It stumbles across Cinna the Poet and questions him with unreasoning fury. In a few brief words Shakespeare characterizes him in his dandified reply:

> What is my name? Whither am I going? Where do I dwell? Am I a married man or a bachelor? Then to answer every man directly and briefly, wisely and truly; wisely I say, I am a bachelor. (13-16)

The plebeians mistake him for Cinna, one of the conspirators:

> 1 PLEB:  Tear him to pieces! He's a conspirator.
> CINNA:  I am Cinna the poet, I am Cinna the poet.
> 4 PLEB:  Tear him for his bad verses, tear him for his bad verses!
> CINNA:  I am not Cinna the conspirator.
> 4 PLEB:  It is no matter, his name's Cinna; pluck but his name out of his heart, and turn him going. (28-34)

He is the first victim of Antony's eloquence as the mob rages on. This mindless murder recalls those grimly comic scenes in *2 Henry VI,* of the uprising of Jack Cade and his English rabble.

### Second Movement: Retribution

The predominant rhythm in the play changes. The civil war is between the armies of Brutus and Cassius on the one hand and Antony, Octavius Caesar and Lepidus on the other. Whereas trumpets, the voices of the crowd, and the storm characterize the first half of the play, here we have the marching rhythms of soldiers, drums and the metallic clash of arms. We are to witness the consequences of the assassination.

> *The triumvirate (Antony, Octavius and Lepidus) plan to*
> *oppose the military threat of Brutus and Cassius (IV.i).*

This is a short but brilliant scene only fifty lines long; Lepidus has only twenty-two words; yet all three characters are clearly etched. The new triumvirate are listing the names of people each wants dead. The triumvirs are unscrupulous, ruthless, and cynical in their shameless bargaining of lives:

> ANT:   These many then shall die; their names are
>              pricked.
> OCT:   Your brother too must die; consent you,
>              Lepidus?
> LEP:   I do consent.
> OCT:                        Prick him down, Antony.
> LEP:   Upon condition Publius shall not live,
>              Who is your sister's son, Mark Antony.
> ANT:   He shall not live. Look, with a spot I damn him.
>
>                                                                    (1-6)

The flat, unemotional tone contrasts with a grisly action. Antony is particularly ruthless: he who saw the murder of one man as the ultimate crime now barters the life of his sister's son for that of Lepidus' brother; and he has no intention of fulfilling the promises in Caesar's will (did he ever intend to?). This is the sort of rule that the benevolent Brutus has let loose on the world. It is irrelevant to the play that the historical events of this scene took place more than a year after the assassination of Caesar; Shakespeare concentrates on the unity of theme and action.

No sooner is Lepidus out of earshot than Antony suggests to young Octavius that the faithful general who has outlived his usefulness to them ought to be put out to pasture like an old horse. "You may do your will," Octavius declares (27). Octavius reveals that their position is dangerous: Brutus and Cassius are recruiting armies and are about to threaten the position in Rome of the triumvirs.

Antony regards power primarily as his own personal possession. He thinks he is the leader of the triumvirate and regards himself as Caesar's heir; but by the end of the play it is Octavius who leads. Here they are suspicious of each other. Their fatal rivalry will be the subject of another play, *Antony and Cleopatra*.

### Brutus and Cassius begin a quarrel (IV.ii).

The civil war begins and continues to the play's end. This short scene introduces us to the conspirators. *Drum. Enter Brutus.* The gentle man is now a general. Brutus and Cassius have recruited armies in parts of Roman Asia Minor. They join up at Sardis to meet Antony and Octavius, marching east across Macedonia.

Brutus reads a letter from Cassius and then turns to Pindarus, a servant of Cassius. Brutus is grave and austere:

> Your master, Pindarus,
> In his own change, or by ill officers,
> Hath given me some worthy cause to wish
> Things done undone ... (6-9)

He makes the unpardonable mistake of criticizing Cassius in front of his own servant. He makes a second mistake by asking his own officer, Lucilius, about his reception by Cassius, and then criticizing him in front of Lucilius:

> Thou hast described
> A hot friend cooling. (18-19)

These lapses are serious breaches of military etiquette.

Shakespeare then creates a remarkable atmosphere in action and sound: *Low march within* is shortly followed by:

> *Enter Cassius and his powers*
> BRUTUS:                        Hark! he is arrived.
>        March gently on to meet him.
> *[We assume Brutus' army marches across the Globe stage to meet Cassius' army entering by one of the doors]*
> CASSIUS: Stand, ho!
> BRUTUS: Stand, ho! Speak the word along.
> 1ST SOLDIER:    Stand!
> 2ND SOLDIER:   Stand!
> 3RD SOLDIER:   Stand! (30-36)

The voices echo, and the drumbeats cease. The armies face each other. At once the furious Cassius accuses Brutus in front of their two armies:

> CAS:    Most noble brother, you have done me wrong.
> BRU:    Judge me, you gods; wrong I mine enemies?
>        And if not so, how should I wrong a brother?

CAS:   Brutus, this sober form of yours hides wrongs;
       And when you do them —
BRU:                    Cassius, be content.
       Speak your griefs softly ...              (37-42)
Brutus invites Cassius into his tent and the armies are led away.

*The quarrel scene of Brutus and Cassius (IV.iii).*

This famous scene is the play's longest. Their quarrel ranges from cold fury, through hot anger, to scorn, defiance, threat and tears; they then renew their warm friendship and, finally, plan their battle strategy. Key to the tense drama is the minute detail of how the two contrasting personalities interact.

The moment the two leaders are in the tent alone they rage at each other. Cassius accuses Brutus of punishing a friend of his for taking bribes, despite Cassius' representations on his behalf:

CAS:                         it is not meet
       That every nice offence should bear his
       comment.
BRU:   Let me tell you, Cassius, you yourself
       Are much condemned to have an itching palm,
       To sell and mart your offices for gold
       To undeservers.
CAS:                   I an itching palm!        (7-12)

Brutus is righteous and scornful. Is the conspiracy on which he staked his life and reputation corrupt? "The name of Cassius honours this corruption" (15). Brutus is thinking of the moral basis of the whole enterprise, as well as Cassius' particular action: "Did not great Julius bleed for justice' sake?" (19) and:

              shall we now
       Contaminate our fingers with base bribes,
       And sell the mighty space of our large honours
       For so much trash as may be graspèd thus?    (23-26)

For Cassius the attack is personal, and he descends to direct insult. He is, he says, an "older" and "abler" soldier than Brutus: "You are not" ... "I am" ... "I say you are not" ... "Urge me no more" (32-35). They are like petulant children.

Some actors wrongly play Brutus as distant here. He is in a towering fury: a cold, deadly rage based on his integrity, his truth to himself, and his simplicity. He has compelling power and taunts Cassius:

Go show your slaves how choleric you are,
And make your bondmen tremble. Must I budge?
Must I observe you? Must I stand and crouch
Under your testy humour? By the gods,
You shall disgest the venom of your spleen,
Though it do split you; for, from this day forth,
I'll use you for my mirth, yea, for my laughter,
When you are waspish. (43-50)

What so annoys the impulsive and imperfect Cassius is Brutus' cold realism:

CAS: When Caesar lived, he durst not thus have moved me.
BRU: Peace, peace! You durst not so have tempted him.
CAS: I durst not?
BRU: No.
CAS: What, durst not tempt him?
BRU: For your life you durst not. (58-62)

Brutus is supercilious, but he has not forgotten his own moral rectitude:

There is no terror, Cassius, in your threats;
For I am armed so strong in honesty
That they pass by me as the idle wind,
Which I respect not. (66-69)

Yet it turns out that Brutus has asked Cassius for money. Brutus' army needs immediate funds. It is Cassius who must supply him,

For I can raise no money by vile means;
By heaven, I had rather coin my heart,
And drop my blood for drachmas, than to wring
From the hard hands of peasants their vile trash
By any indirection. (71-75)

Although he condemns extortion, he wants some of the profits: Brutus' honour and integrity are accompanied by self-righteousness and muddled thinking. But he is harder than he was. His confidence is now certainty; like Caesar, he is convinced of his own rightness on all topics. Cassius still needs close personal relationships: "A friend should bear his friend's infirmities" (85), he tells Brutus:

CAS:  You love me not.

BRU:                I do not like your faults.

CAS:  A friendly eye could never see such faults.

BRU:  A flatterer's would not ...              (88-90)

Then, complaining like a child that Brutus does not love him any more, Cassius spills forth a torrent of self-pity:

Come, Antony, and young Octavius, come,

Revenge yourselves alone on Cassius,

For Cassius is aweary of the world;

Hated by one he loves; braved by his brother ...

O, I could weep

My spirit from mine eyes! There is my dagger,

And here my naked breast ...

Strike, as thou didst at Caesar; for I know,

When thou didst hate him worst, thou lovedst him better

Than ever thou lovedst Cassius.              (92-106)

His eloquence is now bluster and name-calling. His pride is a mask, and he finally breaks down in misery. Brutus melts, and they are quickly back to their former deep friendship. Brutus even comes close to sharing the blame: "When I spoke that, I was ill-tempered too" (115). Cassius pleads:

CAS:     O Brutus!

BRU:                What's the matter?

CAS:  Have not you love enough to bear with me,

When that rash humour which my mother gave me

Makes me forgetful?              (117-120)

Their reconciliation occurs over a glass of wine. Then comes the beautifully understated revelation of Brutus's heart-felt grief:

CAS:  I did not think you could have been so angry.

BRU:  O Cassius, I am sick of many griefs.

CAS:  Of your philosophy you make no use,

If you give place to accidental evils.

BRU:  No man bears sorrow better. Portia is dead.

CAS:  Ha? Portia?

BRU:  She is dead.

CAS:  How 'scaped I killing, when I crossed you so?

O insupportable and touching loss!     (142-149)

Cassius is astonished at Brutus' iron restraint. Brutus hides his conflict from others; the player requires considerable acting skill to convey this to the audience.* It is this sequence that makes Brutus a tragic character. From this point he goes clear-eyed towards his doom.

Then they plan future action. Brutus' egotism still makes him impose his will on his partners; after listening to Cassius' ideas, he prefers his own views and responds, "Good reasons must of force give place to better" (201). Brutus makes another big mistake: he insists that they advance across the Dardanelles to Macedonia and meet Antony and Octavius at Philippi. Yet he has a feeling of fate hanging over him:

> There is a tide in the affairs of men,
> Which, taken at the flood, leads on to fortune;
> Omitted, all the voyage of their life
> Is bound in shallows and in miseries.          (216-219)

This great metaphor of the human traveller, the sea voyager, who must set sail with the tide or else waste away in shallow waters forever, signifies intellectually that a person must seize opportunity when it presents itself or be content to live with failure forever. But the metaphor also gives emotional and aesthetic meanings: of distance; of the mystery and finality of tides; and of the weed-grown shallow waters. These lead, at a deep level, to the feelings of Brutus and give his words the seriousness of prophecy. Cassius abases himself, "Good night, my lord," which Brutus quickly corrects with "Good night, good brother" (235). Cassius and the others leave.

---

* There is a technical problem here. Brutus reveals the death to Cassius, but later in his talk to Messala he seems to be ignorant of it:

> BRUTUS:    Now, as you are a Roman, tell me true.
> MESSALA:   Then like a Roman bear the truth I tell;
>            For certain she is dead, and by strange manner.
> BRUTUS:    Why, farewell, Portia. We must die, Messala.
>            With meditating that she must die once,
>            I have the patience to endure it now.
> MESSALA:   Even so great men great losses should endure.
> CASSIUS:   I have as much of this in art as you,
>            But yet my nature could not bear it so.
> BRUTUS:    Well, to our work alive. What do you think
>            Of marching to Philippi presently?          (185-195)

As Brutus already knows of Portia's death, Cassius then assists him in his response. Brutus' action is not false; it is virtue — true manhood demonstrating itself for the benefit of others. *He has moved from private to public grief.*

Brutus asks his boy, Lucius, to play to him for a moment or two before he falls asleep. "What, thou speak'st drowsily?" (238) indicates that Lucius yawns — a reminder of Brutus' vanished home life. Peace and harmony settle on the scene: Brutus is gentle with the drowsy Lucius and thoughtful in telling his guards to "sleep on cushions in my tent" (241). He has just ordered the preparations for a battle; but on his own he turns to literature and music. This separation of his inner life from the world of affairs underlies his many mistakes. Shakespeare often uses music as a powerful emotional effect; the song is melancholic and nostalgic, helping to create this moment of quiet.

As those on the stage sleep and the music ceases, the calm, wakeful figure of Brutus sits reading in the silence. Then Caesar's Ghost appears:

BRU:  Speak to me what thou art.
GHO:  Thy evil spirit, Brutus.
BRU:                    Why com'st thou?
GHO:  To tell thee thou shalt see me at Philippi.
BRU:  Well; then I shall see thee again?
GHO:  Ay, at Philippi.
BRU:  Why, I will see thee at Philippi then.     (279-284)

We have been well prepared for the Ghost's presence. It enters as the candle "burns ill"; the Elizabethans believed that the appearance of spirits was accompanied by a wind; it also suggests an effective modern staging. Whether we think the Ghost has an objective reality, or that it is Brutus' mental creation, it is powerful and frightening. One of its purposes (as it is with all the supernatural occurrences and omens in the play) is to bring a sense of impending disaster. Unlike Hamlet or Macbeth, Brutus is inarticulate before the supernatural; then he becomes oracular. What Brutus talks of is less than what we expect from a tragic hero of his calibre.

*On the plains of Philippi the two opposing factions meet prior to battle. Brutus and Cassius make their farewell with the premonition that they may never meet again (V.i).*

The concluding section of the play [Act V] is the final conflict of the two factions. Historically there were two battles at Philippi, about three weeks apart; Shakespeare merges them into one, in five continuous scenes without a break. In this first scene, classical and medieval traditions of warfare are mixed:

the leaders of the Roman armies hold a parley like medieval knights prior to the fighting.

Antony and Octavius are very confident because in Brutus' error to meet them at Philippi "our hopes are answerèd" (1). Shakespeare also shows a shift in power from Antony to Octavius:

> ANT: Octavius, lead your battle softly on
>  Upon the left hand of the even field.
> OCT: Upon the right hand I. Keep thou the left.
> ANT: Why do you cross me in this exigent?
> OCT: I do not cross you; but I will do so. (16-20)

Antony does not argue, and four lines later he calls Octavius "Caesar" for the first time in the play. Then the rival army arrives.

This parley, which can look absurd in a scenic theatre, admirably suits the Elizabethan unlocalized stage [see *End Notes*]. Mutual recriminations follow. To Brutus' comment that his enemies make threats, Antony says:

> Villains! You did not so, when your vile daggers
> Hacked one another in the sides of Caesar:
> You showed your teeth like apes, and fawned like hounds,
> And bowed like bondmen, kissing Caesar's feet;
> Whilst damnèd Casca, like a cur, behind
> Struck Caesar on the neck. (39-44)

This is the final clash between the idealism of Brutus and Antony's contempt for it. Cassius says (of Antony):

> Now, Brutus, thank yourself:
> This tongue had not offended so today,
> If Cassius might have ruled. (45-47)

The practical Octavius is impatient of such childishness:

> Come, come, the cause. If arguing make us sweat,
> The proof of it will turn to redder drops.
> Look,
> I draw sword against conspirators.
> When think you that the sword goes up again?
> Never till Caesar's three and thirty wounds
> Be well avenged; or till another Caesar
> Have added slaughter to the sword of traitors. (48-55)

This is the first time he has spoken out, and he does it well. Cassius jeers:

A peevish schoolboy, worthless of such honour,
Joined with a masquer and a reveller.          (61-62)

"Old Cassius still!" mocks Antony.

When the rival armies divide, Cassius' violent outburst is despairing:

Why now, blow wind, swell billow, and swim bark!
The storm is up, and all is on the hazard.          (67-68)

Despite this, Cassius bravely proclaims himself

fresh of spirit, and resolved
To meet all perils very constantly.          (90-91)

Now Brutus and Cassius say farewell. Brutus rises to the height of Stoic dignity:

But this same day
Must end that work the ides of March begun;
And whether we shall meet again I know not.
Therefore our everlasting farewell take:
For ever, and for ever, farewell, Cassius.
If we do meet again, why, we shall smile;
If not, why then this parting was well made.          (112-118)

Cassius echoes the refrain:

For ever, and for ever, farewell, Brutus.
If we do meet again, we'll smile indeed;
If not, 'tis true this parting was well made.          (119-121)

As the battle is about to begin, Brutus expresses his anxiety about the outcome in words that could be said by Hamlet:

O, that a man might know
The end of this day's business ere it come!
But it sufficeth that the day will end,
And then the end is known.          (122-125)

They do not meet again.

*Brutus sends Messala to Cassius with an urgent plea for him to move in a decisive thrust at Octavius' forces (V.ii).*

In one corner of the battle, Brutus breaks Octavius' army for the moment. He sends Messala, liaison officer from Cassius, with a message for Cassius to bring his forces in against Antony's wing:

Ride, ride, Messala, ride, and give these bills
Unto the legions on the other side.          (1-2)

There might be a chance of victory.

> *Cassius thinks he is defeated and makes Pindarus stab
> him. Messala finds Cassius' body and Titinius kills him-
> self. Brutus pays his friend a sad farewell (V.iii).*

We now have a series of short and swift episodes in the battle. Cassius' army retreats before Antony's:

> O Cassius, Brutus gave the word too early,
> Who, having some advantage on Octavius,
> Took it too eagerly; his soldiers fell to spoil,
> Whilst we by Antony are all enclosed. (5-8)

Pindarus, Cassius' servant, rushes in: Antony's men are plun-
dering his tents; he must escape quickly or he will be captured.
Cassius gets far enough away for a view and sees his tents on
fire with a body of cavalry approaching in the distance. He
sends Titinius to find out who they are. Pindarus gets to an
even higher vantage point to see what happens.

In the confusion friend cannot be told from foe. Cassius
assumes that Titinius has been captured and that the enemy
has won. Cassius cries:

> O, coward that I am, to live so long,
> To see my best friend ta'en before my face! (34-35)

Cassius asks Pindarus to run him through with his own sword.
His death has the pattern of his reckless life: he dies because he
will not wait to verify the tale of Titinius' capture. His last words
are bare and ruthless:

> Caesar, thou art revenged,
> Even with the sword that killed thee. (45-46)

He offers Caesar merely a life for a life. His death is a positive
and dynamic life-in-death poetically apprehended, something
which we do not find in the deaths of Brutus and Macbeth.
Pindarus, a captive Parthian, heads for home and is never seen
again.

Titinius enters with Messala. The tale is all a mistake. It was
Brutus' troops that surrounded Titinius excitedly telling him of
their victory over Octavius' wing. Messala finds Cassius dead,
and Titinius says:

> O setting sun,
> As in thy red rays thou dost sink to night,
> So in his red blood Cassius' day is set.
> The sun of Rome is set. Our day is gone ... (60-63)

His final phrase has a three-fold meaning: the passing of the physical day; the end of Cassius' "day" or time on earth; and the passing of an era. Messala goes. Titinius crowns the dead Cassius with the wreath of victory:

> But hold thee, take this garland on thy brow;
> Thy Brutus bid me give it thee, and I
> Will do his bidding. Brutus, come apace,
> And see how I regarded Caius Cassius.               (85-88)

Titinius then stabs himself with Cassius' sword. When Brutus arrives his comment is similar to that of Cassius just before he died: Julius Caesar's spirit is strong and stalking the assassins for vengeance.

What prevents Cassius from converting his dreams into reality are his own limitations. Death mocks Cassius' discrepant role-playing. Cassius alive cannot be the leader he dreams of being, but in death he exists only through Brutus' verbal account of him. When Cassius dies, he becomes in Brutus' words exactly what he had hoped to be:

> The last of all the Romans, fare thee well!
> It is impossible that ever Rome
> Should breed thy fellow.                                 (99-101)

The bodies are carried out in procession with due dignity.

> *As Brutus spurs his men on, Lucilius is captured and mis-taken for Brutus until Antony recognizes him (V.iv).*

> *Brutus wants his friends to help him commit suicide. Strato finally consents. Antony and Octavius enter to find Strato with the body of Brutus. Antony delivers the eulogy, and Octavius orders an honoured burial (V.v).*

A little group of beaten and exhausted men, the torchlight flickering on their faces, watch the defeated Brutus and his chief aides arrive.

> BRU:   Come, poor remains of friends, rest on this
>               rock.
> CLI:    Statilius showed the torch-light; but, my lord,
>               He came not back: he is or ta'en or slain.
> BRU:   Sit thee down, Clitus. Slaying is the word;
>               It is a deed in fashion.                        (1-5)

He has lost the battle because, although he defeated Octavius's wing of the army, he neglected Cassius's failure against Antony.

There is silence on the empty battlefield. We cannot even hear Brutus as he whispers first to Clitus, next to Dardanius; aloud he asks Volumnius to hold his sword while he runs on it but is refused. There are threatening low alarums; Antony and Octavius are closing in. His followers cry to him to save himself. Surrounded by loyal and loving friends, he reasserts his belief in the rightness of his part in the conspiracy as he saw it:

> My heart doth joy that yet in all my life
> I found no man but he was true to me.
>
> I shall have glory by this losing day         (34-36)

which is ironic. He praises his colleagues' loyalty; then at his command they leave him. Brutus approaches his body-servant, Strato:

> BRU:  I prithee, Strato, stay thou by thy lord.
>        Thou art a fellow of a good respect;
>        Thy life hath had some smatch of honour in it.
>        Hold then my sword, and turn away thy face,
>        While I do run upon it. Wilt thou, Strato?
> STRATO:   Give me your hand first. Fare you well, my lord.
> BRU:   Farewell, good Strato. — Caesar, now be still;
>      I killed not thee with half so good a will.    (44-51)

And acknowledging the power of "the spirit of Caesar," Brutus dies.

Octavius, Antony and their armies arrive. Octavius is clearly in charge, and Antony is present only to pay tribute to Brutus:

> This was the noblest Roman of them all.
> All the conspirators save only he
> Did that they did in envy of great Caesar;
> He only, in a general honest thought
> And common good to all, made one of them.
> His life was gentle, and the elements
> So mixed in him, that Nature might stand up
> And say to all the world, 'This was a man!'     (68-75)

Finally there is the play's formal close: the ceremonial lifting of the body, the apostrophe to the dead, and a view of the living future. For these events, Octavius is in charge.

## STYLE

The speech style of *Julius Caesar* is the clearest in Shakespeare's plays. There is little variation in the talk of people; from "You blocks, you stones, you worse than senseless things"* at the opening, everyone finds it easy to say what he thinks. The phrasing for stage speech is invariably flawless: pauses are accurately placed for breathing, and no thought is too long or short for its words.

What people say in the play grows out of rhetoric, originally the art of oratory. Written words, Socrates says, are not alive. ** If you put a question to them, there is only one reply. But, as Agricola also comments, speech is different; listeners are listening not reading — they can answer back. Shakespeare inherits the verbal formulaic techniques (figures) of Agricola and Erasmus, which are part of a still essentially oral age. Shakespeare's figures grow out of understanding language through sound (oral and aural). In *Julius Caesar,* the most important figures are: the *anaphora,* as when Marullus addresses the commoners ("And do you now put on your best attire?" etc.); *alliteration* (repeating an initial consonant), which creates an aural effect, such as Calphurnia's description of disturbed nature ("graves have yawned and yielded up their dead" (II.ii.18); the *pun,* intensifying meaning or mood — found less here than in, say, *Romeo and Juliet;* the *double epithet,* which links two words of roughly the same meaning — "O insupportable and touching loss" (IV.iii.149); a word of Anglo-Saxon origin linked to a Latinate word — "insupportable" (Latin) explained by "touching"; *apostrophe,* as when the speaker turns away from his audience and makes an abstract comment to intensify the emotional tone — when Cassius says, "O ye gods, ye gods! Must I endure all this?" (IV.iii.41) he turns from Brutus and addresses the gods; *hyperbole* ("overstatement"), heightening many effects — "The last of all the Romans, fare thee well" (V.iii.99)

---

* This uses *onomatopoeia:* it suggests actual blows by the blunt, strong monosyllables, and the repeated "s" suggests the hiss of a whip.

** *Phaedrus* 275c.

(he is not the last); and *axiomatic brevity* — Calphurnia warns Caesar not to go to the Capitol: "Your wisdom is consumed in confidence" (II.ii.49).

*Julius Caesar* is notable for its use of monosyllables. No Shakespearean play uses so many nor uses them so superbly. What Julius Caesar and Mark Antony say is often entirely monosyllabic.

Compared to many Shakespearean plays, *Julius Caesar* is largely unmetaphorical and unlyrical. Its stylistic power comes from its strong sentence structure, clarity of meaning, and simple rhythms rather than from associative richness, complexity and allusiveness, as in *Romeo and Juliet*. Nor has *Julius Caesar* the complex imagery of the earlier tragedy. Yet its poetry has major and minor image patterns in simile, metaphor, or description of an event; these appear in ideas that are verbally expressed or embodied in the stage actions.

There are various forms of "extended imagery": a series of related figures of speech. Those focussed on animals ("the dogs of war") and "ambition" are obvious. But the most significant centres on the ritual meal, as with Brutus' "Let us carve him as a dish fit for the gods" (II.i.173). It can appear in verbal expressions: e.g., Cassius asks, "Upon what meat doth this our Caesar feed" (I.ii.148), which is about his source of power; and Caesar sees Cassius as "lean and hungry" (I.ii.193) and thus dangerous to his power. Or the imagery can focus on the action: e.g., the assassination. The pagan atmosphere can blend with a more ethical tone: "Let us be sacrificers, but not butchers, Caius" (II.i.166). In all of these cases the imagery heightens and directs the feelings of the audience.

Most of these images are embedded in political and personal conflicts; they tie them together, giving each additional perspectives. Thus "blood" has two knots of complex meaning: first, *the blood of sacrifice*. To Brutus, blood is the regrettable result of a necessary sacrifice to save the body politic of Rome. It is associated with images of value, of metallic hacking and cutting, or of animals, stag-hunting or bleeding carcasses. These are given direct embodiment, and thus more power, when Caesar's mutilated body lies before the audience for the double climax of III.i-ii.

Second is *the blood of guilt*. To Antony, the conspirators wantonly spilt the blood of the noblest man of all. Thus the blood signifies their guilt: smeared on their arms "Up to the elbows" (III.i.107); it is associated with false humility ("kissing Caesar's feet" (V.i.42)), curs and other fawning animals, and the elixir to make sacred the handkerchiefs dipped in it.

## PLAYING THE PLAY

*Julius Caesar* is a magnificent play for actors. Every role, including the tiniest, is the kind that players like to get their teeth into. The only drawback is that there are but two female roles; neither is large, yet both require good acting.

Every character in the play is affected by a major decision of the director who must answer the questions we posed at the beginning of this chapter. Does the play have one tragic hero? If so, who is it? If it has more than one, who are they? The director's answers will result in a particular interpretation.

Today, most productions have Brutus as the main tragic hero, with one or more others having tragic qualities. Then the question for the director becomes how effective an innocent person can be in moral action. This question addresses the ambiguity of innocence, and this tragic problem goes far deeper than the relation between private and public virtue (also present in the play). Innocence plays into the hands of evil. How it does so affects everyone in the cast.

Brutus is a liberal intellectual caught in a world of *realpolitik* — familiar enough to us from Shakespeare's early histories as well as in modern life. "Honour" for Brutus is moral purity and integrity. Yet Antony may be right when he implies that "honour" is merely an empty word for Brutus. He gives little thought to it. It becomes a catch-phrase to him: because he *believes* he is "honourable," whatever he *wishes* to do will be honourable. This is false. By playing the role of the honourable man, he deceives himself and others. The central quality of Brutus is not his virtue but his will: his virtue is a mask that hides his will from others; they mistakenly believe that his egotistical willfulness is incorruptible principle. His mask of virtue fools everyone, even himself. As a result he is both unworldly and obstinate. In his quarrel with Cassius, Brutus is as arrogant as Caesar at his worst; he sees himself as different from and superior to other men. Yet privately, with Portia and his boy, Lucius, he is a kindly man. It is in public terms that he is the supposed "noble Brutus."

It is his false role that gives Brutus his tragic qualities. He suffers an inner conflict, is worked on by outside forces, and is torn between two parts of himself: his personal relationships and the public good. He is forced to make a huge irrevocable moral choice. The play then traces the hideous interim between the "first motion" and "the acting of a dreadful thing" (II.i.63-64), followed by its consequences, and finally the tragic disillusionment. But as Shakespeare has shaped the play's action and characters (particularly Caesar) with deliberate ambiguity, no one in the play (including Brutus) is a tragic hero in the same sense as Hamlet or Othello.

To find the tragedy of Brutus in his rigid devotion to justice and fair play is too simplistic. Audiences at the Globe believed that his virtues were complicated by self-deception and doubtful principle. To Elizabethans, the conspiracy against Caesar represented a flouting of unitary sovereignty, the basis of Tudor policy. They saw in Brutus a conflict between questionable goals and honourable action. Like Othello, Brutus has an integrity of conduct which leads him into evil; with Othello it is his face, but with Brutus it is his mask.

But Cassius, too, is tragic. And with the example of Gielgud's superb Cassius before us (on stage or film), the director might be led to see Cassius as the central character. Cassius, as a skilled politician, has no scruples in manipulating Brutus's finer feelings to get him into the plot. Cassius' philosophy is Machiavellian — more Renaissance than Roman — and he has a personal animosity behind his drive to murder Caesar. Yet he is no Iago. Caesar's brief description of Cassius is reasonably accurate. He is an "unharmonious" man "who hears no music" (I.ii.203), so Cassius is a figure of disorder in two ways: personally, his hatred of Caesar is grounded in envy at beholding one greater than himself; and politically, his abhorrence is based on his belief in a free, republican Rome. Once Caesar is murdered, Cassius so admires Brutus that he allows him moral ascendancy, and this gesture destroys both them and their republican ideal. Moreover, Cassius the

Epicurean becomes like Brutus the Stoic when he commits suicide, because he is ashamed of having lived "so long, To see
my best friend ta'en before my face!" (V.iii.34-35). It is Cassius'
suicide, even more than the military defeat, that ends the
republican cause. Nor is Cassius so unlike Brutus: he is
shrewder and more practical, but he is basically an idealist too,
an intellectual, whom Caesar had come to suspect because
"He thinks too much" (I.ii.194).

Cassius is like a babe in arms compared to Mark Antony, a
man with no innocence. Antony, the man-of-the-world, viva-
cious and deep-feeling, is the master of "practical knowledge":
he has the "know how" to manipulate people and events to
his own advantage. He is not evil, like the Machiavels in
Shakespeare's early histories: he is generous, kind-hearted
and noble. Antony's success is as a dramatist: he creates
playlets for others and lets them act them out like puppets.
While Cassius creates a Brutus playlet so that he will join the
conspiracy, Antony shows in his famous oration that he is a
great dramatic artist, even superior to Richard III, Iago, and
Edmund in *King Lear*. He is no villain but the tarnished sensual man, halfway between innocence and evil. Above all,
Antony is the compromiser: he finds the possible between his
self-interest and his ideals — he works with what is practica-
ble. The initial impression of him as a harmless playboy wears
off after the assassination when he secures permission to
make the crucial funeral address that sways the populace to
riot. Then we know him for what he is and for what Cassius
always suspected him to be.

What of Julius Caesar himself? After all, the play bears his
name. Curiously, while he is on the stage, he is not tragic. We
see three sides of him: the bombastic ruler who likens himself
to a god; the sick old man with many ailments; and the husband who is willing to be persuaded by his wife — at least, at
first. These three elements are not fully integrated into a living
whole; rather, each one, as it is presented to us, has the appearance of a caricature. The actor, in making the role effective,
needs to cultivate some distance between himself and the ordinary people around him. In my all-male production (1953), I
asked the player to create the character on the basis of the
Colossus metaphor, and it was most effective.

Although Octavius has fewer lines than the other four main characters, no other Shakespearean role is better done within its limitations: he appears three times, speaks some thirty lines, and not one of them is wasted. Antony at Philippi saves the political fortunes of the young Octavius Caesar, who is his nemesis in *Antony and Cleopatra*. Here, however, Octavius is shrewd, cool-headed, incisive and cold. We can well imagine him maturing into the powerful Emperor Augustus. But he is certainly not the tragic hero of *Julius Caesar*, practical success was not, for Shakespeare, the greatest thing in life. Octavius Caesar simply acts; since he exists only in what he does, he is less a character than an embodiment of history.

If in doubt, the director should let the actors fully play their roles to mutually discover the play's tragedy. The brilliance of the play allows for such an uncovering.

# HAMLET

## THE PLAY AND POSSIBILITY

*amlet* is the world's most famous play. It triumphs over time. It is a living organism, never the same from one moment to the next. Each succeeding generation re-creates it.

Today when we read or perform the play we must interpret it for our own time and understand what it means for us here and now. We need to know the meanings gathered by those who have come before us, how these have come into the present day, as well as the meanings specific to our own age. *Hamlet* has been discussed by the greatest critics; yet it defies final analysis, and it permits constant new interpretations. At the same time, actors and directors continuously re-think *Hamlet* and play it in every conceivable way.

*Hamlet* marks a major cultural and historical change in human life, a dramatic world where, for the first time, personality is understood in modern terms. The noble Dane, a solitary figure dressed in black, appears at the moment when "modern" man is born, even though "modern" woman has to wait a few centuries. In the Renaissance, people had struggled out of the collectivity of the Middle Ages and were now free, sceptical and complex individuals. In the person of Hamlet, a modern individual supremely confident of his power over nature, but uncertain of himself and his relations with other people, is given artistic embodiment.

Hamlet is not a self-portrait of Shakespeare. But both the character and the play represent a huge step in his artistic development: they gather together many of the significant themes and ideas of his previous plays, and they are also the beginnings for the great plays that are to follow. *Hamlet* is a watershed for Shakespeare. He creates it halfway through his career, and it is a new departure that is also a culmination.

*Hamlet* the play and Hamlet the person are creations of the theatre. Through Hamlet, Shakespeare understands human beings as actors with true or false masks: honest men or counterfeits, idealists or madmen — but what is "mad," after all? In the playhouse we can see through people's roles. The theatre, as someone once said, is "two boards and a passion." And on the boards, the passion hinges on the actor and his art. In *Hamlet*, Shakespeare, with Burbage and their players, changes the nature and function of theatrical art — and they reveal a new perspective on human nature.

When Shakespeare began writing, the actor's identity with the character was still not quite complete. It was the time of the great clowns, like Tarleton and Kempe, whom the audience knew whatever character they played. The leading London player was Edward Alleyn; life was displayed in his heroic acting. He performed Tamburlaine superbly for the Lord Admiral's Men, but Marlowe had created a character more to be exhibited than acted. So Alleyn "ranted": he went through the motions at a distance from the character. This was not "distancing" in Brecht's sense; Alleyn was more like a puppet than an actor, at least as we would conceive the actor today.

By the time we reach *Hamlet*, Shakespeare has instituted a change. When acting the Dane, Burbage identifies himself with the character he plays. Shakespeare and the company have slowly led up to this development, and it is a conscious decision. The beginnings are in Launce, in the Nurse and in Dogberry, among the broad characters, and in the disguised heroines of the comedies. The next step is Brutus and Cassius, and Hal and Falstaff. But in *Hamlet* the change is complete. The actors forget themselves in their characters, and then the spectators can more easily forget their own world for the *play world*. Much of the appeal of the man, Hamlet, occurs because we so directly experience his intimate feelings. *We see the actor as Hamlet* — it is as though Garrick, or Irving, or Gielgud is appealing to us in his own person. But the actor does not *totally* become Hamlet. Rather, we know Hamlet *through* the actor — much as we know others in life through their social roles. The player analyses Hamlet and then reconstructs the Dane in terms of his own personality.

Shakespeare discovers how to write for performances of this kind. He learns that the actors and their acting are the dramatist's living medium, just as paint is for the visual artist and music is for the composer. Acting is the essential element which Shakespeare must not let his glorious verse, or his company's splendid costumes and pageantry, overshadow.

Shakespeare in his plays is not just a great poet, despite some critics. Dramatic poetry, as Granville-Barker said, is not primarily a matter of words.* Rather, it centres on the poetic conception of character and action: the drama of the theatre. This is nowhere better exemplified than in the opening of the first scene on the battlements in *Hamlet*. A clock strikes. There are brief words — questions — the movement of soldiers in armour — whispers — the gloom and mystery of the night — and then the appearance of the Ghost! In these minimal elements, Shakespeare's actors embody the figures of his imagination. Through words and actions together, they create the profundity of a moment in human life.

Hamlet is the most lifelike and original of Shakespeare's people. He has previously used the "melancholy man," with whom many Elizabethans identified, for Romeo, Orsino, Jaques and others. Now he mixes this figure with many seeming contradictions and with such superb theatrical craft that he strikes a chord among the Elizabethans, as he does among modern audiences. Shakespeare learned how to do this in rehearsal and performance: to think directly in the medium in which he worked; to design the movement of the play as a whole and the rhythms of which it was constituted; to plan the material to give to the actors of his characters; and to focus on the humanity of the actors and their acting. It is in this sense that *Hamlet* is a creation of the theatre, and this must be the basis of any interpretation.

## THE ORIGINAL *HAMLET*

*Hamlet* is a revenge tragedy first presented at the Globe in the daylight of a London afternoon. When was the script written, and how did Shakespeare and his fellows interpret it?

---

* Granville-Barker (1963).

*Hamlet* belongs to 1600 or the early months of 1601. At this time Shakespeare was much concerned with the relationship between the mind, the whole reflective personality, and the world it engages. In the plays written in this period, he addresses the distortions in people's way of looking at the world: the relation of "knowledge" to the knower, to what a person *is*, and to the true or distorted imagination.

Shakespeare was also preoccupied with a troubled father-son relationship. Was this because his own father died in September 1601? In the *Henry IV* plays Northumberland and Hotspur, father and son, parallel the King-Hal and Falstaff-Hal pairings. *Julius Caesar* (1599) is a very different revenge play which emphasizes Caesar and his protegés Brutus and Mark Antony. In *Hamlet,* the killing of Caesar is remembered at two significant moments (I.i.113-120; III.ii.112-113); both plays have a vengeful ghost. *Hamlet* stresses the father-son motif by using three pairs: old Hamlet and the Prince, old Fortinbras and his son, and Polonius and Laertes. All three fathers die violently, and while their sons wish to avenge them, their actions are very different. Hamlet's father was a medieval-style hero, with a love of honour and courtly demeanour. Shakespeare had shown in *Richard II* and *1 and 2 Henry IV* that this world is obsolete and faintly absurd. In *Hamlet* too, the new young men in Norway and Denmark are not in the heroic mould; and Hamlet admits that he, unlike his father, is no Hercules (I.ii.153).

By 1600 Shakespeare was well aware of the contradiction and ambiguity of contemporary attitudes to revenge. In Elizabethan England, the retaliation for murder was solely the business of the state and the law, but this clashed with an irrational but powerful feeling that people cannot be blamed for taking revenge into their own hands to make the punishment fit the crime. Shakespeare must also have known the many plays which refer to revenge: the Roman plays of Seneca and imitations of them in English tragedies, like *Gorboduc.*

In revenge tragedy, the virtuous revenger (unlike villainous Machiavels such as Iago) attracts audience sympathy until he resolves his problem and actually kills; the audience then turns on him, believing that he is contaminated by the deed. Only in *Hamlet* does the audience retain sympathy for the hero from beginning to end. Hamlet is not the usual revenge hero; he cannot act in a brutal, uncomplicated way, yet he cannot ignore the Ghost's command. Until Act IV, he lacks real evidence of his uncle's villainy, but Hamlet's self-accusations show that this is not the whole explanation for his delay. He can, on impulse, kill an invisible foe like Polonius, and he can destroy Rosencrantz and Guildenstern by signing a paper. What Hamlet cannot do is the thing Hieronymo, Titus, and the other revengers do: look in the face of another human being and deliberately kill him. Hamlet is not able to deceive himself, like Laertes, that revenge by itself is a real solution. In fact, Shakespeare extends to the limit the revenge play as a form to inquire into the self and a person's place in society.

His principal source, almost certainly, was a lost Elizabethan play, the so-called *Ur-Hamlet*. Probably written by Thomas Kyd prior to 1589, it is known to us indirectly through a German *Hamlet* and Shakespeare's first Quarto. Philip Henslowe, the manager of the Lord Admiral's Men, refers in his diary to a performance of it on June 11, 1594. The original tale has its roots in the ancient stories, legends and folk tales re-written by Saxo Grammaticus (c. 1180-1208). There is no evidence that Shakespeare read Saxo. But there is every indication he knew Kyd's Hamlet play along with his immensely successful revenge play, *The Spanish Tragedy* (1587), which Shakespeare had already drawn on for his early plays.

Shakespeare also drew on the folk traditions he knew and the ritual dramas performed in the Elizabethan countryside. This tradition is less obvious in *Hamlet* than in other plays such as *The Merry Wives,* but it affected the deep layers and the unconscious structure of the play. For example, the names of both Hamlet and Brutus, Shakespeare's most intellectual characters, signify "the stupid one." Shakespeare knew that in history both boys, after the murders of their fathers, escaped death by pretending to be fools — by putting on "an antic disposition." Indeed, the Hamlet tale has its remote origins in the great world myths: the emergence of a dark wisdom from riddles and apparent folly, a son's revenge for his dead father, and the cleansing of a polluted house.

Robert Ornstein shows how this deep level of Shakespeare's meaning in the ancient scapegoat is reflected in today's juve-

nile delinquent. Hamlet is the victim of a bad home environ-
ment where his stepfather is an alcoholic criminal, and his
mother is a shallow, good-natured creature too easy with her
affections. Unable to communicate with his parents, Hamlet
seeks affection with a youthful companion. Like many young
people, Hamlet is maladjusted and emotionally unstable; he is
moody, hostile, withdrawn, and cynically contemptuous of
authority. Ornstein goes on to say:

> He has homicidal and suicidal tendencies. He is
> abnormally preoccupied with sex and yet incapable
> of returning the love of the girl he sadistically mal-
> treats. He is an exhibitionist in speech and clothing
> ... Deprived of status in his society, he seeks atten-
> tion through acts of violence. But after creating a
> scene in the theatre and killing Polonius, he is sent
> away for radical therapy ... In sum he is, as T. S. Eliot
> brilliantly observed, a rebel without a cause, con-
> sumed with an unfathomable hatred of a world in
> which he never had a chance.*

It is little wonder that the play is highly popular now, at the end
of the twentieth century.

## THE SCRIPT
We are not at all sure that Shakespeare's final script is available
to us. *Hamlet* exists in three substantive texts: the first Quarto
(1603; Q1), the second Quarto (1604; Q2), and the First Folio
(1623; F1). Each gives a reading different from the others.

Q1 was piratically printed and is a puzzling travesty of what
the printer said was a "true and perfect Coppie." Perhaps Q1
was pieced together by an actor with a poor memory who
played the part of Marcellus. He probably wrote down a short-
ened version of the play to be used in the provinces, adding
hints of the *Ur-Hamlet*.

Q2 is a "good" quarto: almost twice the length of Q1, it has
the true Shakespearean ring in almost every line. F1 lacks some
200 lines found in Q2, and it has about 85 new lines; perhaps F1
was used for the Company's established practice at a later date.

---

* Ornstein (1960).

There are many differences between the two texts. Modern editors usually prefer Q2, adding the new lines from F1. The result is a script that was not acted in Shakespeare's time.

*Hamlet* is easily the longest of Shakespeare's plays. When acted, even the shorter F1 is a great length. During much of the year it would have been impossible to fit an uncut *Hamlet* into the number of daylight playing hours available for an ordinary afternoon at the Globe. When the entire tragedy is attempted in the modern theatre, it is an endurance test for players and audience alike. An uncut performance of *Hamlet,* even of the shorter F1, is rarely seen today. Which parts are cut depends on the director's interpretation of the play.

## THE FIRST PERFORMANCES

Richard Burbage was about thirty years old when he first performed Hamlet to much public acclaim. He had already developed the skills to deliver the varied art of the reflective soliloquy as Henry V and Brutus. It is theatre lore that Shakespeare was the first to play the Ghost. John Heminges played Polonius; he had previously created old Capulet, Richard II's Uncle York, Egeus, Glendower, Leonato, and others — a fact more important than that old Lord Burghley might have been the model from life. Robert Armin, the chief comedian of the company since Will Kempe left, was the Gravedigger. Kempe had played the first Launce and Dogberry, but Armin brought a new dimension of fooling seen in Feste and Touchstone, noble ancestors of the Gravedigger.

T. W. Baldwin has conjectured the cast-list for Hamlet during the summer of 1603:*

| Hamlet | Burbage | Claudius | Lowin |
|---|---|---|---|
| Horatio | Condell | Polonius | Heminges |
| Laertes | Sly | Ghost | Shakespeare |
| 1 Gravedigger | Armin | Osrick | Cowley |
| Rosencrantz | Cooke | Fortinbras | Gilburne |
| Gertrude | Crosse | Ophelia | Wilson |

The manner of performance was of rapid, uninterrupted continuity, sweeping on from scene to scene without a break. This

---

* Baldwin (1961).

onward motion is inherent in Shakespeare's dramatic narrative, action and sound, the speech of the actors supported by the sounds of trumpet, drum, or cannonade.

The play requires few objects: no scenery apart from the backing of the tiring-house; and furniture and properties that are functional or evocative: the council-table (I.ii), the two thrones, the players' own cart-load of properties, the pick, spade and skull for the graveyard, and the elaborate paraphernalia of the final duel, listed in the stage directions of Q2 and F1.

When modern productions of *Hamlet* use Shakespeare's own form of staging, the only difficulty is Ophelia's burial. Shakespeare used a trap door in the floor for the grave: Laertes and (perhaps) Hamlet jumped down into it, and Ophelia was buried there. Without some form of lower level, the men cannot jump into it, and Ophelia's body must be carried off-stage again — which looks strange.

Costumes were probably Elizabethan: a few hints suggest a contemporary style (e.g., Hamlet's doublet and stockings), while others (a sea-gown, a suit of sables, a bonnet) are of no specific period. They were also sumptuous for at least the principal characters. Shakespeare's keen eye for the dramatic is shown in the startling contrast of Hamlet's "inky cloak" with the glorious finery of Claudius' courtiers (I.ii); in the Ghost's first martial attire and the pathetic contrast of his visit to his widow's closet in his night gown (given in Q1); in the different uniform of Fortinbras's Norwegian army; and in the dandified caricature of young Osrick, the "water-fly."

## THE GREAT TRADITION

In interpreting *Hamlet* we discover much from past performances that can help us.* From Burbage's time to today, the play's widespread appeal shows that there is a core of meaning that all audiences share. Paradoxically, various changes by individual actors have immediately appealed to spectators at a particular moment in history.

---

* For stage history see Salgado (1975), Sprague (1944, 1953) and Sprague and Trewin (1970).

## FROM BETTERTON TO GARRICK

*Hamlet* was played fairly consistently from the Restoration to Garrick's retirement. The tragedy was one of intrigue and irony, according to Hames Drake (1699), who wrote the first extended criticism of the play. The play was altered less than others, though it was cut to get rid of "irrelevant" matter and to make it conform to usual length. Scenes were transposed, supposedly to achieve unity. Later a happy ending was added, with Hamlet living.

The most important actor to interpret the role in the Restoration was Thomas Betterton, the leading member of the Duke's Company. Betterton had the benefit of the advice of Lowin, who had created the original Claudius. In 1709, Steele in the *Tatler* said of Betterton's last recorded performance in the role at the Haymarket:

> Had you been to-night at the play-house, you had seen the force of action in perfection: your admired Mr. Betterton behaved himself so well, that, though now about seventy, he acted youth; and by the prevalent power of proper manner, gesture, and voice, appeared through the whole drama a young man of great expectation, vivacity, and enterprise.

Here was a Hamlet who was a "hero." Colley Cibber said that when Betterton as Hamlet saw the Ghost, "he open'd with a pause of mute amazement! then rising slowly to a solemn, trembling voice, he made the ghost equally terrible to the spectator as to himself!"

Hamlet continued to be played by such tragedians as Robert Wilks and Barton Booth. One critic reported of James Quinn that he was in such a rage at his father's ghost that he stamped and raved at it.

The great David Garrick made *Hamlet* (Drury Lane, 1772) into one of his finest successes. At first he tried to remove the Gravedigger's scene and the fencing-match in deference to pseudo-classical prejudice, but the public objected. Garrick added a melancholy asked for by Aaron Hill: it was meditative, with little bitterness in it: half thought and half feeling in the period style. Garrick had the inner energy to make Shakespeare's words his own. He also organized a Jubilee at Stratford-upon-Avon in September 1769, the first of the

Shakespearean festivals now held each year in many places throughout the world.

## FROM KEMBLE TO IRVING

Garrick's great shadow fell over the later Hamlets of Spranger Barry, John Henderson and even the brothers Kemble, who around the turn of the century tried to restore Shakespeare's text. John Philip Kemble devised more historically accurate costumes, starting a return to studying the play as Shakespeare wrote it. Kemble's famous portrait by Lawrence, with his hat of plumed feathers and long cloak, shows him wearing the miniature which he displays to Gertrude in the closet scene, a tradition that Gielgud and many modern Hamlets continued.

No one noticed that Hamlet was delaying his revenge until Goethe and other late eighteenth-century romantic critics began exploring the Prince's psyche.

> The time is out of joint. O, cursèd spite,
> That ever I was born to set it right!     (I.v.188-189)

When Goethe said that these words held the key to Hamlet, he began an international tradition for interpreting the play. In the romantic period, Edmund Kean was a bravura Hamlet who overshadowed the characterizations of other major actors like Charles Young. Romantic actors were occupied with the question, why does Hamlet not act immediately?

Coleridge thought that all hangs on the "To be or not to be" soliloquy:

> Thus conscience does make cowards of us all;
> And thus the native hue of resolution
> Is sicklied o'er with the pale cast of thought ...
>
>                                          (III.i.83-85)

In other words, the balance between the real and the imaginary worlds is disturbed. This new concept slowly infused the performances that followed.

After 1837 William Macready began to act and direct the play using the restored text, trying to realize Shakespeare's intentions. By mid-century, Charles Kean, like his father Edmund, dominated *Hamlet* as the "star" and carried Kemble's historical staging and costuming to extremes. Whether Hamlet was actually mad or only pretending to be became a major issue. The Victorians were much concerned with madness.

Charles Fechter, a French actor, appeared as a most romantic Hamlet who only pretended to be mad (1861); unfortunately his foreign accent and frequent error of emphasis stood in the way of his success.

The climax of nineteenth century Hamlets was Henry Irving's (Lyceum, 1874). Irving tailored the play to highlight his role, yet as he was an artist concerned with the integrity of the entire performance, his production became world renowned. Ellen Terry (whose Ophelia was "a wonder") minutely described Irving's appearance as Hamlet. The pale face, disordered black hair, simple tunic edged with fur: "No bugles, no order of the Danish Elephant — he did not wear the miniature of his father obtrusively round his neck." Perhaps she was thinking of Fechter, who played Hamlet with her sister Kate (John Gielgud's grandmother) as Ophelia.

The influence of Henry Irving was and continues to be enormous. H. B. Irving copied his father's make-up and costume and looked extremely like him. Johnston Forbes-Robertson, who had played continually with Irving, also wore much the same attire in his *Hamlet* with Mrs. Patrick Campbell (1897). She played Ophelia as really mad. Forbes-Robertson introduced the idea of the actor lying exhausted and supine, after the Ghost's revelation, and he looked up at the stars as he said, "O all you host of heaven." This action was repeated by John Barrymore, Donald Wolfit, and by many others. There was also a series of famous Hamlets who conformed to a more traditional performance of the Prince: Salvani and "the divine" Sarah Bernhardt (1899) from the continent; Edwin Booth, Edward Sothern and Walter Hampden in America; and in London, Herbert Beerbohm Tree (1892) and Wilson Barrett.

To get *Hamlet* into three hours, with the elaborate scenic changes of the times, meant so much cutting that managers had to solve the problem as best they could. When Frank Benson gave the whole text at Stratford-upon-Avon (1899), he performed it in two sections, going in the afternoon to the end of the Play Scene, and at night beginning with Claudius' prayer.

## PSYCHOLOGISTS

In the 1880s British universities broke philology into its component parts, and the discipline of English Literature, which included plays, emerged, though drama as a separate university discipline had to wait for many years.

By 1900, authoritative scholars examined plays as literature. Thus A. C. Bradley's *Shakespearean Tragedy* (1904) begins, like Irving, from Hamlet as a man of exquisite moral sensibility: his melancholy is not the madness which he feigns. Hamlet is a well-liked man of action whose sensitivity is over-strained by his task, and the result is his inaction.

Bradley published his psychological approach at roughly the same time as Freud became famous for psychoanalysis, the effect of the unconscious on conscious life. Ernest Jones's Freudian view of *Hamlet* comes fifty years later,* but it describes what psychoanalysts had been discussing — namely, that Hamlet suffers from an Oedipus complex. Hamlet becomes conscious of this with the Ghost's revelations: "O my prophetic soul! My uncle?" Hamlet sees his duty to avenge his father's murder, but his mother's guilty sexual conduct is horrifying. And Bradley agreed. Jones says that Hamlet's conflict lies in his wish for the death of his father at the hands of a jealous rival, and an unconscious jealousy at his mother giving herself to another man. The result is an intense sexual revulsion; Hamlet's obscene jests with Ophelia become intelligible when we remember that they take place in front of Gertrude. His sense of his own evil prevents him from denouncing his uncle. As Claudius incorporates the deepest and most buried part of his own personality, he cannot kill him without killing himself.

These psychological explanations are far from Shakespeare's humours, around which he created Hamlet. But they are ways in which people at the beginning of the twentieth century were coming to understand themselves. These views are reflected in the performances of Gielgud and Olivier, Finney and Schofield, Redgrave and Jacobi, and other Hamlets of our time.

## HAMLET IN THE 20TH CENTURY

With many variations, the Irving style continued in the first quarter of the century with the Hamlets of Henry Ainley, John

---

* Jones (1954).

Barrymore (whose "O Vengeance" rang to the ceiling for a full minute), John Martin-Harvey, Ernest Milton, and Godfrey Tearle. Nor is it forgotten today.

## DESIGNS AND STAGING

As a young man, Edward Gordon Craig (Ellen Terry's son) had acted for Irving. Craig's stage designs for *Hamlet,* with their unlocalized setting, and carried out by him in Stanislavsky's Moscow production in 1911, had a tremendous influence on later productions. Impressionist and symbolic, they led to a violent reaction against the old-fashioned realistic settings. In the Hamlets of Martin Harvey, Barrymore, and Gielgud, the influence of Craig was obvious. It was seen in the permanent set Tyrone Guthrie employed for Olivier's *Hamlet* at the Old Vic (1937). And it had a profound effect on Olivier's 1948 movie which, after its simplistic opening stating it was a play about "a man who could not make up his mind," also revealed obvious Freudian motifs.

William Poel presented *Hamlet* and other Shakespeare plays in Elizabethan dress from 1881. An even earlier attempt had been made by Benjamin Webster in 1844. But the first production to make a stir in England in sixteenth century costume was that of J. B. Fagan at Oxford in 1924. The method was followed at the Old Vic and elsewhere on various occasions. The first time John Gielgud played Hamlet (Old Vic, 1929), Harcourt Williams also used this period. Productions in a simulated Elizabethan playhouse were directed by Nugent Monk at The Maddermarket, Norwich, for many years.

Basil Sydney in America, Colin Keith-Johnston in London, Moissi in Vienna, together with Sir Barry Jackson's production in 1925, used modern dress. They were forerunners of Tyrone Guthrie's famous modern dress production (Old Vic, 1938) with Alec Guinness as Hamlet, and Andrew Cruickshank as the greatest Claudius in living memory. But for Leslie Howard's *Hamlet* (1936), H. B. Irving designed a striking archaeological production based on Saxo Grammaticus. Michael Benthall put his Freudian production (Stratford-upon-Avon, 1948) into early-Victorian costume. Since then the play has been set in all manner of historical periods and in theatres of all shapes, without losing its inherent power to move the audience.

## THEATRE AND THE CRITICS

Early in the century, Harley Granville-Barker led the professional theatre to re-interpret Shakespeare. However, he retired
early as a director to devote himself to writing his famous
*Prefaces* to Shakespeare. He brought out the *vitality* of
Shakespeare's plays and stressed the idea that a Shakespeare
script could only be finally interpreted when played in the theatre. Although he never directed *Hamlet,* his views of the play
were very influential:

> Shakespeare does marvels with this Hamlet who is
> neither mad nor sane, both "mad in craft" and
> "punished with sore distraction"; the victim — as we
> all at some time feel we are — of the world's "sane"
> view of his "insane" perplexities; the man — as
> which of us has not been? — at war within himself;
> and a traveller, with that passport, into strange twi-
> light regions of the soul. But he cannot, for all his
> skill, so assimilate character and story that no incon-
> gruities appear. For the two are of a different dra-
> matic nature.*

This interpretation of the Prince has been seen in many
Hamlets, notably those of John Gielgud and of Christopher
Plummer (Stratford, Ontario, 1957).

Where Granville-Barker was an actor-director turned scholar, T. S. Eliot was a poet and playwright who wrote criticism,
and G. Wilson Knight was a scholar and an actor-director. Eliot
wrote an introduction to Knight's masterpiece, *The Wheel of
Fire,*** but they hold contrasting views of Shakespeare. With
*Hamlet,* however, they are in surprising agreement. For Eliot,
the problem is the play ("undoubtedly a failure") not the character, and this encourages critics to be creative: Coleridge
"made of Hamlet a Coleridge." In *Hamlet* "the delay in revenge
is unexplained on grounds of necessity or expediency; and the
effect of the 'madness' is not to lull but to arouse the King's
suspicion." For Eliot, Hamlet is dominated by an emotion
which is inexpressible, because it is in excess of the facts as they
appear. Eliot agrees with the psychologists that Hamlet's disgust

---

* Granville-Barker (1953).
** Knight (1930).

is sexual, but "his mother is not an adequate equivalent for it; his disgust envelops and exceeds her."* As Hamlet cannot objectify the feeling, it poisons his life and obstructs the action. The effect of this view in the playhouse is to give more dramatic weight to Claudius.

This is also the effect of G. Wilson Knight's view, but for very different reasons: "Except for the original murder of Hamlet's father, the Hamlet-universe is one of healthy and robust life, good-nature, humour, romantic strength, and welfare: against this background is the figure of Hamlet pale with the consciousness of death. He is the ambassador of death, walking amid Life."** Knight says there is much that is likeable in Claudius and much that is questionable in Hamlet who watches, analyses, and torments others: "They are dreadfully afraid of him."

The effect of this critical view in the theatre is to provide a balance between Hamlet and Claudius, protagonist and antagonist. This was seen in Knight's own production of the play (Rudolf Steiner Hall, London, 1935), and it gave rise to the great performances of Claudius by Andrew Cruickshank (1938), Alec Clunes (1955), Douglas Campbell (Stratford, Ontario, 1957) and Timothy West (Prospect Theatre, 1977).

## GIELGUD AND HIS INFLUENCE

It is generally agreed by both critics and audiences that John Gielgud's Hamlet (New Theatre, London, 1934; Empire Theater, New York, 1936) was the most remarkable of the century: reflective, intellectual, and melancholic. But for Gielgud, Claudius did not have the same power; this is Hamlet's play.

As befitted a member of the Terry family, Gielgud approached his role in a consciously traditional way, with elements from Irving and others. But he also used the new psychological understandings of the prince. Of the American production, Rosamund Gilder reported:

---

* Eliot (1951).
** Knight (1930).

> The generation he has grown up in is one which knew in its childhood that nobility and brutality were not legends but common facts recorded for four years in daily torrents of blood [e.g., in World War I].
>
> ... Gielgud's performance gives a sense of an almost intolerable tension. Waves of emotion mount in a continuous progression ... until finally in the closet scene the last crest is reached, the last crash carries all before it ... This is the climax, the turning point of the play.*

All subsequent Hamlets have been measured against Gielgud's, from Donald Wolfit's sympathetic view of a young man troubled by externals, in a production of Q1 (1937), to the contemporary performances of Derek Jacobi (Prospect, 1977; BBC-TV, 1987) and Albert Finney (National Theatre, 1986).

Peter Brook's production of *Hamlet* at the Phoenix Theatre (1955), following its tour of England and Russia, was fundamentally a re-working of Gielgud's interpretation by Paul Scofield and a remarkable cast. Gielgud also directly influenced Richard Burton's Hamlet. When Burton first performed it (Old Vic, 1953) it was as a full-blooded melodrama. In America, however, Burton was directed by Gielgud in a contemporary stage-rehearsal production (1964) which was a more subtle interpretation. For example, two lines which have been much varied, are:

> There are more things in heaven and earth, Horatio,
> Than are dreamt of in your philosophy.     (I.v.166-167)

They had usually been delivered with the snubbing intonation, "*your* philosophy." John Gielgud in 1934 chose "your *philosophy,*" but in the New York production Burton said, "Than are *dreamt of* in your philosophy".

While London audiences compared Gielgud's Hamlet with that of Alexander Moissi who appeared in an adjacent theatre, American audiences in 1936 compared the Hamlets of John Gielgud and Leslie Howard. In the Mousetrap scene, Gielgud merely drew his dagger at the climax, but Howard thrust frantically at the throne — an action that went back at least to

---

* Gilder (1960).

Beerbohm Tree and has reappeared with variations. Thus the Prince has driven his dagger into a table (John Neville); beaten with his hands on the seat of the throne (Richard Hampton); torn to pieces the Player's manuscript containing the Hecuba speech (Ian Bannen); overturned and then replaced the throne (David Warner); and kicked down the throne from the dais (Richard Pasco).

Claudius' prayer scene also has been strongly affected by Gielgud. As Claudius kneels, he lays aside his sword. Hamlet, entering behind him, picks it up, carries it with him and uses it, later, to kill Polonius. Gielgud introduced this device in 1934, took it to America in 1936, and used it many times subsequently. In practice, it relieves the actor from carrying a sword in the Players' scene where it is awkward for him, and gives him one in the Closet scene where it is necessary. The business has subsequently been popular with many Hamlets. Gertrudes and Ophelias have become increasingly sexual in their interpretation, with the Ophelia of Simone Valere (with Jean-Louis Barrault, Ziegfeld Theatre, New York, 1952) becoming tragic because of this emphasis.

## A VARIETY OF PERSPECTIVES

A major element in Gielgud's Hamlet was the the idea of relativity. There was a high level of uncertainty both in the hero's motives and in all the action. Compared with Irving's, the Gielgud production did not have strong cause-and-effect. The play's very lack of causal logic was a part of its point. Hamlet's theatre world reverberated with questions: fearful, alarmed, anguished, clichéd, conversational, meditative and intellectual. Then there were ominous questions, like the tense challenges with which the play begins: "Who's there?" Questions feel out the darkness, searching for identities and assurance. "Bernardo?" ... "Have you had quiet guard?" ... "Who hath relieved you?" ... "What, is Horatio there?" ... "What, has this thing appeared again tonight?"

The emphasis on uncertainty becomes a major quality of *Hamlet* in the contemporary theatre. A very different production from Gielgud's was that of Michael Langham with Christopher Plummer as Hamlet. Yet, like Gielgud's, questions led to hints and guesses passing through the darkness on the battlements: "At least, the whisper goes so" ... "I think it be no other but e'en so" ... "I have heard that on the crowing of the cock ..."

In more and more productions, uncertainty is everywhere. The causal world of Isaac Newton that underpinned Irving's thinking has given way to the uncertain universe of Einstein and Heisenberg. At the heart of the play today lies "To be, or not to be, that is the question." Thus relativism is basic to understanding Ophelia's Mad Scene (IV.v). Until Ellen Terry, her lunacy was always sweet and tender. Mrs. Patrick Campbell finally broke that mould in 1897, and modern psychology has led performers to realize that there is no single way to perform the role. The player's interpretation will be reflected in her costume. Traditionally she wore white muslin to indicate her innocence and gentleness, possible in an expurgated text. Black, as mourning for her father, appeared around 1900. Only much later began her deliberate indecency of dress, emphasizing the sexual aspects of her madness. Now the scene is often one of horror, as was the interpretation of Rosemary Harris (National Theatre, Old Vic, 1963). All will depend on the pointing of the lines,

> Thought and afflictions, passion, hell itself,
> She turns to favour and to prettiness        (IV.v.188-189)

for these lie at the core of the scene.

Some Hamlets perilously play the King's game — but beat him at it. Then the game becomes Hamlet's own. He keeps secret his revengeful purpose from everyone — even from Horatio until near the end of the tragedy. Such an approach is more literary than psychological. This was the effect of Derek Jacobi's interpretation: his madness was clearly false as he maintained his plan to the very end. It echoed that of William Hutt's Hamlet (Canadian Players, 1956). He was clearly a heroic revenger, a procrastinator, lost in thought and weak of will.

In contrast, Hamlet was played as an egomaniac by David Warner (it was also Madariaga's critical view). His contradictory extremes of conduct were reminiscent of the Elizabethan accounts of melancholy, and Warner acted more like the hero in Marston's *Antonio's Revenge* (1599). Such an approach makes Hamlet mostly mad and rarely sane.

For Nicol Williamson (Roundhouse, 1969), Hamlet was a haunted man with his mind on the frontier of two worlds, unable either quite to reject or quite to admit the supernatural. He struggled to get something done but could not because of his inability to understand himself, his fellows, or the universe. His hesitation was the fear of being dead. When Williamson said, "Such fellows as I," he meant human beings, creatures shaped in sin, and the audience felt they were in a charnel-house.

Critics especially, and theatre people less so, are inclined to see that *Hamlet* reflects ancient ways of thought. Thus Francis Fergusson sees in *Hamlet* a living myth (story) and a ritual (action); every generation has interpreted the play according to its own myths and rituals.* This is opposite to the theories of Eliot and the psychologists, who describe Hamlet as a man who has lost both a throne and a social, publicly acceptable persona — a local habitation and a name.

Fergusson shows that much of the medieval religious culture was still alive in Shakespeare's time. Over the whole of the Globe stage was a permanent canopy, painted to represent the heavens, and the Ghost's "cellarage" below the stage was sometimes called Hell. This symbolic stage brings the theatre near to ritual. H.D.F. Kitto sees an uncanny resemblance between the openings of *Hamlet* and of the *Agamemnon* (c. 458 B.C.), the earliest extant Western European play: both tragedies involve the shameful killing of a great king, the adultery of his consort, and the demand upon the son of the dead man a task which, whether or not he fulfils it, will destroy him. Kitto parallels the *structures* of the two plays. Effects of this interpretation were seen in the production of Peter Hall and Peter Brook's revealed ritual elements in the play.

## THE CHANGING HAMLET

Performances of Hamlet still begin, now and again, with a clock striking. It is perfectly in keeping with the soldiers' lines:

> FRAN: You come most carefully upon your hour.
> BERN: 'Tis now struck twelve.                    (I.i.6-7)

As very shortly it is one o'clock when the Ghost appears, we rarely hear the clock on the second occasion. Today the Ghost and the First Player are often doubled. It is said that this cast-

---

* Fergusson (1949).

ing went back to Shakespeare, yet there is no trace of it before the 1930s when Mark Dignam twice doubled the roles.

Polonius is a rewarding part for a good actor. The most famous Polonius early in the century was A. Bromley Davenport in Sir Barry Jackson's modern-dress *Hamlet* (1925). Davenport was the first to combine the diplomatic manner of the court official with the strict attitude of a loving parent to conceal his true character: an inquisitive, pompous, sly and spying old fox. The most famous recent Polonius, more vacuous and less of a loving father, was Hume Cronyn in Gielgud's 1964 New York production.

Osricks of the Victorian stage were simply court popinjays, for example Martin Harvey in Forbes-Robertson's production. Twelve years before this, he had played the role with Irving at the Lyceum. When John Barrymore brought his *Hamlet* to London (1925), Frederick Cooper was a charming little fop. But by Hugh Hunt's revival (New, 1950), Osrick was a sly, saturnine figure, a sinister accomplice of the King, a messenger of death.

The inevitable cutting of the script has led some characters to disappear for generations. Fortinbras was usually cut until Forbes-Robertson's *Hamlet*; this meant the loss of IV.iv and Hamlet's "How all occasions" soliloquy. Frank Benson kept Fortinbras after 1899, but he was missing from the *Hamlet* of Ernest Milton and of others. Today Fortinbras is usually reinstated, but we hardly ever see Voltimand and Cornelius. Reynaldo, Polonius's servant, rarely appears: he was brilliantly played in full by the young Alec Guinness in Guthrie's revival at the Old Vic and Elsinore (1937). An unexpected cut in Tony Richardson's production, with Nicol Williamson's prosaic Hamlet, was the Second Gravedigger. Memorable First Gravediggers have included Cedric Hardwicke, Ralph Richardson and, in Olivier's film, Stanley Holloway, the most humorous of them all. Deliberately "contemporary" productions, like Joseph Papp's *The "Naked" Hamlet* (with Martin Sheen and Ralph Waite, New York, 1968), have cut and added to the script with impunity but have been unable to destroy the play.

In earlier performances, the end of the play was not always as Shakespeare had intended. It often closed on "The rest is silence." Beerbohm Tree preferred to end with Horatio's "Flights of angels sing thee to thy rest." At this moment an angelic choir was heard faintly to echo the phrase, "Good night, sweet Prince," which visibly affected the audience. Such music is unlikely today although there were great cannon, far downstage, in Peter Hall's production (Stratford-upon-Avon, 1965). Perhaps the most significant quality of *Hamlet* is its end-less suggestiveness: it provides innumerable perspectives on the nature of human life as a whole.

## THE PLAY WORLD

A basic theme in all Shakespeare's tragedies is the protagonist's response to his loss of identity. In *Othello, Macbeth, King Lear* and *Timon of Athens* the appropriate response controls the dra-matic action. This does not quite happen in *Hamlet* because of its abundance of action. But the use of roles by Hamlet and others is central to the play; it derives from the theatre and focusses upon acting.

In *Hamlet,* the world of the play is a metaphor for life. The play combines two metaphors: the theatre metaphor — Jaques' "All the world's a stage" *(As You Like It,* II.vii.140); and the drama metaphor — Prospero's

We are such stuff

As dreams are made on ...     *(The Tempest,* IV.i.156-157)

Life is not only like the theatre, it *is* a play. During his career, Shakespeare moves from the first metaphor to the second. *Hamlet,* midway in his career, uses both.

This tragedy strikes a significant chord today, more so than in any other era. This is because modern thinking continuously uses the metaphor for creativity in the sciences, social sciences, the arts, and the mundane and practical — in all human endeavours. Einstein, for example, worked with visual metaphors in his scientific discoveries — picturing two trains passing each other at high speeds, and the like. In our post-Einsteinian world, all things and all events are explicable through the relative perspectives of metaphors: in models, par-adigms and so forth.

Shakespeare believed that the *play world* had its own power, particularly power over people. Thus Hamlet says that the play-within-the-play, *The Murder of Gonzago,* will have power over Claudius:

> The play's the thing
> Wherein I'll catch the conscience of the King.
>
> (II.ii.602-603)

Both the play and the play-within-the-play describe the dissembler, the Player King. The actor holds a mirror up to nature; the world and the stage world are analogues — they reflect each other — and control over one means control over the other.

These issues were not uppermost in the minds of Victorian actors. For Irving and Forbes-Robertson the key question was, is Hamlet mad? Yet the seeds of new thinking were beginning to appear. For example, Ivan Turgenev in his essay, *Hamlet and Don Quixote*,* says Hamlet is an egoist and so has no faith in himself. Hamlet clings to his "I," this self in which he has no faith, and he uses the "mask" of madness. He is preoccupied with his own personality. The distinction between the "I" and the "not-I" (self and other) is fundamental to later psychology. Martin Buber notes that Hamlet uses "I" and "It," while good social relations are based on "I" and "Thou."** In the dramatism of Kenneth Burke, life and all human works hinge on the relation of "I" to my role;*** and human relations are dramatic because, if they are to be effective, I must put myself in your place. These contemporary forms of thinking lead to different ways of directing *Hamlet in* comparison to those at previous eras.

## DRAMATIC TERMINOLOGY

The world of the London theatre is embedded in Shakespeare's imagination, and it becomes fundamental to his dramaturgy. It is there from his first works: the linguistic types of play metaphor in the use of "acts," "scenes" and "tragedies" found in *Titus Andronicus* and *1 and 2 Henry VI*. But after *The Shrew*, the metaphor becomes increasingly complex. In *Hamlet* the major instances are show, act, play, seem, assume, put on, and shape.

"Show" is the unifying image in *Hamlet,* giving a single focus to much of the diverse material in the play: the images of clothing, painting, mirroring; the episode of the dumb show and

---

* Turgenev (1930).
** Buber (1958).
*** Burke (1968).

*The Murder of Gonzago;* the leap of Laertes into Ophelia's grave; the final sword fight. Many characters are drawn into its implications.

"Act" is the play's radical metaphor. It re-focusses the problems about reality into questions about the nature of an act. The play asks, what is an act, and what is its relation to the mental act (its purpose)? "If I drown myself wittingly," says the Gravedigger, "it argues an act, and an act hath three branches — it is to act, to do, and to perform" (V.i.10-12). How does a mundane act such as sitting or eating relate to a fictional act (a pretence, or dramatic act)? There could be many answers, e.g.:

- An action may be entirely fictional, as when Polonius prepares Ophelia to meet Hamlet with "pious action" that "sugar[s] o'er The devil himself" (III.i.48-49).
- An action may not be a pretence but yet not be what it appears: Hamlet spares Claudius when he finds him in an act that has some "relish of salvation in't" (III.iii.92).
- An action may be a fiction that is also the start of a new reality, as when we assume a virtue we do not have.
- An action may be a pretence that is actually a mirroring of reality, like *The Murder of Gonzago* or the tragedy of *Hamlet.*

Shakespeare hints that in a *significant* act the purpose is imaginative, and the external action is dramatic (or fictional) — a position held by some contemporary philosophers.

"Play" in Elizabethan parlance has two primary meanings: children's "play" and a more precise word for all the elements in a stage play that make up the art of the theatre. In the latter sense it is so extended that every major person in the tragedy is a player in some way, and every major episode is a playlet within the play. Thus there are various kinds of play, e.g.:

- The court plays and Hamlet plays.
- Rosencrantz and Guildenstern try to play on Hamlet, though they cannot play on his recorders — an extension to a musical sense.
- The play-within-the-play itself suddenly dissolves the normal barriers between the actual and the fictional. The travelling players are like those who entertain Sly in *The Shrew,* but here things are more complex. On the stage before us is a play of false appearances in which an actor called the Player King is playing. Yet also on the stage is Claudius, a

second Player King, who is a spectator of the first. Finally, an actual audience watches the spectators who are also players.
- The duel becomes itself a playlet in which everyone but Claudius and Laertes plays a role in ignorance: "The Queen desires you to show some gentle entertainment to Laertes before you fall to play." "I ... will this brother's wager frankly play." "Give him the cup" ... "I'll play this bout first." (V.ii.247-278)
- The professional actors play the roles of the courtiers, Hamlet, and the travelling players.

The tragedy is riddled with theatrical language that is similar to "play": the various uses of "play the part," "perform," "pro-logue," "applaud" and other phrases which are either overtly or covertly theatrical.

The ambiguities of "seem" are wound within *Hamlet*. On Hamlet's first appearance, he seizes upon his mother's thoughtless "seems" and says bitterly:

These indeed 'seem';
For they are actions that a man might play.
But I have that within which passes show —
These but the trappings and the suits of woe.
(I.ii.83-86)

He contrasts real grief with the marks of sorrow which a trage-dian might employ to create an illusion of grief.

"Assume" is also significant. What we assume to be so, may not be so:

the devil hath power
T'assume a pleasing shape ...                (II.ii.597-598)

But it may be a good Ghost; when Horatio tells Hamlet of the apparition he has seen, the Prince answers cautiously:

If it assume my noble father's person,
I'll speak to it ...                (I.ii.244-245)

But what we can assume may be what we are not yet, but for which we have the potential — as when Hamlet advises his mother, "Assume a virtue, if you have it not" (III.iv.161).

The terms "put on" and "shape" have similar effects. Shape is form, the form in which we normally meet the thing or event: "Do you see yonder cloud that's almost in shape of a camel?" (III.ii.382). Hamlet says to the Ghost, "Thou comest in such a questionable shape" (I.iv.43), echoing Horatio (I.i.46-49). But "shape" may also indicate a disguise: an actor's costume or an actor's role, as when Claudius, plotting against Hamlet's life, says to Laertes:

> Weigh what convenience both of time and means
> May fit us to our shape.                    (IV.vii.148-149)

"Put on" has a further ambiguity. "Put on" in *Hamlet* can mean to assume a role, a mask, a frock, a livery or an antic disposition. It is clearly a meaning derived from the actors. By understanding the human being as an actor, Shakespeare recognizes the flexibility within human performance.

These ideas are also very contemporary. In the late twentieth century, Marshall McLuhan expanded Shakespeare's meaning of "put on" and used it to show that we "put on" media; that the pen is an extension of the hand, the wheel is an extension of the foot, and so forth.

## THEATRE AND LIFE

Metaphors are not merely linguistic. They exist in all media. The theatre and drama metaphors are centred in actors, human beings representing other human beings: we are all "costumed players."

In *Hamlet* the themes of disorder, futility, and pride emerge as surrounding the actor and the *play world*. But such themes were also traditional in the history of the theatre itself. Since Roman times, a theatrical life had not been respectable. In the Middle Ages, the actor abandoned his proper place in God's order: he disturbed the social hierarchy [see *End Notes*] and represented disorder. Craftsmen, acting in the Cycles who deserted their trade for the stage invoked the wrath of moralists.

In *Hamlet,* these issues of order are central; the play is riddled with comments about plays and actors. Like the Londoners who came to the Globe in 1600, it seems to Shakespeare and Hamlet that "both at the first and now" (III.ii.21) the purpose of playing is to hold a mirror up to nature. Hamlet speaks as though this Elizabethan idea is part of some given order of things, like the enjoyment that the actors bring with them into Elsinore. And the idea included the medieval technique of giving the theatre audience the role of a crowd of onlookers within the play. This device remained popular, but it was specifically Shakespearean. He makes it more subtle than his contemporaries did, when Hamlet addresses

You that look pale and tremble at this chance,
That are but mutes or audience to this act ...

(V.ii.328-329)

He has used this technique in *Julius Caesar* (III.i.111-113), but here it is simpler and more effective.

*Hamlet* is dominated by the idea of the play. The play metaphor appears in many forms: as the dissembler, the Player King, appearance and reality, falsehood and truth, and the theatrical nature of certain moments of time. The world and the stage have a double relationship, one that is reciprocal: the actor holds a mirror up to nature, while nature reflects the features of the play. Thus the entire tragedy is filled with the presence of the London theatre and its peculiar, shifting sense of time: it occurs in the present tense, yet it unites the past and the future. The crowing of the cock sends the mind of Marcellus back a thousand years; the reign of the dead Hamlet is constantly remembered in the reign of Claudius. The past haunts Hamlet. His concern for the future, for the survival of his "story," seems to reach out to the players in the Globe who are then engaged in telling it and to the audience as they witness it.

REALITY AND ILLUSION

Two key questions in *Hamlet* are the nature of reality and the relation of reality to appearance. Illusion and reality meet throughout the play, and it is this intersection which makes Hamlet pause.

The play begins with an illusion, an "apparition" as Marcellus says, the Ghost. Is the Ghost real, or is it a diabolical illusion? This dilemma is inherent in the revelation: if the apparition is an illusion it is a devil that has assumed the shape of Hamlet's father. This type of issue recurs in the play.

Hamlet, in such a shifting world, pretends to be mad, and his pretence allows him to wait. From his point of view, if the Ghost is only an appearance, then is the King's appearance reality? He tests out this dilemma by means of another kind of illusion, the play-within-the-play.

Clothes reveal the world of surfaces, of illusion: "the apparel oft proclaims the man," Polonius assures Laertes (I.iii.72). Similarly Polonius takes Hamlet's vows to Ophelia as false apparel. They are bawds, he tells her, in masquerade,

Not of that dye which their investments show,
But mere implorators of unholy suits ...   (I.iii.128-129)
The difference between the inner and outer (the real and the
appearance, the self and clothes) is at the core of Hamlet's
dilemma. Only recently his mother was in widow's weeds, yet
now within a month, a little month, before even her funeral
shoes are old, she has married his uncle. Her mourning clothes
were an appearance, not reality. His own are no appearance, as
he tells her when she asks him to cast his "nighted colour off"
... "'Tis not alone my inky cloak, good mother" (I.ii.77).
Hamlet's visible image gives the verbal image a theatrical reality. His inky cloak is a dramatic metaphor for three things: his
grief for his father, his person as melancholy, and his presence
as death. Later, Shakespeare creates a metaphor whereby both
his mind and his costume are disordered, as Ophelia describes
so vividly to Polonius:

Lord Hamlet, with his doublet all unbraced,
No hat upon his head, his stockings fouled,
Ungartered, and down-gyvèd to his ankle ...   (II.i.78-80)
Still later, he has a third costume, the simple traveller's garb in
which he has come from the ship: a metaphor for a change in
his character.

The problems of reality and illusion also occur in the
metaphors of art. For example, in the paints, the colourings,
the varnishes that may either conceal (illusion) or, in the
painter's hands, reveal (reality). Claudius' art is to conceal:

The harlot's cheek, beautied with plastering art,
Is not more ugly to the thing that helps it
Than is my deed to my most painted word.   (III.i.51-53)
Ophelia looks beautiful to Hamlet: "the celestial, and my soul's
idol, the most beautified Ophelia," he calls her in his love letter
(II.ii.109). But even Polonius wonders about "beautified." Does
it mean her innocent beauty? Or "beautied" like the harlot's
cheek? Later Hamlet comments, "I have heard of your paint-
ings too, well enough. God hath given you one face, and you
make yourselves another" (III.i.143-144).

Theatrical art may also conceal or reveal. In the play-within-
the-play, Hamlet uses an "image" (his own word) of Gonzago's
murder to uncover Claudius' guilt: it holds, "as 'twere, the mirror up to nature" (III.ii.21-22). Similarly in his mother's bed-

room he makes her recoil in horror from his "counterfeit presentment of two brothers" (III.iv.55) by (at least, in stage tradition) showing her his father's picture beside his uncle's.

Deception is a way of life in Hamlet's Denmark. Polonius lovingly gives his son Laertes permission to return to France and then directs his servant to spy on him. From the Ghost, Hamlet learns that a man "may smile, and smile, and be a villain" (I.v.108). He feels betrayed by Ophelia who allows herself to be used against him. He is spied on by Rosencrantz and Guildenstern. And Laertes, professing to accept Hamlet's offer of love with an open heart, conspires with Claudius to kill him in the fencing match with a poisoned foil. Except for Hamlet's friendship with Horatio, virtually every human relationship in the court of Denmark is to some degree false.

## ROLES

The people in *Hamlet* continually play roles: the travelling players take theatrical roles; acts of deceit and spying transform other occasions into playlets where people use roles; and there are countless examples of people miscast in roles or violating and misperforming them. In an extraordinary dialogue (III.ii), Hamlet explains to the professional players both the theoretical basis of their art and the practical ways to play their roles. How to play a role is a primary issue in the play.

Claudius doubly embodies the false role: his true self and the role he exhibits publicly; and his qualifications for the kingship and the role-status he has obtained through murder. Claudius as King symbolizes how roles are used in Denmark: the standard family and social roles are no longer valid because they have been violated and can no longer be effectively performed. Claudius' act of murder violates his roles of brother, of subject to the king, of brother-in-law, and of uncle. The murder also corrupts marital roles, so Hamlet cannot play his role as son to both his father and mother. Hamlet comments on this complete corruption of roles when he talks of his "uncle-father and aunt-mother" (II.ii.374-375), and when he calls Claudius "dear mother" (IV.iii.51).

Hamlet refuses to play the parts that others try to force on him. He rejects the demands of Claudius and Gertrude to change his role (I.ii). He later refuses the efforts of Rosencrantz and Guildenstern to define him and to play upon him as on a pipe (III.ii.358-368). His rejection of imposed roles is clear in his failure to perform the role of revenger given to him by his father's Ghost, despite his declaration that he will assume the role at once and immediately carry out its demands. Hamlet acts as if all roles are suspect; he can no longer accept any role as a valid expression of himself or trust himself to any role and feel secure.

This resistance by Hamlet suggests that he does not see the world as the others do. Although no role seems valid any more, Hamlet has the need for some kind of role so that he can once again acquire an identity. Thus he constantly grasps at substitute roles, e.g.:

- *The mourner*: this cannot last long; he is pressured to abandon it.
- *The "antic disposition"* which is far more flexible.
- *Brief performances,* one after the other, of his fellow characters' various ideas about him, particularly in III.ii before, after, and even during *The Murder of Gonzago*. Here he expands the framework of his "antic disposition."
- *The dramatist:* as he busies himself with the damnation of Claudius and the salvation of his mother (III.ii-III.iv), he suspends the "antic disposition" and tries to control others.

Ultimately, Hamlet ceases to play these substitute roles because he finds a role seemingly imposed from outside which at last he can accept and to which he can willingly submit. The experiences of his sea-voyage convince him that there is, after all, "a divinity that shapes our ends" (V.ii.10).

Almost everyone within this *play world* tends to take the role of dramatist, or stage director: each tells other people what roles they should play and how they should play them, starting from the beginning when Horatio tries to control the Ghost, and Claudius and Gertrude try to persuade Hamlet to mourn no longer. Many of Hamlet's fellow characters falsely believe that they can understand and explain him. As a dramatist Hamlet is quite unlike Claudius, Polonius, or Laertes. They try to manipulate experience by planning large playlets. Hamlet cannot do this. He acts spontaneously or not at all; his stage directions must include his participation, as with his involvement in *The Murder of Gonzago*.

## THE PLAY AND THE DREAM

Shakespeare's other plays show that he thought that the imaginative creation (the play) is related to the real world in much the same way that dream is related to the *play world* [see *End Notes*]; and that there are degrees from reality to illusion: the real world-the *play world*-the dream world. Both the *play world* and the dream world are created by imagination; but a play is nearer than a dream to reality.

Hamlet, however, seems to think that drama and dreams are similar (II.ii.549). But can plays and dreams be trusted? Hamlet uses such questions to ponder human life: "what is this quintessence of dust?" He concludes that people have two alternatives: either they use their capability and godlike reason, or they become beasts who simply sleep and feed. People, says Hamlet, are noble in reason but are the paragon of animals when they find

> quarrel in a straw
> When honour's at the stake. (IV.iv.55-56)

For Hamlet, truth lies in the idea that all that people know is that they exist; truth is divorced from substance and from the means by which substance appears. When "All the world's a stage," truth emerges as our roles engaged in moral acts. If "We are such stuff As dreams are made on," then dreams and plays provide criteria for us to make a judgment of reality. They are ways to tell the true from the false.

## STRUCTURE

For such a long and seemingly unwieldy play, the structure of *Hamlet* is strong and sturdy. Stage directors discover this when they try to cut; to remove any section changes the balance of the performance.

### RHYTHM AND WAVES

Shakespeare structures his plays around a rising action followed by a fall. He never fears an anti-climax. This curve-like structure gives an undulating movement of tension and relaxation. A change in rhythm does not break the action; it is both a continuation and a change. In *Hamlet* the curving structure dominates all others. G. Wilson Knight says that the primary rhythm is of "speed-waves." Thus, from the play-within-the-play scene, the speed increases to Hamlet's meeting Gertrude and the rapid dialogue leading to Polonius' death. There is a pause, but it quickly gains pace as Hamlet loses control; the action gathers, rises to a climax, and the Ghost enters: "Hamlet is now limp, his bolt shot, the Queen too: the whole action is limp. The scene drags on like a wounded snake, with repetitions: an intentional anti-climax."*

Because the play centres on Hamlet, it takes the rhythm of his personality as he wavers between action and inaction, the heaven of grace and the hell of cynicism. This see-saw motion is shaped by his emotions: Hamlet cannot feel anything strongly for long, for passion implies purpose, and he does not have one aim for any length of time. His sudden bursts of energy (at Ophelia's grave) and decisive yet unthinking action (the death of Polonius) are brief moments in his sea of despair. The play has a continuous undulating rhythm of stops and starts, of negatives and positives, of death and life. The stage director must find how plot, time, space and sequence interweave in the rhythmic curves of the production.

## THE PLOT STRUCTURE

Shakespeare customarily uses a main plot and one or more minor plots. In the tragedies, a minor plot is usually comic; this is not merely "comic relief" but is essential to the whole play.

In *Hamlet*, the way the plots are structured is unique and extraordinary. The stories are tightly woven together, but they are causally and logically interdependent. The stories, however, are ironically parallel: Polonius, for instance, plays the "clown" to Hamlet's "hero"; and Hamlet frequently feels himself in the role of clown to Fortinbras and even Laertes. Shakespeare continually shifts between viewpoints throughout the play: e.g., from the soldiers of I.i, to the hypocritical Claudius of I.ii; from the shrewdness of Polonius, to the intuitions of Ophelia. The action is seen from so many angles that we can say that *the plot has an internal relativity.*

In the main plot, Hamlet tries to find and destroy the hidden evil that is poisoning the life of Claudius' Denmark. All of

---

* Knight (1930).

the characters help in his task, consciously or unconsciously, and in comic evil or inspired ways. *The plot structure is one of contrasts.* The contrasts between the perspectives of the various characters are more important than their overt struggles. Structurally those contrasts are brought out by the order of the scenes, as we shift from comic to tragic versions of the main action.

We can use the first scenes of the play as a simple example. I.iii is simultaneously a comic parallel to the beginning of the main plot (I.i-I.ii) and the prologue to the story of Polonius and Laertes. The Laertes-Polonius story is analogous to that of Hamlet and his father-figures (the Ghost and Claudius): the fathers set spies on their sons: Reynaldo by Polonius, Rosencrantz and Guildenstern by Claudius. These first scenes are also contrasted: the divided world of Polonius-Laertes is minor compared with the divided world of the Ghost-Hamlet; yet the minor plot shows more about Hamlet's problem and the true sickness of Denmark than any fact could.

Shakespeare's use of ceremony is structural. From his first plays he is a master at this technique, and the scenes of pageantry are vital to *Hamlet*. They are all civic, military or religious rituals: the changing of the guard on the battlements; the formal assembly of the court of Denmark (three times); the funeral of Ophelia; the duelling ritual. Each is relevant to a specific story, but its chief purpose is to reflect the action of the main plot at a specific step in its development. Then the various plot-lines are gathered together in the ceremony; all else waits for a moment as we are reminded of the social values important to the plot.

From the start, the ceremonials are invocations for the well-being of society (the mythological level) and the secular or religious devices for securing it (the ritual level). When Hamlet refuses to take Claudius' first court at its face value (I.ii), we doubt its efficacy. The rituals alter from the honest changing of the guard (I.i), through Ophelia's mock rites (IV.v), to the full inversion of values (what Fergusson calls the "black Mass") of Claudius' last court (V.ii).

There is also a plot structure of the particular to the universal. *Hamlet* ends in the utter destruction of the two families:

Hamlet-Claudius-Gertrude and Polonius-Laertes-Ophelia. The architectonic pattern is so vast that *Hamlet* is both the individual tragedy of a person and something more like religious drama that indicates the design of providence. The idea that unites the characters in one coherent catastrophe is that evil works to attack and overthrow both the good and the bad. Providence is central to this action, so Shakespeare makes us feel that, as with Greek tragedy, the particular event is also universal. Claudius, the arch-villain, driven by crime into further crime, meets manifestly divine justice.

ACTION AND REACTION

Throughout the play, action is followed by reaction. A character's action backfires or reacts against him, a pattern that the Greeks called *nemesis*. Some obvious instances: Hamlet's unsuspicious generosity is certainly mistaken in the last scene — he ought to have known his uncle by this time; and Polonius' passion for spying brings about his own death.

TIME

Time in the play is not objective but subjective. It is primarily Hamlet's own time: time that is significant to him. As the Ghost leaves, Hamlet announces he will put on an antic disposition; then we see the initial consequences — he has frightened Ophelia. The length of clock time between the two events is irrelevant. Hamlet feels that one event logically follows the other. In the theatre, and particularly in *Hamlet*, dramatic time is the duration of the action, not necessarily plot time.

In *Hamlet*, the present is infected with the past. Hamlet is haunted by past events: the shock of the murder and more importantly his horror at his mother's acts make him forget his vengeance. His mother's acts taint his thought like a disease. The future tense within the play is very near to the present: will the Ghost speak to Hamlet, and how will Claudius respond to *The Murder of Gonzago*? The issues of the short-term future are immediate and powerful, but those of the long-term future feel distanced from the action: e.g., who will be the next king of Denmark?

The sound of *Hamlet* gives the play its temporal dimension, while movement establishes its spatial significance. Although the play contains some of Shakespeare's greatest poetry, on the stage sound and movement must be balanced. The sound includes the speech, the silences, and the sound-effects. Sound-effects are frequent and of great importance: trumpets, alarums, drums, cannon, tolling bells, the thunder-tempests and music. On these two latter, the time of the Shakespearian world revolves: they are basic to the play. Music in Shakespeare is always harmonious, contrasting with civic and cosmic disorder.

The versions of the script show Shakespeare's precision with what is said: the balance of word against word, phrase against phrase; the deliberate antithesis used when Claudius first expresses the contrived formality of diplomacy; and the way one speaker picks up and reinterprets the words of another — as when Horatio says of the Ghost that "this is wondrous strange," and the Prince replies, "And therefore as a stranger give it welcome" (I.v.165). The director needs to grasp the sense as Hamlet's swift intellect uses a vast array of verbal devices; he needs to "hear" the sound of the script in speech and time.

The slow, contemplative verse of the soliloquies brilliantly expresses changes of thought. "O, what a rogue and peasant slave am I" (II.ii.547-603) is in iambic pentameter, blank verse whose language is personal and direct with a flowing effect of unrehearsed spontaneity. In

> For murder, though it have no tongue, will speak
> With most miraculous organ            (II.ii.591-592)

murder is personified, and the "m" alliteration sustains the effect. The contrast of the two voices of Hamlet: the calm, reasonable aristocrat ("O, what a rogue ... ") and the passionate man ("this slave offal"), mixes courtly vocabulary and syntax with household cursing. This contrast emphasizes time.

## SPACE

The director pictures the events and movements indicated in the script and conveys them to the audience. All occurs in and around the Castle at Elsinore. There are interiors like Gertrude's closet and exteriors like the graveyard, all easily staged in the Globe by using the medieval *house* and *place* [see *End Notes*]. Thus after *The Murder of Gonzago* Hamlet converses with others, delivers his soliloquy, and exits [R] to find his mother.

The rear curtain opens to reveal Claudius. Hamlet, going to his mother, enters [R] on the main stage, pauses at Claudius' room but cannot kill him and exits [L]. Claudius' scene ends, and the curtains are drawn. Polonius going to Gertrude's closet enters [R], and (possibly after business to cover the momentary property changes backstage) the curtains open; he enters the Queen's closet. With Polonius behind the arras, Hamlet enters [L] and begins the scene with his mother.

*Hamlet* used the full physical resources of the Globe: the upper levels of the tiring-house for the battlements; and the trapdoor for the Ghost's cellarage and Ophelia's grave. Today's director using a thrust stage is at an advantage in comparison with one who must work on a proscenium stage. A thrust stage brings the play's space *towards* the audience whereas a proscenium platform takes the space *away* from them. The director interprets the play in spatial levels (e.g., segments of the play that are "near" or "far" from the audience) and arranges them on the acting area.

SEQUENCE

Like most of Shakespeare's plays, the act divisions of later editors have little relation to the play's structure, and there is no break between some scenes. In production terms, *Hamlet* has three major Movements:

- *Movement One* (I.i-I.v).

    This Movement sets the action in motion in three main rhythms: (1) the Ghost (I.i) and the revelation of Claudius' villainy to Hamlet (I.iv-I.v); (2) the Court, the main characters and their interaction (I.ii); (3) the family of Polonius, Laertes, Ophelia (I.iii).

- *Movement Two* (II.i-IV.iii).

    This Movement is one great sweep of action balanced between Hamlet's growing attack upon Claudius and Claudius (with others) spying on Hamlet. It reaches a climax in the play-within-the-play, Claudius' prayer, and the closet scene with Gertrude where Hamlet kills Polonius (III.ii-iv). Then Claudius sends Hamlet to England. The main action has within it many other rhythms: the breakdown of the Hamlet-Ophelia love story; the hustle and bustle when the travelling players

arrive; the differences between Hamlet's friends —
Horatio versus Rosencrantz and Guildenstern; and
many other secondary rhythms.
* *Movement Three* (IV.iv-V.ii).

   This runs until the end of the play. The King's
   "counter-action" is the main motive force; Hamlet, until
   the last scene, is almost a passive figure.

   Eight days are represented on the stage, as follows:
   Day 1:  I.i-I.iii.
   Day 2:  I.iv-I.v.
   Brief Interval.
   Day 3:  II.i-I.ii.
   Day 4:  III.i-IV.iii.
   Day 5:  IV.iv.
   Brief Interval.
   Day 6:  IV.v-IV.vii.
   Day 7:  V.i.
   Day 8:  V.ii.

## ACTION

### First Movement: Exposition

*Hamlet* opens with such a huge effect that the rest of the play
reverberates with it. Shakespeare reverses the usual process and
starts with a climax: the Ghost. From then on Hamlet is affected by the Ghost's shattering revelation — the key to the whole
play. But in a masterly piece of construction, Shakespeare
divides this effect into two parts: the Ghost is introduced in I.i,
but Hamlet only encounters it in I.iv.

The opening is perhaps the most famous in Shakespeare.
Its only rival is the start of *Macbeth* with the three witches. The
two darkest of Shakespeare's tragedies begin with supernatural
figures that prompt the bloodshed. They are seen at first by
more than the hero but later only by the hero; at the end they
no longer exist. This view of the supernatural is different from
that commonly held in Shakespeare's time.

The action begins "above," on the tiring house: the soldiers
tell Hamlet they saw the Ghost "upon the platform where we
watch" (I.ii.213).

*Elsinore, the Castle. The sentries are armed in case of an attack by Fortinbras, Prince of Norway. Recently a Ghost looking like the late King of Denmark has appeared to them. Horatio is brought to meet it. It appears and disappears. They resolve to tell young Hamlet of the matter (I.i).*

On the battlements, Francisco is on guard. Barnardo approaches so nervously that he does not wait to be challenged but cries:

BAR:   Who's there?

FRA:   Nay, answer me. Stand and unfold yourself.

BAR:   Long live the King!

FRA:   Barnardo?

BAR:   He.

FRA:   You come most carefully upon your hour.

BAR:   'Tis now struck twelve. Get thee to bed, Francisco.

FRA:   For this relief much thanks. 'Tis bitter cold,
　　　　And I am sick at heart.

BAR:   Have you had quiet guard?

FRA:　　　　　　　　Not a mouse stirring.　　　　(1-11)

In this brilliant and swift exchange, Shakespeare tells us the place, time and season. Barnardo is nervous and tense; his prompt arrival is lest the Ghost appear to Francisco, who evidently knows nothing. Francisco, the "honest soldier," is brusque and terse; he accounts for feeling "sick at heart" by the fact that "'tis bitter cold." In the still night ("not a mouse stirring"), men's voices ring out sharply in subdued fear. The stage is darkly lit. Perhaps there is a whining wind, not too loud and repeated at intervals.

Francisco leaves as Horatio arrives with Marcellus who, as well as Barnardo, has seen the Ghost. Horatio's scepticism is clear: "Tush, tush, 'twill not appear." In Reinhardt's *Hamlet* with Moissi (London, 1929), the soldiers who warmed their hands over a brazier of coals were not raw young actors but old and bearded veterans whose terror was moving and convincing. Barnardo catches the audience's attention with his story, leading almost to the point where yesterday the Ghost appeared:

Last night of all,
When yond same star that's westward from the pole
Had made his course t'illume that part of heaven
Where now it burns, Marcellus and myself,

The bell then beating one —                    (35-39)
The chill of Barnardo's tale falls on his listeners and the audience. Their flesh is already creeping when (his sentence incom-
plete) the story becomes reality: "Peace, break thee off. Look
where it comes again" (40).

. The Ghost enters in full armour: his beaver (the visor of his
helmet) is raised so that his face is visible. Horatio tries to get
the Ghost to speak:

> What art thou that usurpest this time of night,
> Together with that fair and warlike form
> In which the majesty of buried Denmark
> Did sometimes march?                    (46-49)

But the Ghost disappears. The three men react differently.
Barnardo is matter-of-fact; he observes the "thing," when it
appears, more exactly than the others do, and teases the con-
verted sceptic:

> How now, Horatio! You tremble and look pale.
> Is not this something more than fantasy?         (53-54)

Marcellus is on edge, and he is anxious for Hamlet to be told.
Horatio's scepticism vanishes; the portent can only bode "some
strange eruption to our state" (69). We glimpse a political and
moral uncertainty: the whispered rumours, the underhand
diplomacy and ruthless action that pervade the Danish court.

When the Ghost reappears, Horatio stands in its path and
begs it to speak. In spite of the danger ("though it blast me")
and the menace of the Ghost's spread arms (Q2 has the stage
directions), Horatio holds his breath three times on a half-line
(in the pause we hear the iambic line ticking):

> If thou hast any sound or use of voice,
> Speak to me.
> If there be any good thing to be done
> That may to thee do ease and grace to me,
> Speak to me.
> If thou art privy to thy country's fate,
> Which happily foreknowing may avoid,
> O, speak!                    (129-136)

On Horatio's final, "Speak to it," the Ghost lifts up its head,
"like as it would speak," but a distant cock crows and causes it
to shrink "in haste away" (I.ii.215-218) —

> it started, like a guilty thing
>
> Upon a fearful summons.            (149-150)

They try to stop it. Their shouts, "'Tis here," "'Tis here," "'Tis gone," are variously spoken about the stage: "It faded on the crowing of the cock" (158). The scene began at midnight: now it is dawn:

> But look, the morn in russet mantle clad
>
> Walks o'er the dew of yon high eastward hill.  (167-168)

So much has happened in the interval that the transition seems natural.

> *The King and Queen settle political issues; agree that*
> *Laertes, Polonius' son, can go to Paris; fail to persuade*
> *Hamlet out of mourning but do persuade him not to*
> *return to Wittenberg. After Hamlet's soliloquy, Horatio*
> *and the soldiers tell him of the Ghost. Hamlet will join*
> *them tonight (I.ii).*

In sharp contrast to the dark night on the battlements, the court is dazzlingly costumed and lit as it bustles to prepare for a Council meeting. Hamlet, an incongruously black-clad figure, sits at one end of the council-table. Trumpets herald the King and Queen. Claudius is a brilliant figure, a "very, very peacock" as Hamlet later says. The visual effect here is important. The stage direction of Q2 hints that, at the Globe, the back curtains opened, and a council-table is discovered.

The King addresses his Council, dispatching business:

> Though yet of Hamlet our dear brother's death
>
> The memory be green, and that it us befitted
>
> To bear our hearts in grief, and our whole kingdom
>
> To be contracted in one brow of woe,
>
> Yet so far hath discretion fought with nature
>
> That we with wisest sorrow think on him
>
> Together with remembrance of ourselves.            (1-7)

He speaks of his brother's death with dignified sorrow, and of

> our sometime sister, now our Queen,
>
> Th'imperial jointress of this warlike state ...            (8-9)

as if the marriage is chiefly a dynastic matter. But he and his smooth verse rhythms repulse us. Marriage with a dead brother's wife was thought incestuous and violated canon law; yet their subjects seem to support the marriage, incestuous or not.

Both in Norway and Denmark, the crown was not necessarily inherited; and a brother rather than a son has been elected king. Hamlet has not been denied the Danish throne.

In foreign affairs the king is a good diplomat. A Norwegian army led by young Fortinbras menaces Denmark. Claudius sends ambassadors to the sick King of Norway to suppress the raid.

Claudius is then affectionately gracious: "And now, Laertes, what's the news with you?" (42) The indulgent King grants the young man's suit to visit Paris almost before it is presented, as a gift to the loyal Polonius. But from the start, Claudius resents Hamlet's defiant mourning. It is almost an insult which the subtle King first belittles by ignoring it. Then four lines of alternate speech open the conflict of Claudius and Hamlet:

> KING: But now, my cousin Hamlet, and my son —
> HAM: A little more than kin, and less than kind!

Despite the provocation in Hamlet's muttered reply, Claudius is mild:

> KING: How is it that the clouds still hang on you?
> HAM: Not so, my lord. I am too much in the sun. (64-67)

This dialogue is masterly: the King identifies the Prince and shows his ambiguous relationship: cousin-nephew and son-stepson. Hamlet gives a riddling retort. The answer to Claudius' question of Hamlet's black costume shows he is "too much in the sun" or "too much in the son," meaning don't try to usurp my father's place with me! (F1 prints "Sun," Q2 has "sonne.") Gertrude says:

> Good Hamlet, cast thy nighted colour off,
> And let thine eye look like a friend on Denmark.   (68-69)

The Queen contrasts appearance and reality: if death is common, "Why seems it so particular with thee?" Hamlet replies, "'Seems,' madam? Nay, it is. I know not 'seems'" (76), stressing his disgust in "k" and "s" sounds:

> 'Tis not alone my inky cloak, good mother,
> Nor customary suits of solemn black ..."          (77-78)

He establishes his role: if the external signs of his mourning are "actions that a man might play," he has "that within which passes show" (84-85); he can express his feelings in the role of the public mourner, but aware it is histrionic, he feels partly separated from it. He decisively refuses to play the parts Claudius and Gertrude give him.

Claudius gives him a veritable sermon, full of banal piety:

> Fie, 'tis a fault to heaven,
> A fault against the dead, a fault to nature,
> To reason most absurd, whose common theme
> Is death of fathers, and who still hath cried,
> From the first corse till he that died today,
> 'This must be so.'                    (101-106)

As the audience is lulled by his soft words, his fangs suddenly show:

> For your intent
> In going back to school in Wittenberg,
> It is most retrograde to our desire ...     (112-114)

Claudius' excesses of speech and smiling kindness show that he feels his role to be false. He implies that the succession is the problem with Hamlet. Gertrude knows better. More important than his father's death is her marriage. The King and Queen still have their secret (the adultery) to keep from Hamlet, and Claudius guards a deadlier one (the murder) from her.

Gertrude begs Hamlet to "stay with us. Go not to Wittenberg." She wins only a cold, "I shall in all my best obey you, madam" (with a slight emphasis on the second-person pronoun). Claudius quickly takes this as "a loving and a fair reply ..." (which it is not), and declares that:

> This gentle and unforced accord of Hamlet
> Sits smiling to my heart ...               (119-124)

Play-acting is forced on the fastidiously honest Hamlet who is surrounded by the deceiving court. He can only unburden his inner thoughts when he is alone. The first of Hamlet's seven soliloquies begins:

> O that this too too sullied flesh would melt,
> Thaw, and resolve itself into a dew;
> Or that the Everlasting had not fixed
> His canon 'gainst self-slaughter. O God, God,
> How weary, stale, flat, and unprofitable
> Seem to me all the uses of this world!
> Fie on't, ah, fie, 'tis an unweeded garden
> That grows to seed. Things rank and gross in nature
> Possess it merely.                         (129-137)

His revulsion for life and longing for death are so intense that only religious awe lies between Hamlet and suicide. His flesh is sullied because it is the flesh of a woman who, only weeks after the death of her first husband, has married her husband's brother:

> O God, a beast that wants discourse of reason
> Would have mourned longer ...                    (150-151)

Hamlet's bitter judgment on himself is also because he has no role to help him deal with the situation. He has lost his father through death and his mother through transformation: she is now something other than his mother. Without identity, Hamlet is no longer at home in the world and is a mere object; so he yearns for the non-existence of death. He feels at the end of things. "It is not, nor it cannot come to good." What can he do? "But break, my heart, for I must hold my tongue" (158-159).

He sees three sober figures waiting for him: Horatio and the soldiers. The play's action re-starts, and from here to the end of the scene the pulse beats more strongly. Hamlet speaks before he has seen who his visitors are: "I am glad to see you well" (160). Immediately he recognizes Horatio, and his welcome is spontaneously affectionate. Then:

> HOR:  My lord, I think I saw him yesternight.
> HAM:  Saw? Who?
> HOR:  My lord, the King your father.          (189-191)

Following the shock is a segment of superb dialogue, a four-voiced exchange, swift, vivid, simple, and tight. Hamlet questions them briskly:

> HAM:  Then saw you not his face?
> HOR:  O, yes, my lord. He wore his beaver up.
> HAM:  What, looked he frowningly?
> HOR:  A countenance more in sorrow than in anger.
>                                               (229-232)

Horatio is calm. Hamlet is tense. Marcellus and Barnardo supply support.

> HAM:          I will watch tonight.
>               Perchance 'twill walk again.
> HOR:          I warrant it will.
> HAM:  If it assume my noble father's person,
>       I'll speak to it though hell itself should gape
>       And bid me hold my peace.          (242-246)

As they leave, Hamlet gives us the first hint of the truth: "I doubt some foul play" (256).

> *Laertes, leaving for France, gives his sister Ophelia advice before Polonius gives him advice. Polonius orders Ophelia to end her relationship with Hamlet (I.iii).*

Ophelia, as Ellen Terry observed, only "pervades" her early scenes, and they are notoriously difficult both for actress and director. Too much must be told in the First Movement of *Hamlet* for there to be any mention of Ophelia until now. Here she has little opportunity to be anything but a charming sister and an obedient daughter. Her father and brother act as playwrights to her; they work successfully to hinder the fulfilment of Hamlet's and Ophelia's roles as lovers. Laertes' warning to his sister, Polonius' "few precepts," and his repetition, with emphasis, of Laertes' warning contain little but advice.

In a fine high school production this scene opened as two sailors, carrying a sea-chest (bearing some of the "necessaries" of which Laertes speaks), crossed the stage. This was a typically Elizabethan way to establish the acting area as the quay-side for the moment; later it is said, "The wind sits in the shoulder of your sail, And you are stayed for" (56-57).

The talk of Laertes with Ophelia is of a brother anxious for the sister's welfare while he is away. He tells her to be wary of Hamlet:

> Perhaps he loves you now,
> And now no soil nor cautel doth besmirch
> The virtue of his will. But you must fear,
> His greatness weighed, his will is not his own ...
> Then weigh what loss your honour may sustain
> If with too credent ear you list his songs,
> Or lose your heart, or your chaste treasure open
> To his unmastered importunity.
> Fear it, Ophelia, fear it, my dear sister.          (14-33)

Ophelia only knows the Hamlet who has approached her "with love in honourable fashion." But she is not without spirit. She charmingly bursts Laertes' sermon with her comparison to an ungracious pastor, begging him not to

> Show me the steep and thorny way to heaven
> Whiles like a puffed and reckless libertine
> Himself the primrose path of dalliance treads ...   (48-50)

Polonius' "precepts" to Laertes are good conservative counsel in his long-winded style. The speech is memorable for its last lines that, although ironic, suggest a deeper thoughtfulness.

> This above all: to thine own self be true,
> And it must follow, as the night the day,
> Thou canst not then be false to any man.          (78-80)

With Laertes gone, Polonius lectures Ophelia about Hamlet's courtship. The locality of the scene becomes neutral; the quayside is forgotten. Polonius commands her "in plain terms" to have no further communication with Hamlet. Unlike Juliet and Desdemona, Ophelia obeys.

### The Ghost reappears and Hamlet follows it (I.iv).

This and the next scene are in reality one and should be played together. We are aloft on the tiring-house, but the main stage is used for I.v (although Leslie Howard played the scene in a crypt and Moissi by a large cross in a churchyard).

Hamlet, Horatio and the night sentries watch in the night cold. It has struck twelve, and the time is near "Wherein the spirit held his wont to walk" (6). We expect this to be the Ghost's cue, but suddenly somewhere below the battlements comes the sound of the King's revelry, trumpets and gunfire. Hamlet complains that Danish drunkenness has ruined his country's reputation and says that a character flaw may be present in a person from one inborn defect, "some vicious mole of nature":

> the o'ergrowth of some complexion, [humour]
> Oft breaking down the pales and forts of reason (27-28)

which may damn the reputation of a man like himself.

Suddenly the Ghost is here, silently standing in relief against the darkness. The effect on Hamlet is enormous. His immediate response is the breathless panic of the opening prayer:

> Angels and ministers of grace defend us!
> Be thou a spirit of health or goblin damned,
> Bring with thee airs from heaven or blasts from hell,
> Be thy intents wicked or charitable ...          (39-42)

He gets no answer. He repeats, "Say, why is this? Wherefore? What should we do?" (57). The Ghost keeps us in suspense, then beckons Hamlet to follow. Horatio tries to dissuade

Hamlet, describing the dangers of walking at night on the parapets as he, in the Globe, looks downward over the rail of the upper level:

> What if it tempt you toward the flood, my lord,
> Or to the dreadful summit of the cliff
> That beetles o'er his base into the sea,
> And there assume some other, horrible form,
> Which might deprive your sovereignty of reason
> And draw you into madness? Think of it.
> The very place puts toys of desperation,
> Without more motive, into every brain
> That looks so many fathoms to the sea
> And hears it roar beneath.                    (69-78)

His warning to Hamlet is a form of playwriting. But Hamlet struggles free:

> HAM:       It waves me still.
>        Go on. I'll follow thee.
> MAR:   You shall not go, my lord.
> HAM:       Hold off your hands.
> HOR:   Be ruled. You shall not go.
> HAM:       My fate cries out
>        And makes each petty artere in this body
>        As hardy as the Nemean lion's nerve.
>        Still am I called. Unhand me, gentlemen.
>        By heaven, I'll make a ghost of him that lets me!
>        I say, away! Go on. I'll follow thee.
>        *Exeunt Ghost and Hamlet*                    (78-86)

As the Ghost and Hamlet disappear, the terror of Horatio and the soldiers increases. They have five lines more, just time for the Ghost and Hamlet (Shakespeare and Burbage) to go from the tiring house to the stage.

> *The Ghost tells Hamlet it is the spirit of his father, murdered by his brother, Claudius, who committed adultery with Gertrude. Hamlet is to set things right but to leave Gertrude's punishment to heaven (I.v).*

Now the Ghost tells Hamlet its tale. Probably Shakespeare himself stood on the Globe stage and first spoke the sonorous lines on which depends the whole action of the play. The Ghost's denunciation of his "most seeming-virtuous Queen" (46) has a great impact on Hamlet's already explicit disgust at the hasty marriage; now he is told that there was adultery before her husband's death. The Ghost is interrupted by "the morning air" (58), so it moves to a vivid account of the murder, unmasking Claudius as "that incestuous, that adulterate beast" (42):

> And in the porches of my ears did pour
> The leperous distilment; whose effect
> Holds such an enmity with blood of man
> That swift as quicksilver it courses through
> The natural gates and alleys of the body,
> And with a sudden vigour it doth posset
> And curd, like eager droppings into milk,
> The thin and wholesome blood. So did it mine.   (63-70)

The Ghost died unshriven of his sins, and so the doom it suffers "to walk the night" and "fast in fires" results from the treachery of Claudius. The Ghost's final injunction is characteristic of its nobility:

> But howsomever thou pursues this act,
> Taint not thy mind, nor let thy soul contrive
> Against thy mother aught.                        (84-86)

Its story peaks at the triple cry of "horrible." As "The glow-worm shows the matin to be near" (89), the Ghost once more shrinks in haste away, with its fading cry of "Adieu, adieu, adieu. Remember me." It descends into the trapdoor (the "Hell"). Hamlet is left on his knees, calling upon his sinews to "bear me stiffly up" (95). Echoes of the terrors beyond the grave run from here to the Graveyard scene as Hamlet becomes obsessed with hideous thoughts of the body's decay:

> O all you host of heaven! O earth! What else?
> And shall I couple hell? O, fie!                 (92-93)

From now until he sets out for England, Hamlet is "mad." Yet how mad is he? He will also *pretend* to be mad, but the role and the reality are not easily distinguished. Caught in a maze of deceit, Hamlet takes refuge in an illusion he devises. He becomes an actor and, from his "antic disposition," he bides his time for vengeance:

> Remember thee?
> Yea, from the table of my memory
> I'll wipe away all trivial fond records,
> All saws of books, all forms, all pressures past
> That youth and observation copied there,

> And thy commandment all alone shall live
> Within the book and volume of my brain,
> Unmixed with baser matter.                    (97-104)

His next thought is of his mother: "O most pernicious woman!"
(105). Then of Claudius: "That one may smile, and smile, and
be a villain" (108).

Suddenly the stage is full of shouts and rapid movements as
Horatio and the soldiers rush about the night looking for
Hamlet. He is unstable in his cunning and in taking refuge in a
torrent of words as he greets them. He appeals to his "friends,
scholars and soldiers" never to reveal what they have seen. They
agree, but Hamlet wildly insists again, "Nay, but swear't ... Upon
my sword" (145-147). The Ghost under the stage several times
cries, "Swear" (149), and they do. Hamlet calls, "Rest, rest, per-
turbèd spirit!" and when he says:

> So, gentlemen,
> With all my love I do commend me to you,
> And what so poor a man as Hamlet is
> May do t'express his love and friending to you,
> God willing, shall not lack.

the Hamlet they know speaks again. Then with the sudden cry:

> The time is out of joint. O, cursèd spite,
> That ever I was born to set it right!              (182-189)

he faces a new dawn.

### Second Movement: Development and Complications

The Second Movement consists of the main body of the play.
All the major issues, themes and people of the plot have
already been introduced.

> *Polonius sends Reynaldo to Paris with money for Laertes
> and to spy upon him. Ophelia tells how Hamlet has sud-
> denly appeared in her closet — "mad for thy love," says
> Polonius and goes to tell the King (II.i).*

The opening of the scene is domestic comedy, a welcome
relief from the previous tension. The dialogue elaborates the
portrait of Polonius, showing his habit of going round about in
pursuit of his object. No less characteristic is his stubbornness
in sticking to his wearisome exposition in spite of his hearer's

impatience. His directions to Reynaldo are a form of playwriting and indicate his deviousness.

When Reynaldo leaves, Ophelia in a distressed state reports to her father that she has been frightened by the sudden appearance in her room of

> Lord Hamlet, with his doublet all unbraced,
> No hat upon his head, his stockings fouled,
> Ungartered, and down-gyvèd to his ankle,
> Pale as his shirt, his knees knocking each other,
> And with a look so piteous in purport
> As if he had been loosèd out of hell ...          (78-83)

This took place just after the cellarage scene, so it shows the intensity of his feeling then. It is no play-acting on Hamlet's part.

> At last, a little shaking of mine arm
> And thrice his head thus waving up and down,
> He raised a sigh so piteous and profound
> As it did seem to shatter all his bulk
> And end his being.          (92-96)

His "piteous" sigh shows that he realizes her failure, and that all is over between them. He waits for the help that never comes:

> That done, he lets me go; ...
> He seemed to find his way without his eyes;
> For out o'doors he went without their helps
> And to the last bended their light on me.          (96-100)

We feel the finality of Hamlet's farewell to his love; the picture is almost unbearably poignant. Twice during Ophelia's account, an eloquent "thus" shows that her words are embodied in action.

Polonius thinks that Hamlet is mad with love-sickness because Ophelia has rejected his attentions. She returns his letters and refuses to speak to him; when a distracted Hamlet forces his way into her presence, she apparently sits staring at him in terrified silence; then she immediately tells Polonius. Docility is her major characteristic: in the third act she allows herself to be used as a pawn against him and lies to him; at *The Murder of Gonzago* she passively faces Hamlet's indecencies; and when her father is killed, she disintegrates into a gentle madness.

> *Rosencrantz and Guildenstern start work. Fortinbras is diverted. Polonius plans to show that Hamlet is mad for the love of Ophelia. The Players arrive. The Hecuba soliloquy: Hamlet will prove Claudius' guilt in the play-within-the-play (II.ii).*

Rosencrantz and Guildenstern, Hamlet's friends, will serve their King loyally. Claudius thanks "Rosencrantz, and gentle Guildenstern." The Queen graciously echoes: "Thanks Guildenstern and gentle Rosencrantz." The King sets the pair, unaware of his real motive, to spy on their friend. This starts the contrary movement of the play: Hamlet's against Claudius is stalled; now the King's against Hamlet begins.

News comes that Fortinbras will not attack Denmark, but to invade Poland, he wants to march over Danish territory. Claudius agrees. The acts of Fortinbras contrast with Hamlet's inaction. Polonius tells of Hamlet's love and reads his love letter. Polonius' repetitions seem endless: thus "What do you think of me?" is picked up by "But what might you think ... what might you, Or my dear majesty your Queen here, think ... What might you think?" (129-139).

We do not know at what moment Burbage made his entry, but this issue becomes vital to interpreting the play. Both Q2 and F1 *(Enter Hamlet reading on a Booke)* put it after the King's line: "We will try it" (167), in which case Hamlet has overheard nothing. Dover Wilson* argues persuasively for an earlier entry (160) so that Polonius'

> he walks four hours together
>
> Here in the lobby                                                    (160-161)

draws our attention to Hamlet's presence at that point. He then overhears,

> I'll loose my daughter to him.
>
> Be you and I behind an arras then.                     (162-163)

This will affect how Hamlet plays the "fishmonger" and "nunnery" scenes. Gielgud tried it both ways, settling on the second.

Hamlet proceeds to act the role of madman with Polonius:

POL:   How does my good Lord Hamlet?
HAM.   Well, God-a-mercy.

---

* Wilson (1940).

Polonius treats him as a harmless lunatic. He mischievously plays the part:

POL.   Do you know me, my lord?

HAM.   Excellent well. You are a fishmonger.

POL.   Not I, my lord.

HAM.   Then I would you were so honest a man.

POL.   Honest, my lord?

HAM.   Ay, sir. To be honest, as this world goes, is to be
one man picked out of ten thousand.

POL.   That's very true, my lord.

HAM.   For if the sun breed maggots in a dead dog, being a good kissing carrion — have you a daughter?

POL.   I have, my lord.

HAM.   Let her not walk i'th sun. Conception is a blessing. But as your daughter may conceive, friend,
look to't.                                         (171-186)

Hamlet detests Polonius: the "tedious old fool," loyal to
Claudius, made Ophelia jilt him. Overhearing his proposal to
loose his daughter to him, Hamlet is furious. From behind his
"antic" mask he lashes Polonius with ironic double meanings:
"fishmonger" is a pander or procurer; "carrion" is carnal
"flesh"; and the quibble on "conception" is obvious. It is all lost
on Polonius. He also misses Hamlet's other veiled warning: "O
Jephthah, judge of Israel, what a treasure hadst thou!" (402-
403). There is method in Hamlet's madness: his surface talk is
nonsense, but his words make deeper if ambiguous sense.

Hamlet greets his old friends, Rosencrantz and
Guildenstern, as warmly as he greeted Horatio: "Good lads,
how do you both?" (226)

HAM:   What have you, my good friends, deserved at
the hands of Fortune that she sends you to
prison hither?

GLD:   Prison, my lord?

HAM:   Denmark's a prison.                         (239-243)

Rosencrantz tries to trick him: "Why, then your ambition makes
it one ..." (251), and both harp on "ambition." Hamlet challenges them: "what make you at Elsinore? ... I know the good
King and Queen have sent for you ... be even and direct with
me whether you were sent for or no." Their embarrassment
shows: "a kind of confession in your looks, which your mod-

esties have not craft enough to colour." They agree, "My lord, we were sent for" (270-292). He tells them what to report: he gestures to the visible "frame" of the earth (the playhouse), which he shrinks to the "promontory" of the stage, and over it the Heavens, "This most excellent canopy, the air, look you, this brave o'erhanging firmament, this majestical roof fretted with golden fire," which he reduces to a "foul and pestilent congregation of vapours" (299-303). The play is a world where humanity falls to "this quintessence of dust" (308). Shakespeare starts a deliberate digression. Hamlet hides himself from the pair's prying through theatre gossip: the "little eyases" of the children's companies rival the Chamberlain's Men — "the boys carry it away?" (338-359).

The trumpets sound, and Polonius hurries in to announce that the Players are arriving at Elsinore. There are sinister overtones in Hamlet's initial cry: "He that plays the king shall be welcome" (319). The colourful tradition of the Players enters the tragedy, deflecting its course, and the dark castle fills with sound, colour, drums, trumpets and the garish robes of the city actors, Hamlet's old friends. Treachery and vengeance are forgotten. Polonius, recalling his own ill-omened appearance as Julius Caesar at the university, is excited: his absurd catalogue of plays is curiously joyous. Hamlet is enthusiastic, a surprising reaction that brings variety to his role. The tempo of the scene quickens as the action of the tragedy pauses. Hamlet welcomes his old acquaintances with pleasure. He begins a favourite speech, taken over by the First Player in an older theatrical convention which is still very moving. His words ironically apply to Hamlet's condition:

> So as a painted tyrant Pyrrhus stood,
> And like a neutral to his will and matter
> Did nothing. (478-480)

Hamlet urges the Player to "Say on; come to Hecuba." (Hecuba was a widowed queen, like Gertrude.) Hamlet, the mask of madness forgotten, notices the emotion of the performer; even Polonius says "Prithee no more" (518), and he sees real tears in the Player's eyes. Hamlet tells Polonius to treat the actors well, for "after your death, you were better have a bad epitaph, than their ill report while you live." When Polonius replies: "My Lord, I will use them according to their desert," Hamlet angrily retorts:

God's bodkin, man, much better! Use every man
after his desert, and who shall 'scape whipping? Use
them after your own honour and dignity.  (527-529)

Hamlet detains the First Player: "Dost thou hear me, old friend?
Can you play *The Murder of Gonzago*?" We have not heard that
word since the Ghost used it. "You could for a need study a
speech of some dozen lines or sixteen lines, which I would set
down and insert in't" (534-539). From the power of the actor
the idea of *The Mousetrap* arises. The actors will perform that
play tomorrow night, and the tragedy is back on course.

"Now I am alone," says Hamlet. It is a long time since he
was so.

O, what a rogue and peasant slave am I!
Is it not monstrous that this player here,
But in a fiction, in a dream of passion,
Could force his soul so to his own conceit
That from her working all his visage wanned ... (546-551)

"This player here": Burbage gestures to where he has performed. He re-plays it for us: the "visage wanned," the "tears,"
and so forth. But he did it "all for nothing. For Hecuba!" (554-
555). The irony has many levels:

- Real and imaginative passion differ; the player is a
  dream maker. The actor's art and the world it creates
  are dreams.
- The Player is play-acting a "fiction" of tragedy; what
  would he do if his tragedy were real, like Hamlet's?
- Hamlet is performed by an actor, as is the First Player:
  are we not all (including the audience) then actors?
- The First Player's speech and action are excessively
  histrionic, whereas, by contrast, the violent emotion of
  Hamlet's soliloquy is more spontaneous and "natural;"
  but what is "natural"?
- In the play itself, Hamlet is not active, and Shakespeare
  wants us to be conscious of Hamlet's inaction here. He
  also wants to show us that Hamlet is aware of his inaction, that he is impatient of it, and that he is proposing
  to do something about it.

In these levels of irony, we forget that it is Burbage, or Garrick,
or Irving, or Gielgud pretending to be Hamlet. He seems as
real as we are. But he must be sure of his uncle's guilt before
he acts: the test will be tomorrow night:

> About, my brains. Hum — I have heard
> That guilty creatures sitting at a play ...            (586-587)

By getting the Players to act before the King a replica of his
father's murder, Hamlet becomes a dramatic artist:

> The play's the thing
> Wherein I'll catch the conscience of the King.    (602-603)

> *Rosencrantz and Guildenstern report to the King and*
> *Queen. Hamlet soliloquizes, "To be or not to be." He and*
> *Ophelia talk as Claudius and Polonius eavesdrop.*
> *Polonius persuades Claudius to let Gertrude interview her*
> *son; if she cannot find the cause of his madness, Hamlet is*
> *to go to England (III.i).*

As Hamlet exits, the King and Queen enter at a slower
rhythm; their spies report events. Claudius and Polonius plan
to eavesdrop on Hamlet when he takes his habitual walk.
Polonius gives Ophelia her stage directions: she must carry her
prayer-book as a plausible reason for being alone.

When Polonius remarks on the hypocrisy of mankind, quite
unexpectedly Claudius betrays to us the "heavy burden" on his
conscience. He murmurs:

> O, 'tis too true.
> *(Aside)* How smart a lash that speech doth give my con-
> science!
> The harlot's cheek, beautied with plastering art,
> Is not more ugly to the thing that helps it
> Than is my deed to my most painted word.
> O, heavy burden!                                      (49-54)

The audience knows that Claudius is guilty, with a guilty conscience. The King and Polonius slip behind the arras as
Ophelia waits for Hamlet.

"To be, or not to be — that is the question ..." (56). Hamlet
walks slowly on stage, reading a book, and then looks up to
deliver the most famous lines in drama. His previous resolution
has evaporated with his mood swings, typical of melancholics.
The questions he asks are those we all wrestle with in great
crises; and he typifies all great men whose depth of insight prevents them from acting decisively. His first question is ambiguous: on the surface it means, "To live or to die by suicide?" But it
also questions present Being. Shakespeare, like Boethius, uses
the words "to be," "are" and "is" to indicate essential Being.

Actors dismiss such problems in the immediacy of the stage. They notice that the soliloquy is full of long vowels (sleep, heartache, dream, pause); the thought interrupts them for a while, but they return (again, weary life, bourn). His initial question becomes whether he should be passive or fight and risk his death:

> Whether 'tis nobler in the mind to suffer
> The slings and arrows of outrageous fortune
> Or to take arms against a sea of troubles
> And by opposing end them. To die, to sleep —
> No more ...                                        (57-61)

If he could make death and sleep one, he might evade ("shuffle off") the pain of consciousness:

>                and by a sleep to say we end
> The heartache and the thousand natural shocks
> That flesh is heir to. 'Tis a consummation
> Devoutly to be wished.                              (61-64)

The wish is for both the body's death and the soul's. Suicide raises "the dread of something after death" (78). The question of bodily disintegration and personal survival is horrible to Hamlet; he would welcome death if death were all and begins philosophic speculation:

> Thus conscience does make cowards of us all;
> And thus the native hue of resolution
> Is sicklied o'er with the pale cast of thought,
> And enterprises of great pitch and moment
> With this regard their currents turn awry
> And lose the name of action.                        (83-88)

The speech, as G. Wilson Knight tells us, "is built up on two contrasted sets of metaphors. Life, 'this mortal coil,' is at best something which hampers and impedes. Death, on the other hand, is presented simply as a relaxing of tension and an abandonment of the struggle."* What Hamlet needs is not less conscience but more.

Granville-Barker rightly says that the soliloquy "is passion at a still, white heat, fused into thought."** But Hamlet has no solutions. We are asked not to judge but to understand.

---

\* Knight (1930).
\*\* Granville-Barker (1963).

He sees Ophelia at her devotions. He asks her to pray for
him too:

> Nymph, in thy orisons
> Be all my sins remembered.                              (89-90)

For a brief instant we see them as two shy young lovers, tongue-
tied in each other's company, both in reproachful sorrow.

She brings back his gifts. That wounds him, and he roughly
denies them; she then accuses him of unkindness. Her trite
aphorism and the too neat rhyming of "noble mind" with
"unkind" are obvious echoes of her father. In disgust he proceeds to bewilder her with his riddling wit:

> HAM: ... if you be honest and fair, your honesty should
> admit no discourse to your beauty.
>
> OPH:  Could beauty, my lord, have better commerce
> than with honesty?
>
> HAM:  Ay, truly. For the power of beauty will sooner
> transform honesty from what it is to a bawd than the
> force of honesty can translate beauty into his like-
> ness. This was sometime a paradox, but now the
> time gives it proof. I did love you once.
>
> OPH:  Indeed, my lord, you made me believe so.
>
> HAM: You should not have believed me. For virtue
> cannot so inoculate our old stock but we shall relish
> of it. I loved you not.
>
> OPH:  I was the more deceived.
>
> HAM: Get thee to a nunnery. Why wouldst thou be a
> breeder of sinners? I am myself indifferent honest,
> but yet I could accuse me of such things that it were
> better my mother had not borne me. I am very
> proud, revengeful, ambitious, with more offences at
> my beck than I have thoughts to put them in, imagi-
> nation to give them shape, or time to act them in.
> What should such fellows as I do crawling between
> earth and heaven? We are arrant knaves all. Believe
> none of us. Go thy ways to a nunnery.    (107-130)

As he turns to leave her, he sees the arras and remembers
Polonius' plot. He suspects that their conversation is overheard
and asks, "Where's your father?" (There is no need for a clumsy
movement of betrayal by Polonius or the King, which often
occurs in the theatre). To Hamlet, Ophelia has become poten-

tially a danger, perhaps allied with his enemies.

"Where's your father?" is his crucial test of her. She lies, and Hamlet takes her answer to be a lie. It is his second wound of this kind. The first named his mother an adultress. He still believed in Ophelia's seeming innocence, but now he knows that he has been set up, and he explodes with a devastatingly cruel anger. His violent railing convinces her that he is mad indeed. In his eyes, she is now as wanton as his mother and all womankind. He repeats his cry "to a nunnery," "nunnery" meaning "brothel."

> I have heard of your paintings too, well enough. God
> hath given you one face, and you make yourselves
> another. You jig and amble, and you lisp. You nickname
> God's creatures and make your wantonness your igno-
> rance. Go to, I'll no more on't. It hath made me mad.
>                                                      (143-148)

Ophelia has acted the role of his mother, the harlot, so Ophelia is a scapegoat. His parting shot of "Those that are married already all but one — shall live" (148-149) is directed at his uncle behind the arras. Then he is gone, and their romance is in ruins. In a famous theatrical moment, Edmund Kean as Hamlet, having left the stage, electrified the audience by returning, tiptoeing across the stage, and kissing Ophelia's hair.

Ophelia's bewildered, heart-broken outcry when he leaves her:

> O, what a noble mind is here o'erthrown!
> The courtier's, soldier's, scholar's, eye, tongue, sword,
> Th'expectancy and rose of the fair state ...      (151-153)

reveals her remorse over her lost love.

The King is now sure that Hamlet is neither in love nor mad. Claudius' disquiet is visibly increased, for he is beginning to smell the truth:

> There's something in his soul
> O'er which his melancholy sits on brood,
> And I do doubt the hatch and the disclose
> Will be some danger ...                          (165-168)

and he has begun to act:

> which for to prevent,
> I have in quick determination
> Thus set it down: he shall with speed to England ...
>                                                      (168-170)

Ophelia may well overhear these words since the matter is not secret. Polonius has an alternative plan: after the play, let his mother "be round with him" (184) as Polonius eavesdrops; if that produces nothing, send him to England; and the more sinister

> or confine him where
>
> Your wisdom best shall think.                              (187-188)

The minds of Claudius and her father are on Hamlet. They ignore the miserably sobbing girl, now that she has served her turn. Nor do they notice the horror on her face at her father's callousness.

> *Horatio is to observe the King's reaction to "The Murder of Gonzago." During the play, Claudius rushes away.*
> *Gertrude wishes to see Hamlet who soliloquizes: ""Tis now the very witching time of night" (III.ii).*

The action is continuous as some of the Players begin to set up the stage for *The Murder of Gonzago*. Hamlet arrives. His mood has changed again: now he is unmistakably sane. The actors gather round to listen to him. He lectures them on their skill, attacking extravagance in writing and performing. In explaining the theoretical basis of theatre art, he defines for another person how he should play his part — the most characteristic act of the play as a whole. Hamlet stresses "naturalness" in speech and gesture:

> Speak the speech, I pray you, as I pronounced it to you, trippingly on the tongue. But if you mouth it as many of our players do, I had as lief the town crier spoke my lines. Nor do not saw the air too much with your hand, thus.                              (1-5)

He claims for dramatic art a new dignity and importance. Burbage, as Hamlet, has sharp words for the "groundlings": he rails at the "unskilful" for their unsympathetic laughter but compliments the "judicious" whose opinion is vital to the actor and the author. The advice to the players is often slightly embarrassing for the actor because he feels the audience is only waiting to catch him doing all the things he has told the players not to do.

Then comes a tiny but brilliant piece of Shakespearean stagecraft:

> *Exeunt Players. Enter Polonius, Rosencrantz and Guildenstern.*

HAM:  How now, my lord? Will the King hear this piece
      of work?
POL:  And the Queen too, and that presently.
HAM:  Bid the players make haste. *Exit Polonius*
      Will you two help to hasten them?
ROS:  Ay, my lord. *Exeunt Rosencrantz and Guildenstern*
HAM:  What, ho, Horatio! *Enter Horatio*
HOR:  Here, sweet lord, at your service.          (56-63)

In this minor moment, why does Shakespeare not use a messenger? He added meaning: Polonius gives his own self-impor-
tance to the message, and the mischievous Hamlet enjoys using
him as a lackey; Hamlet's distrust of Rosencrantz and
Guildenstern shows in their fast dismissal, and he mocks them
in the triteness of their errand, "Will you two help to hasten
them?" They are replaced by the true friend.

> Horatio, thou art e'en as just a man
> As e'er my conversation coped withal.          (64-65)

This is the most sane Hamlet so far. He confesses with great del-
icacy how much Horatio's friendship has meant to him. Hamlet
explains his plan: in the speech he has inserted, if the King's

> occulted guilt
> Do not itself unkennel in one speech,
> It is a damnèd ghost that we have seen,
> And my imaginations are as foul
> As Vulcan's stithy.          (90-94)

Horatio agrees to watch the King during the play.

The King and Queen arrive with splendid pageantry, ani-
mation and colour to see the play. Before our eyes Hamlet puts
on (like a mask) his "antic disposition"; it disguises his excitement at his ambush — "I must be idle" (100). Claudius asks:
"How fares our cousin Hamlet?" (102). The Prince corrupts
the verb "fare" by using it (in the Vice's fashion; see *End Notes*)
in the sense of eating, not in its general meaning (of "how do
you do"):

> Excellent, i'faith; of the chameleon's dish. I eat the
> air, promise-crammed. You cannot feed capons so.
>           (103-104)

Hamlet is often impertinent, but he is no Vice. Polonius
becomes the butt of Hamlet's outrageous punning.

HAM:  My lord, you played once i'th'university, you say?
POL:  That did I, my lord, and was accounted a good actor.
HAM:  What did you enact?
POL:  I did enact Julius Caesar. I was killed i'th'Capitol.
      Brutus killed me.
HAM:  It was a brute part of him to kill so capital a calf there.

(107-115)

If he is to watch the King, he cannot respond to his mother's affectionate "Come hither, my dear Hamlet, sit by me" (118). So he strikes at Ophelia. Bradley notes: "The disgusting and insulting grossness of his language to her [is such] as you will find addressed to a woman by no other hero of Shakespeare's, not even in that dreadful scene where Othello accuses Desdemona."* Hamlet has a savage side, as Rosencrantz and Guildenstern will discover.

The Players mime a brief summary of the story they are about to present. When the King sees the Dumb Show he is at once alert. Hamlet's "The players cannot keep counsel. They'll tell all" (150-151) announces the trap which he has laid. *The Murder of Gonzago,* compared to *Hamlet,* is slightly old-fashioned. As it unfolds, the King and Queen are dragged into it like a nightmare. The Player King and Queen reach out to threaten the reality of their audience.

Claudius thought his poisoned killing was his secret; yet it seems that Hamlet knows it. On the Player Queen's couplet,

In second husband let me be accurst!

None wed the second but who killed the first ..." (189-190) his comment of "That's wormwood" (191) shows he believes his mother to have been an accomplice in the murder. "If she should break it now!" (234) is aimed straight at his mother. At the Player Queen's exit, he asks:

HAM:  Madam, how like you this play?
GER:  The lady doth protest too much, methinks.
HAM:  O, but she'll keep her word.

When Claudius joins issue, we think that he may stop the show.

HAM:  No, no, they do but jest, poison in jest. No
      offence i'th' world.
KING: What do you call the play?

---

* Bradley (1978).

HAM:  *The Mousetrap* ... 'Tis a knavish piece of work.
But what of that? Your majesty, and we that have
free souls, it touches us not.          (239-252)

The speech Hamlet has written is half-way through: the
Murderer bends over the sleeping figure of the Player King *[F1: Powres the poyson in his eares]*, and Claudius' nerve snaps.
Hamlet, not missing his triumph, shouts:

'A poisons him i'th'garden for his estate. His name's
Gonzago. The story is extant, and written in very choice
Italian. You shall see anon how the murderer gets the
love of Gonzago's wife.          (270-273)

The King rises from his throne and staggers out. The great climax: "Give me some light. Away!" (278), is rarely staged today
with any great invention, though it worked well with Gielgud,
Redgrave, and Burton (in New York). Sarah Bernhardt
snatched a torch from an attendant and held it to the King's
face on "What! frighted with false fire?" and Moissi did much
the same with a large candelabrum. Irving created the business
of lying on the floor with the manuscript in his hand and of
squirming on his stomach across the stage. He also played with
a fan of peacock's feathers which Ophelia let drop, and which
he tore to pieces, as he lay exhausted on the throne, and flung
away on the words, "A very, very — peacock" (293).

The sudden collapse into general confusion is a brilliant
stroke of theatre. The Queen and the courtiers follow the King,
the startled Players "strike" their show, and in a great swirl of
colours and light, the stage empties in a confusion of cries.
With Horatio, Hamlet is left at centre stage triumphant. He has
learned all he needs to know about his uncle:

HAM:  O good Horatio, I'll take the ghost's word for a
thousand pound. Didst perceive?
HOR:  Very well, my lord.
HAM:  Upon the talk of the poisoning?
HOR:  I did very well note him.          (295-299)

Now he is exhilarated by his momentary triumph over his enemies.

Rosencrantz and Guildenstern hurry back with an urgent
message from the Queen who wishes to see Hamlet. A Player
returns with recorders. Hamlet politely begs Guildenstern to
play one. When he cannot, Hamlet issues a sharp warning:

Why, look you now, how unworthy a thing you make of

me! You would play upon me. You would seem to know
my stops. You would pluck out the heart of my mystery.
You would sound me from my lowest note to the top of
my compass. And there is much music, excellent voice,
in this little organ. Yet cannot you make it speak. 'Sblood,
do you think I am easier to be played on than a pipe?
Call me what instrument you will, though you can fret
me, you cannot play upon me.                    (371-379)

With the entry of Polonius to reinforce his mother's command,
Hamlet takes his "antic disposition" to absurdity. The old man
humours the madman:

HAM:   Do you see yonder cloud that's almost in shape
       of a camel?
POL:   By th'mass, and 'tis like a camel indeed.
HAM:   Methinks it is like a weasel.
POL:   It is backed like a weasel.
HAM:   Or like a whale.
POL:   Very like a whale.
HAM:   Then I will come to my mother by and by. (383-390)

Then, with "Leave me, friends," Hamlet rids himself of them
all. Polonius, Rosencrantz and Guildenstern are frightened by
Hamlet's behaviour at the play and anxious to get him to his
mother as quickly as possible. It is this feeling of being hustled
that makes Hamlet delight in ridiculing them and in forcing
them to leave him to come in his own time. He suddenly transforms the playhouse to a sinister and threatening midnight:

'Tis now the very witching time of night,
When churchyards yawn, and hell itself breathes out
Contagion to this world. Now could I drink hot blood
And do such bitter business as the day
Would quake to look on.                    (395-399)

But he has a duty to do:

Soft, now to my mother ...
Let me be cruel, not unnatural.
I will speak daggers to her, but use none.    (399-403)

*Acting Areas and Staging:*
In the next group of scenes, performance reveals Shakespeare's
use of space at the Globe. From the area where *The Mousetrap*
play was performed (the hall), Hamlet passes through the

King's chapel or private chamber on his way to his mother's closet. On his return, his journey is reversed: Hamlet is pursued from the closet through the lobby (where he disposes of the body, lugging the guts into "the neighbour room" (III.iv.213)) and down the stairs where he is caught and arraigned before the King. Asked about the body, he says, "you shall nose him as you go up the stairs into the lobby" (IV.iii.35ff.) — i.e., the body will be smelled going up the stairs but found in the lobby. There are three acting areas for both the forward and backward journeys.

In modern practice, an open stage satisfies Shakespeare's conditions easily: Hamlet moves from one unlocalized area to another. On a stage with a proscenium arch, the journey will probably be indicated by exits and entrances.

> *Claudius tells Rosencrantz and Guildenstern they will take Hamlet to England soon. Claudius prays. Hamlet enters but will not kill him: he must die in a state of sin (III.iii).*

Claudius, characteristically resolute, takes action to rid himself and Denmark of his "dangerous" nephew. He will send Hamlet to England with the faithful Rosencrantz and Guildenstern as escorts. The possible assassination of Elizabeth I occupied her subjects, just as Hamlet threatens the King's life and thus the realm:

> The cess of majesty
> Dies not alone, but like a gulf doth draw
> What's near it with it ...                      (15-17)

As they hurry off, Polonius warns the King that Hamlet is going to his mother's closet; he will eavesdrop on their conversation.

For the first time we see Claudius alone. A kindly man and a good king who gained his throne and queen by murder, he sheds his usual hypocrisy in a revealing and moving scene. Surprisingly he has a powerful conscience: he knows he is a criminal ("O, my offence is rank ..."), guilty of the "primal eldest curse" of Cain — "A brother's murder" — but "Pray can I not" (36-38).

> What if this cursèd hand
> Were thicker than itself with brother's blood,
> Is there not rain enough in the sweet heavens
> To wash it white as snow? Whereto serves mercy
> But to confront the visage of offence?            (43-47)

How can he pray for forgiveness and still cling to the rewards of crime:

> My crown, mine own ambition, and my Queen.
> May one be pardoned and retain th'offence?      (55-56)

He pathetically wants forgiveness, but he is not prepared to alter his way of life. Few of us are. Claudius' "offence" is the sin and its "effects":

> In the corrupted currents of this world
> Offence's gilded hand may shove by justice;
> And oft 'tis seen the wicked prize itself
> Buys out the law. But 'tis not so above.      (57-60)

The image of heavenly justice is central to *Hamlet*. Judgment Day is here and now. The pace quickens to the climax of rhetorical apostrophe:

> What then? What rests?
> Try what repentance can. What can it not?
> Yet what can it when one cannot repent?
> O, wretched state! O, bosom black as death!      (64-67)

He does not attempt to pray until the end of his soliloquy when, wavering between hope and despair, he is most moving:

> Help, angels! Make assay.
> Bow, stubborn knees, and, heart with strings of steel,
> Be soft as sinews of the new-born babe.
> All may be well.      (69-72)

The question for us all is, shall we try to get rid of our committed sin, or shall we admit that it was a part of ourselves? We all find that difficult.

Hamlet appears, intent upon converting his mother before killing his uncle. Confronted by the kneeling King, he has his first opportunity for revenge:

> Now might I do it pat, now 'a is a-praying.
> And now I'll do't. And so 'a goes to heaven.
> And so am I revenged. That would be scanned.   (73-75)

His sword is poised. But he hesitates: "that would be scanned."

> To take him in the purging of his soul,
> When he is fit and seasoned for his passage      (85-86)

is no revenge when Claudius did not do the same for his father. He spares the King lest, killed at prayer, his enemy should escape everlasting damnation. Hamlet shows no Christian charity. Dr. Johnson has a famous observation on this passage: "This speech, in which Hamlet, represented as a virtuous character, is not content with taking blood for blood, but contrives damnation for the man that he would punish, is too horrible to be read or uttered."* But being who he is, Hamlet cannot kill him now. So he leaves.

Claudius is unaware of Hamlet, but he faces the truth about himself:

My words fly up, my thoughts remain below.

Words without thoughts never to heaven go.      (97-98)

The irony is that Claudius strives to pray but cannot, and Hamlet spares him because he thinks he is praying. Presumably, as Granville-Barker said, if Hamlet knew what was in the King's mind, he would kill him on the spot.**

The directors must remember that the King's incriminating soliloquy is heard only by the audience. Not until Hamlet unseals the royal commission entrusted to Rosencrantz and Guildenstern, on the voyage to England, does he or anybody else in the play have positive proof of his uncle's villainy. For the greater part of the tragedy Hamlet possesses only the word of a possibly unreliable Ghost, plus his own instinctive dislike of Gertrude's second husband, as a basis for revenge. It is not much justification for suddenly stabbing a man in the back as he kneels at his devotions.

Many critics believe that this scene is really the climax of the entire play, but it is not for Gielgud. To him as an actor, the following scene and the killing of Polonius are the climax of Hamlet's long inaction; it is this physical act that seems to break the spell of doubt in Hamlet's mind and unloose his stream of repressed anguish and revenge.

> *The Closet Scene. Polonius hides behind the arras. Hamlet speaks roughly to Gertrude, she cries for help, Polonius shouts out, and Hamlet kills him. Hamlet scourges his mother. The Ghost appears, unseen by the Queen. Hamlet takes Polonius' body away (III.iv).*

Polonius is in haste — the Prince is coming — but he has time to give the Queen some quick advice: "Look you lay home to

---

* Johnson (1908).
** Granville-Barker (1963).

him." Before he hides, Polonius cannot resist the further direction: "Pray you be round with him." As Hamlet calls, "Mother,
mother, mother," the old man darts behind the arras (1-8).

What is Gertrude's age? In life, she might be fifty and look
quite matronly. But not on Shakespeare's stage. Played by a
boy, sensual enough to make Claudius commit murder for her,
she is "young" — yet with a son of Hamlet's age. The play is
rooted in Hamlet's reproach that at her age

> The heyday in the blood is tame; it's humble,
> And waits upon the judgement ...                    (70-71)

when she is, in fact, young enough that her blood is not tame.

Mother and son are alone together for the first time in the
play. The interview begins in heat, Gertrude trying hard to be
round with him, and Hamlet bitterly parodying each phrase of
her rebuke:

> HAM:  Now, mother, what's the matter?
> GER:   Hamlet, thou hast thy father much offended.
> HAM:  Mother, you have my father much offended.
> GER:   Come, come, you answer with an idle tongue.
> HAM:  Go, go, you question with a wicked tongue.
> GER:   Why, how now, Hamlet!
> HAM:                                  What's the matter now?
> GER:   Have you forgot me?
> HAM:                                  No, by the Rood, not so!
>     You are the Queen, your husband's brother's wife,
>     And, would it were not so, you are my mother.
> GER:   Nay, then I'll set those to you that can speak. (9-18)

She rises but is flung back in her chair again and so menaced
by his:

> You shall not budge.
> You go not till I set you up a glass
> Where you may see the inmost part of you       (19-21)

that she cries aloud for help.

Polonius echoes her cry. Instantly Hamlet draws his sword
and plunges it through the arras with a mad cry: "How now? A
rat? Dead for a ducat, dead!" (25). It is, he thinks, the perfect
revenge, although hidden, like so much else in the play, behind
an arras. He pierces it, thinking he has at last got to the heart
of the evil. Yet it is the wrong man, and now he himself is a

murderer. However, his intention is plain:

HAM:               Is it the King?

GER:  O, what a rash and bloody deed is this!

HAM:  A bloody deed — almost as bad, good mother,
          As kill a king and marry with his brother. (27-30)

It may have been Bernhardt as Hamlet who first made the killing of Polonius the crux of the play. She achieved a tremendous theatrical effect in her cry at "Is it the King?" (27) when his sword, held above her head, made Hamlet's figure into a great interrogation mark. The next lines must be strongly pointed by the actors so that the audience may not miss their significance. In her bewildered horror she can only echo vaguely, "As kill a king!" which suggests she is not implicated in her late husband's murder. She has a dawning knowledge of what he implies Claudius has done. Mrs. Patrick Campbell said, "The point about Gertrude in the closet scene is not that she didn't know Claudius was a murderer, but that she doted on him so much that she wouldn't have minded if he had been." In a few seconds Hamlet has to understand and convey clearly to the audience three things: that he realizes his mother did not know Claudius was a murderer; that she set someone to spy on him behind the arras; and that it is evident from her cry that it is not, as he imagined, Claudius whom he has killed. Hamlet draws aside the curtain and sees what he has done:

Thou wretched, rash, intruding fool, farewell!

I took thee for thy better. Take thy fortune.

Thou findest to be too busy is some danger.     (32-34)

If Hamlet's violence terrified Gertrude, his killing of Polonius breaks her nerve. Believing him a raving lunatic, she is cowed as he says:

               Peace, sit you down,

And let me wring your heart.                 (35-36)

"What have I done ...?" she cries, and his reply is withering:

               Such an act

That blurs the grace and blush of modesty;

Calls virtue hypocrite; takes off the rose

From the fair forehead of an innocent love

And sets a blister there ...                (41-45)

The word "blister" also means the branding of a harlot. Heaven's face, he tells her, is "thought-sick at the act" (52).

"What act ...?" she cries again. The answer is adultery. As
Hamlet puts it,

> Look here upon this picture, and on this,
> The counterfeit presentment of two brothers.
> See what a grace was seated on this brow:
> Hyperion's curls, the front of Jove himself,
> An eye like Mars, to threaten and command,
> A station like the herald Mercury
> New lighted on a heaven-kissing hill —
> A combination and a form indeed
> Where every god did seem to set his seal
> To give the world assurance of a man.          (54-63)

Here stage tradition has two miniatures pendant round the
necks of son and wife. She cries:

> O Hamlet, speak no more.
> Thou turnest mine eyes into my very soul          (89-90)

and then he tramples her down:

> Nay, but to live
> In the rank sweat of an enseamèd bed,
> Stewed in corruption, honeying and making love
> Over the nasty sty —          (92-95)

Hamlet hideously presents her incestuous union with "A king
of shreds and patches" (103) as she, in tears, pleads guilty.

Then, in an astonishing climax, the Ghost reappears. *Enter
the ghost in his night gowne,* says Q1. With its appearance,
Hamlet's anger goes. It has come to whet his "almost blunted
purpose," unable to rest, we suppose, until it is avenged. It is
natural that the Ghost should be in this room; father, mother
and son are together in a domestic scene suggesting a family
life that no longer exists.

> GER:   To whom do you speak this?
> HAM:         Do you see nothing there?
> GER:   Nothing at all. Yet all that is I see.
> HAM:   Nor did you nothing hear?
> GER:         No, nothing but ourselves.     (132-134)

For Gertrude can see nothing. What else can she not see? With
the Ghost's exit, she thinks that her son is mad again, which
Hamlet indignantly denies:

> Lay not that flattering unction to your soul,
> That not your trespass but my madness speaks. (146-147)

The Ghost has commanded him to "step between her and her fighting soul!" (114), so he tries to rescue her from her sin. He has, she tells him, cleft her heart in twain. He responds

> O, throw away the worser part of it,
> And live the purer with the other half          (158-159)

as a prelude to

> Good night. But go not to my uncle's bed.
> Assume a virtue, if you have it not.          (160-161)

Suddenly he sees her in a terrible clarity: she cannot renew her virtue, and he has no faith in her repentance. Having stripped one mask from her he bids her wear another. He must be Heaven's "scourge and minister," yet he loves her still, with a love which makes him be "cruel, only to be kind ..." He turns bitter. Answering her miserable, "What shall I do?" he is sarcastic:

> Not this, by no means, that I bid you do:
> Let the bloat King tempt you again to bed,
> Pinch wanton on your cheek, call you his mouse,
> And let him, for a pair of reechy kisses,
> Or paddling in your neck with his damned fingers,
> Make you to ravel all this matter out,
> That I essentially am not in madness,
> But mad in craft.          (182-189)

She promises she will not betray him to Claudius. He thinks she will, but he is wrong. She is repentant, and she does not betray him. Hamlet's vivid picturing of his mother's sex life with Claudius is pathological; it is adolescent for a man of thirty. His illness is melancholia (Elizabethan), or clinical depression (modern psychiatry), with wild swings of mood due (in modern terms) to a chemical imbalance of the neuro-transmitters in the brain. He has deep incongruities. His emotions circle endlessly, without direction. He takes refuge in postures. The problem facing the actor is which facet of Hamlet is uppermost at any one time.

The repetition of "Good night ... once more goodnight ... so again, good night ..." hints to us of earlier days when the son would say good-night to his mother before going off to sleep; and this mood carries the unexpected sequel to "And when you are desirous to be blest" in the sudden charm of "I'll blessing beg of you" (172-173).

Seeing Polonius behind the arras brings back the reality of the old man's death. His rage gone, Hamlet speaks of him with dignity and penitence, rather than personal compassion:

> For this same lord,
> I do repent. But heaven hath pleased it so,
> To punish me with this, and this with me,
> That I must be their scourge and minister.
> I will bestow him and will answer well
> The death I gave him.                                    (173-178)

In Elizabethan terms, Hamlet is a doomed man: blood demands blood, and a mistake does not excuse him.

He takes up Polonius's body, and with a last repetition of "Mother, good night," he goes, lugging the guts into the neighbouring room (213-218).

> *Gertrude tells the King about the events. Rosencrantz and*
> *Guildenstern find Hamlet (IV.i).*

This scene is continuous with the last. After Hamlet goes, the Queen is distraught: shall she keep her promise to Hamlet, or shall she tell her husband the truth? She makes up her mind as Claudius enters:

CLAU: What, Gertrude? How does Hamlet?
GER:   Mad as the sea and wind ...                      (6-7)

To Claudius, Polonius's death indicates his own danger: "It had been so with us, had we been there" (13). His nerve is shaken: "His liberty is full of threats to all" (14). To hurry him from Denmark is now urgent. Rosencrantz and Guildenstern find Hamlet and — speaking fair, as they have been told to do — summon him to the King. He pretends to comply but suddenly turns and runs, an obvious lunatic; and they all have to chase after him. Then follows a macabre torchlight hue and cry through the darkened castle after a lunatic killer.

> *Hamlet refuses to tell Rosencrantz and Guildenstern where*
> *Polonius' body is (IV.ii).*

There is no break in the action as the thrilling game of hide-and-seek continues until they corner Hamlet. Suddenly, with a "Hide fox, and all after," he bolts away down the dark corridors, madder than ever. The hue and cry goes on.

> *Hamlet eventually tells Claudius where Polonius' body is.*
> *Hamlet is to go to England with Rosencrantz and*
> *Guildenstern. Alone, Claudius reveals that Hamlet will be*
> *put to death there (IV.iii).*

This is also continuous with the previous scene. This sequence, by contrast with the earlier long scenes, gives the impression of great speed. The King, surrounded and supported by courtiers and guards, says:

> How dangerous is it that this man goes loose!
> Yet must not we put the strong law on him.
> He's loved of the distracted multitude ...
>     To bear all smooth and even,
> This sudden sending him away must seem
> Deliberate pause. (2-9)

For the first time we hear of the populace and their love, soon to be fastened on Laertes. Hamlet now has been secured and brought before his uncle and judge. The tone in the King's first question suggests a formal arraignment: "Now, Hamlet, where's Polonius?" (16). His gruesome but witty responses are insults: "At supper ... Not where he eats, but where 'a is eaten" (17-19). Suddenly, Hamlet capitulates and reveals the whereabouts of the body: "you shall nose him as you go up the stairs into the lobby" (35). The King pronounces sentence: as his concern is for his nephew's safety (he says), he sends him to England.

In his soliloquy, Claudius' purpose is revealed to us for the first time. England owes "homage" to Denmark and cannot disregard the instructions in his sealed letter, carried by Rosencrantz and Guildenstern, for "The present death of Hamlet" (67).

### Third Movement

From here, the play runs continuously to the end. The rhythm changes to the King's counter-attack which largely initiates the action. Hamlet is relatively passive until the end. He leaves Denmark in IV.iv; we do not see him again until V.i.

> *Fortinbras and his army cross Denmark. Hamlet, on his*
> *way to the harbour, meets one of its Captains and then solil-*
> *oquizes, "How all occasions do inform against me" (IV.iv).*

The curtains close on the King, and the bare stage represents open country near Elsinore: Fortinbras with his army marches across, drums beating. We need reminding of Fortinbras now in case his return from Poland, at the end of the play, is implausible. He sends the Captain with a message for the Danish King. Hamlet, Rosencrantz and Guildenstern see the army marching away. Hamlet, impressed, forestalls the departure of the Captain whose frank account of Fortinbras' enterprise astonishes the Prince.

All but Hamlet leave. His soliloquy is a very sane self-analysis. Fortinbras' decisive action reminds him that he has delayed his revenge:

> What is a man,
> If his chief good and market of his time
> Be but to sleep and feed? A beast, no more.
> Sure He that made us with such large discourse,
> Looking before and after, gave us not
> That capability and godlike reason
> To fust in us unused.                    (33-39)

Humanity cannot afford not to use reason.

> Now, whether it be
> Bestial oblivion, or some craven scruple
> Of thinking too precisely on th'event —
> A thought which, quartered, hath but one part wisdom
> And ever three parts coward —           (39-43)

The merciless truth suddenly rings out in the baffled

> I do not know
> Why yet I live to say 'This thing's to do,'
> Sith I have cause, and will, and strength, and means
> To do't ...                             (43-46)

and yet, until now he has done nothing:

> Examples gross as earth exhort me.
> Witness this army of such mass and charge,
> Led by a delicate and tender prince ...
> Rightly to be great
> Is not to stir without great argument,
> But greatly to find quarrel in a straw
> When honour's at the stake.             (46-56)

Is "honour" a mere word, as Falstaff says in *1 Henry IV*, or is it

a plot
Whereon the numbers cannot try the cause,
Which is not tomb enough and continent
To hide the slain?                                      (62-65)

He sees his problem as a "condition" for which he is not responsible, any more than the sick man is to blame for the infection which strikes and devours him. He ends decisively:

O, from this time forth,
My thoughts be bloody, or be nothing worth!     (65-66)

He goes resolutely to the sea-shore and the boat to England.

Curiously, this small scene has had superb décor in the twentieth century. There was a splendid Viking ship in Leslie Howard's production, and Tyrone Guthrie arranged the scene magnificently in his Old Vic production with Fortinbras above on an eminence, in shadow, while Hamlet spoke on the stage below.

*Ophelia's mad scene. Laertes arrives at the head of a mob, set on revenge for Polonius. The sight of Ophelia adds to his grief. Claudius defuses the rebellion (IV.v).*

This scene is one of Shakespeare's most skilled pieces of writing for the theatre. Its linear structure is remarkable: (1) Ophelia's delayed entry; (2) her first mad scene; (3) the King's speech to Gertrude; (4) the messenger's news of the revolution; (5) Laertes' entry and Claudius' brilliant defusing of the situation; (6) Ophelia's second mad scene; (7) Claudius' comforting of Laertes. The undulating rhythm of tension and relaxation, both between and within the segments, is perfectly designed with superb poetry and dialogue.

"I will not speak with her ... What would she have?" (1-4) asks the agitated Queen. Hearing of Ophelia's condition, we realize that the death of her father, killed by her lover, may have unhinged her. "Let her come in," says Gertrude:

To my sick soul, as sin's true nature is,
Each toy seems prologue to some great amiss.     (17-18)

Ophelia enters, gazing for a moment at the Queen, whom she does not recognize in her madness. She says, "Where is the beauteous majesty of Denmark?" (21), but ironically the "beauteous majesty" is now a fearful woman. Ophelia sings. Q1 says she plays a lute which, as Granville-Barker shows, enables her to sit.* She sings bits of traditional ballads, altering them with the thoughts now in her mind. Her songs refer to Polonius' death and the romance denied her: the baker's daughter who became an owl tells of girls who are forbidden to grow up; and the song about St. Valentine's Day hints at her romantic rejection. Clearly she cannot cope with her recent losses. Claudius enters but can do nothing for her.

Then Ophelia startles them with her sudden, "My brother shall know of it" (70). She then mimes her entry into her coach: "Come, my coach! Good night, ladies, good night. Sweet ladies, good night, good night" (71-73). Yet as she leaves there is only one lady present.

Horatio goes to keep a close watch on her. The King turns to the Queen, lamenting the multitude of their recent troubles:

> O, this is the poison of deep grief. It springs
> All from her father's death — and now behold!
> O Gertrude, Gertrude, *[she says nothing]*
> When sorrows come, they come not single spies,
> But in battalions: first, her father slain;
> Next, your son gone, and he most violent author
> Of his own just remove ...                    (76-82)

Ominously, Gertrude is silent throughout. His speech is technically remarkable in setting the scene in appropriate time and context. Polonius' death and Hamlet's departure are quite recent, for

> we have done but greenly
> In hugger-mugger to inter him ...                    (84-85)

We are surprised that the smooth Claudius has foolishly had Polonius buried hastily and secretly, but we are startled by the news that Laertes

> is in secret come from France,
> Feeds on his wonder, keeps himself in clouds,
> And wants not buzzers to infect his ear
> With pestilent speeches of his father's death ...   (89-92)

There is a noise within. A messenger bursts into the royal presence. His speech is typical of a technique in poetic drama which the Elizabethans inherited from the Greeks. Designed to save the company the problems of mounting a mob scene, it

---

* Granville-Barker (1963).

functions to create the emergency of popular revolt, and to hint at a ritualized atmosphere. Laertes raises a rebellion to avenge Polonius, believing the King to blame. The messenger says the mob has broken through the guards and

> They cry 'Choose we! Laertes shall be King!'
> Caps, hands, and tongues applaud it to the clouds:
> 'Laertes shall be king! Laertes king!'                    (108-110)

which is echoed by those back-stage. We hear a noise which is interpreted by the King: "The doors are broke" (113). This technique makes the entry of Laertes very exciting. The crowd want to follow him into the King's presence, but he persuades them through the door to "stand ... all without" (114). Two or three might show their faces, but they retire.

However, the "giant-like" rebellion is stillborn. Once it meets the master politician, Claudius, it becomes a hubbub and a few fierce speeches from a passionate young man. Laertes challenges Claudius: "Give me my father" (118). Then the Queen intervenes, and he violently rounds on her. The King gains our admiration by his cool reception of the young man through his imperious question:

> What is the cause, Laertes,
> That thy rebellion looks so giant-like?
> Let him go, Gertrude. Do not fear our person.
> There's such divinity doth hedge a king
> That treason can but peep to what it would,
> Acts little of his will. Tell me, Laertes,
> Why thou art thus incensed. Let him go, Gertrude.
> Speak, man.                                              (122-129)

As the King's moral position is reasonably secure, he can afford to face Laertes: he was not directly responsible for the death of Polonius.

> KING: Speak, man.
> LAER: Where is my father?
> KING:         Dead.                                      (129-130)

The King courageously states it. "But not by him," the terrified Gertrude intervenes. Claudius confidently says, "Let him demand his fill" (131). The rhythm of this passage is subtle: it is tied together by the repeated "Let him go Gertrude ... let him go Gertrude ... Let him demand his fill." Laertes rants:

> To hell allegiance! Vows to the blackest devil!

> Conscience and grace to the profoundest pit!
> I dare damnation ...
>                     only I'll be revenged
> Most throughly for my father.                    (133-138)

Claudius responds only with a "Who shall stay you?" He so reduces the rebel that he will at least listen to reason. Laertes's tragic position is parallel to Hamlet's: both have a murdered father to revenge, but the direct action of Laertes contrasts with the procrastination of Hamlet. Both see Claudius as their enemy; Hamlet rightly, Laertes wrongly. Both are loved by the multitude. Claudius' playwriting is brilliant: his sympathy and his offer to explain how he himself is guiltless of the murder. We hear another noise outside the door as a voice calls, "Let her come in" (154).

Ophelia returns. She stands silent. She does not know her brother. As they meet again, she chants:

> They bore him bare-faced on the bier,
>         Hey non nony, nony, hey nony,
> And in his grave rained many a tear ...              (166-168)

Laertes is overwhelmed. She is not in the same mood as before. She thinks she is taking part in her father's funeral: she moves singing across the stage in imagined procession ("They bore him bare-faced on the bier"), stands as if by his grave-side ("And on his grave rained many a tear"), and distributes her flowers among the mourners. The symbolism of Ophelia's flowers has great pathos. "Rue" is for Gertrude: it is the "herb of grace," an antidote to carnal lust, and she must wear her rue "with a difference." Then, "There's a daisy. I would give you some violets, but they withered all when my father died" (184-185) — she is associated with violets throughout the play. Her words, "Pray you, love, remember" (177) are almost unbearable, and our last impression of Ophelia is one of pathetic innocence. "God bye you" (200), she says as she departs, head bowed, hands folded, and very quietly.

The King takes advantage of Laertes' grief and leads him away, the rebellion forgotten, as the rest leave.

> *Horatio's letter from Hamlet tells how he has escaped from the ship with the aid of pirates and is in Denmark (IV.vi).*

In this brief bridging scene, sailors bring Horatio a letter from Hamlet; they have letters for the King too. The actor of Horatio has already shown his skill in evocation by speech. He becomes now a good raconteur, making us listen as he reads the letter: the quick-witted Hamlet has managed to elude Rosencrantz and Guildenstern by boarding a pirate ship that was attacking them; the pirates have brought Hamlet back to Denmark and carry these letters. Additionally, "I have words to speak in thine ear will make thee dumb" (23-24). As the scene is short, directors often feel it can be cut. As Gielgud showed, however, it maintains a sense of continuity.

> *The King proves his innocence in Polonius' death to*
> *Laertes. News comes that Hamlet has returned. Laertes*
> *welcomes the chance of vengeance. The King devises a*
> *means for it. The Queen reports that Ophelia has drowned*
> *herself (IV.vii).*

The Victorians often set this scene in a garden or exterior of some sort, presumably to help the idea of Ophelia's flowers and the Queen's description of her drowning. This was part of a decorative tradition and has little place in the modern theatre.

The King has persuaded Laertes that his father's killer is his own dangerous enemy too. But why was Hamlet not put on public trial?

>        The Queen his mother
> Lives almost by his looks, and for myself —
> My virtue or my plague, be it either which —
> She is so conjunctive to my life and soul
> That, as the star moves not but in his sphere,
> I could not but by her.                    (11-16)

The King truly loves his wife. Then news arrives: Hamlet intends to be at court tomorrow. Laertes is delighted. But the King must work fast.

As his manipulation of Laertes is masterly, Claudius becomes a playwright of the scene. First, he plays to Laertes' vanity by saying that Hamlet has praised his swordmanship:

> He made confession of you,
> And gave you such a masterly report
> For art and exercise in your defence,
> And for your rapier most especial,

> That he cried out 'twould be a sight indeed
> If one could match you ...                          (94-99)

Talk of Hamlet's envy of such skill is a clever touch. Then:

> Laertes, was your father dear to you?
> Or are you like the painting of a sorrow,
> A face without a heart?                          (106-108)

In answer to the indignant counter-question, "Why ask you this?" he reveals his feelings for Gertrude:

> Not that I think you did not love your father,
> But that I know love is begun by time,
> And that I see, in passages of proof,
> Time qualifies the spark and fire of it.
> There lives within the very flame of love
> A kind of wick or snuff that will abate it ...   (109-114)

Those "passages of proof" can only be Gertrude's silent obedience to Hamlet's request to deny herself Claudius' bed. The King then pounces:

> KING:          But to the quick o'th'ulcer —
> Hamlet comes back. What would you undertake
> To show yourself in deed your father's son
> More than in words?
> LAE:          To cut his throat i'th'church!    122-125)

The victim is hooked, and Claudius silkily approves Laertes' determination:

> No place, indeed, should murder sanctuarize.
> Revenge should have no bounds.                (126-127)

So successful is Claudius's method that Laertes agrees to a duel with Hamlet but he will use "a sword unbated" (with no button on the point) which he will dip in poison. The crafty King immediately ponders a means of reinsuring against failure:

> I'll have preferred him
> A chalice for the nonce ...                          (158-159)

Jointly, Claudius and Laertes have become dramatists: they define the forthcoming duel as a playlet through the care with which they plot it out.

Technically, the most difficult part of the scene is the entrance of the Queen to tell of Ophelia's death. Laertes' "Drowned! O, where?" (165) has defeated many actors, and if the Queen is a good character actress, she finds it difficult to fit the willow speech (as it is called by actors), which is a sort of cadenza, into the rest of her performance, to which it seems to have no particular relation. But its simple beauty gives a pathetic picture. We hear how

> There on the pendent boughs her crownet weeds
> Clambering to hang, an envious sliver broke,
> When down her weedy trophies and herself
> Fell in the weeping brook. Her clothes spread wide,
> And mermaid-like awhile they bore her up;
> Which time she chanted snatches of old tunes,
> As one incapable of her own distress,
> Or like a creature native and indued
> Unto that element. But long it could not be
> Till that her garments, heavy with their drink,
> Pulled the poor wretch from her melodious lay
> To muddy death. (172-183)

This vivid narrative, with its haunting imagery, creates an atmosphere of flowers and music. It must be conveyed clearly to the imagination of the audience: the performer must not gain special attention for the Queen's personal distress. She uses gesture and mime to help make her tale more graphic rather than to indicate her own feelings.

The effect upon Laertes is interesting too. He has just, for vengeance, committed himself to an act of callous treachery. After the first shock he listens quietly and has no more to say when the story ends than, "Alas, then she is drowned?" (183), and his tears flow.

> *Hamlet, no longer mad, returns with Horatio to Elsinore.*
> *He stops to talk to a Gravedigger. The court arrives for*
> *Ophelia's burial, and Hamlet quarrels with Laertes (V.i).*

This set a serious technical problem for the decorative scene designer in older productions. There is no time for an interval before or after it — yet he had to have a practical set, a grave, a glint of sky, besides some other suggestion of an exterior. Beerbohm Tree indulged in a spring landscape with blossoms, sheep scattered on the hills, and flowers which he picked for Ophelia's grave. In the Reinhardt-Moissi production the scene was played at night by torchlight, and Ophelia was carried on in white robes on an open bier. Unfortunately there was no trap, and having set the bier above the grave, the men fought over her, were parted, the Court retired, and poor Ophelia was left out all night. These problems were not faced at the Globe or on modern thrust stages.

The graveyard of the Castle is symbolic of the play as a whole. In the gruesome horror of burial, Shakespeare signifies the major issues of the play: life and death, good and evil, reality and illusion, and human nature. Evil is symbolized in the universal graveyard where, as the Gravedigger says with grim humour, he holds up Adam's profession. It is sited in the earth to which everyone returns; all come to a place where we might stumble on "Cain's jawbone, that did the first murder!" (77). The graveyard also symbolizes reality and illusion because death puts the question, "What is real?" in its absolute form: "Now get you to my lady's table and tell her, let her paint an inch thick, to this favour she must come" (189-191). Most pervasive of all, the graveyard symbolizes the mystery of the human condition. Human joys and ambitions are grotesque from the perspective of the grave: Yorick who once carried the young Hamlet on his back is now a stinking skull, and the noble dust of Alexander the Great somewhere plugs a bung-hole. As Hamlet says, "That skull had a tongue in it, and could sing once" (75-76).

*Enter two Clowns* — that is, clowns of the company, probably Robert Armin and another. The script does not give them roles, but they exist in every English parish even today: two Gravediggers or the sexton and his assistant. They pierce through the niceties of the play to the heart of the present context with

> 1 CLOWN:   Will you ha' the truth on't? If this had not been a gentlewoman, she should have been buried out o'Christian burial.
>
> 2 CLOWN:     Why, there thou sayst. And the more pity that great folk should have countenance in this world to drown or hang themselves more than their even-Christian.                    (23-29)

For the first time, we meet the simplicity and earthiness of ordinary people. They work with a pick-axe and a spade in the trap door on the stage. They speak wisdom in riddles, like: Who builds stronger than a mason, a shipwright, or a carpenter? and the answer is a grave maker: "The houses he makes last till Doomsday." After that strenuous effort, the Second Clown is sent off to fetch "a stoup of liquor" (58-60).

Shakespeare has learned to blend this kind of low comedy tightly into the play to provide comic relief between two tense scenes; it amuses us with their logical explanation of the outcome of the suicide; it half-revolts us with its ghoulish humour; and it parallels the deep meanings of the play. It is so integral to the play that *Hamlet* is inconceivable without this scene.

The First Gravedigger has no proper name. He is identified in the texts simply as "Clown." He has an occupational obsession: the Gravedigger is interested only in death and burial. His riddles, his jokes, his small talk, and even his songs all end in a hole in the ground.

Unexpectedly, Hamlet appears. He is in his "sea-gown" alongside Horatio. We assume the meeting suggested in his letter has taken place. Hamlet now looks different, and he is in another frame of mind: he confronts, recognizes, and accepts the human condition.

Hamlet and Horatio eavesdrop on the Gravedigger who, busy with his spade, sings a popular ballad. When he throws up first one skull and then another, Hamlet imagines who they were, and the smell of death is brought onto the stage. When Hamlet asks the Gravedigger, "Whose grave's this, sirrah?" we know the answer. So the Gravedigger's whimsy, perversity, and quibbles over words, make us laugh:

HAM: Whose grave's this, sirrah?
CLO: Mine, sir ...
HAM: What man dost thou dig it for?
CLO: For no man, sir.
HAM: What woman then?
CLO: For none neither.
HAM: Who is to be buried in't?
CLO: One that was a woman, sir. But, rest her soul,
        she's dead.        (115-134)

They enjoy this, and the quip at the expense of their English audience when they joke about "young Hamlet" that is "mad, and sent into England," but "'Twill not be seen in him there. There the men are as mad as he" (145-153). We learn old King Hamlet defeated the elder Fortinbras on "that very day that

young Hamlet was born" (142-145), some "thirty years" ago
(160). He will, presumably, complete the circle of interring the
Prince at the end of the play. Meanwhile he proceeds with dev-
astating effectiveness to treat Hamlet linguistically as Hamlet
himself has treated others. The graveyard meditations, though
often beautiful, are remorselessly realistic. The Gravedigger
brings Hamlet face to face with the ultimate reality. Before it,
language fails, and revenge becomes a bad joke. Hamlet asks
about a specific skull; the Gravedigger says it belonged to
Yorick, the king's jester in old King Hamlet's time. Hamlet
remarks:

> Alas, poor Yorick! I knew him, Horatio. A fellow of infi-
> nite jest, of most excellent fancy. He hath bore me on
> his back a thousand times. And now how abhorred in
> my imagination it is! My gorge rises at it.     (181-185)

As a child, the Prince kissed Yorick's lips and laughed with a
child's delight at his pranks, his songs, his jokes. But he has no
jokes now, even though his skull is grinning. Hamlet is suddenly revolted by the contrast between life and death.

The funeral cortège slowly appears. The Gravedigger moves
away as Hamlet and Horatio slip into shadow. The coroner
ruled that Ophelia's death was suicide, but the King has
ensured she will be buried in sanctified ground. Now there are
"maimed rites" at which the Priest expresses his disapproval.
Laertes is distressed: his insistent repetition of, "What ceremony else?" (221) shows him to be near hysteria. As the bearers
lower the coffin, he says:

> Lay her i'th'earth,
> And from her fair and unpolluted flesh
> May violets spring! I tell thee, churlish priest,
> A ministering angel shall my sister be
> When thou liest howling.                    (234-238)

Only now does Hamlet realize whose grave this is. The
Queen strews it with flowers saying, "I hoped thou shouldst
have been my Hamlet's wife" (240). The furious Laertes leaps
down into the open grave, and clutches the dead body of his
sister in his arms. His melodramatic gesture makes Hamlet
angry. With a similar extravagance, he strides to the graveside
declaring his return to Denmark: he is "Hamlet the Dane"
(254). Laertes climbs out of the grave and attacks him. There is

an uproar. The Hamlet who is now master of himself says:

> Thou prayest not well.
> I prithee take thy fingers from my throat.
> For, though I am not splenitive and rash,
> Yet have I in me something dangerous,
> Which let thy wisdom fear. Hold off thy hand. (255-259)

He is not mad but justifiably indignant:

> I loved Ophelia. Forty thousand brothers
> Could not with all their quantity of love
> Make up my sum.                    (265-267)

Laertes, held by others, is silent. Hamlet calls:

> Hear you, sir.
> What is the reason that you use me thus?
> I loved you ever.                    (284-286)

As the scene disintegrates into violence, into something horrifying and wild, it is as if all the hidden corruption and ugliness masked by the unacknowledged play-acting of the preceding scenes suddenly erupts into view.

Hamlet dismisses the histrionic scene and walks away. Claudius has a quiet word with Laertes, reminding him (and us) of "last night's speech" and preparing us for the finale.

> *Hamlet tells Horatio of his sea adventure. Osrick brings Laertes' challenge to Hamlet. The duel follows. The Queen mistakenly drinks the wine poisoned by Claudius. Laertes wounds Hamlet with a poisoned foil which is exchanged, so Hamlet wounds Laertes. Gertrude dies. Laertes denounces the King who is killed by Hamlet. Claudius and Laertes die. Hamlet recommends Fortinbras as king and dies (V.ii).*

From a graveyard, the bare stage returns to being unlocalized. Not until "Sir, I will walk here in the hall" (170) do we have a clear sense of place. Directors vary in the way they interpret this scene:

- Hamlet seemingly purges Denmark of evil: his death is a necessary sacrifice and a triumph in its accomplishments.
- When Hamlet acts with firmness, he accepts a role as others do — his tragedy is his naive acceptance of experience.
- Hamlet thwarts Claudius' play; yet Claudius and Laertes

equally thwart his; the two actions balance each other.

The scene opens with Hamlet's powerful story of his sea adventure. This is Shakespearean narrative at its best: vivid, urgent and witty, with rhythmic variety and vigorous diction. The Prince, at his most energetic and decisive, is the fatalistic Hamlet of V.i as he says:

> There's a divinity that shapes our ends,
> Rough-hew them how we will —                    (10-11)

He is no longer a private revenger; he seeks public vengeance and justice. When he escaped from the ship, he changed Claudius' instructions. He uses the theatre metaphor to describe what happened to the two spies:

> Being thus be-netted round with villainies,
> Or I could make a prologue to my brains
> They had begun the play. I sat me down,
> Devised a new commission, wrote it fair.         (29-32)

He re-framed Claudius' plot into his own playlet. The metaphor makes Hamlet into a Player King: he sends to England a mock royal order sealed with his father's signet so that Rosencrantz and Guildenstern will be executed in England in his place. Hamlet is quite cold-blooded about it:

> HOR:  So Guildenstern and Rosencrantz go to't.
> HAM:  Why, man, they did make love to this employment.
>         They are not near my conscience.          (56-58)

Hamlet's tone towards Claudius has changed:

> He that hath killed my King and whored my mother,
> Popped in between th'election and my hopes,
> Thrown out his angle for my proper life,
> And with such cozenage — is't not perfect conscience
> To quit him with this arm?                        (64-68)

If his revenge is "perfect conscience," then

>             is't not to be damned
> To let this canker of our nature come
> In further evil?                                   (68-70)

Although we know of Laertes' plot, Hamlet is sympathetic towards him because he too has lost a father.

> But I am very sorry, good Horatio,
> That to Laertes I forgot myself.
> For by the image of my cause I see
> The portraiture of his.                           (75-78)

This is the old Hamlet, a role that will get him into trouble.

Young Osrick — "the waterfly" — appears. A fop in appearance and in speech, he is a fantastic with affected court manners, a great character part. T. W. Baldwin suggests it was first played by Cowley who has just been Aguecheek and is about to play Slender;* compared with them, however, Osrick is less of a fool. He brings the King's proposal for a duel between Hamlet and Laertes, but behind his ridiculous gabble about the wager ["six French rapiers and poniards, with their assigns, as girdle, hangers, and so" (147)] lurks death. At Osrick's expense, Hamlet enjoys himself; but as he cannot hide behind "madness," his mockery is brutal. Young Osrick must try to persuade him, so he presses on: he praises the "excellence" of Laertes "for his weapon"; his retinue say he has no equal, "he's unfellowed" (140-141) — just the phrase to arouse Hamlet's interest. Hamlet takes the bait and abruptly replies:

> Sir, I will walk here in the hall. If it please his majesty, it is the breathing time of day with me ... I will win for him an I can. (170-173)

There have been two great Osricks to two great Hamlets: Martin Harvey to Irving and Alec Guinness to John Gielgud.

The King sends an unnamed lord to know if Hamlet is ready now. His reply shows he has serenely accepted that the time has come:

> I am constant to my purposes. They follow the King's pleasure. If his fitness speaks, mine is ready, now or whensoever, provided I be so able as now. (195-197)

Horatio tries to dissuade him:

> HOR: You will lose this wager, my lord.
>
> HAM: I do not think so. Since he went into France I have been in continual practice. I shall win at the odds. But thou wouldst not think how ill all's here about my heart. But it is no matter.
>
> HOR: Nay, good my lord —
>
> HAM: It is but foolery. But it is such a kind of gaingiving as would perhaps trouble a woman.
>
> HOR: If your mind dislike anything, obey it. I will forestall their repair hither and say you are not fit.

---

* Baldwin (1961).

> HAM: Not a whit. We defy augury. There is a special providence in the fall of a sparrow. If it be now, 'tis not to come. If it be not to come, it will be now. If it be not now, yet it will come. The readiness is all. Since no man knows of aught he leaves, what is't to leave betimes? Let be.                    (203-218)

Horatio's playwriting is unsuccessful. Hamlet is ready to meet his death in the role of the avenger, imposed on him by the Ghost. But even the new resolute Hamlet does not *initiate* the action. Instead of acting, he waits patiently.

The state entry interrupts Hamlet and Horatio — trumpets and drums, with courtiers bringing in a prepared table with flagons of wine, cushions, foils, daggers and gauntlets. Osrick presides over the duel and is the judge — Horatio may be another — while Hamlet and Laertes prepare. This is the crisis of the counteraction, the King's plot against Hamlet. Hamlet no longer has a plot, only a role to fulfil and a resolution to do so.

Hamlet apologizes to Laertes. He confesses that he has wounded both the young man's "nature" (his natural affection, for Polonius was his father) and his "honour" (the violent intervention at Ophelia's graveside):

> Give me your pardon, sir. I have done you wrong.
> But pardon't, as you are a gentleman.
> This presence knows, and you must needs have heard,
> How I am punished with a sore distraction.    (220-223)

The courtiers who support the King know Hamlet to have been mad; they must not know that it was pretence. His apology (234-238) is sincere. In contrast, Laertes hypocritically says he is "satisfied in Nature," which we know he is not:

> I do receive your offered love like love,
> And will not wrong it.                        (245-246)

Both men are conscious performers in a staged reconciliation ritual, to be followed by a "show." Hamlet's situation is impossible: he cannot explain; he has to fabricate a fiction in order to satisfy the court. The fiction Laertes counters with is a calculated and treacherous lie, not a despairing evasion.

Osrick brings the foils. The King describes the order of proceedings: if Hamlet scores a hit, Claudius will drink his health:

> Set me the stoups of wine upon that table.
> If Hamlet give the first or second hit,

Or quit in answer of the third exchange,
Let all the battlements their ordnance fire.
The King shall drink to Hamlet's better breath,
And in the cup an union [pearl] shall he throw
Richer than that which four successive kings
In Denmark's crown have worn. Give me the cups,
And let the kettle to the trumpet speak,
The trumpet to the cannoneer without,
The cannons to the heavens, the heaven to earth,
'Now the King drinks to Hamlet.' (261-272)

His overblown words hide Laertes who takes the button off a foil and dips the point in his deadly poison. Hamlet is content with any foil; presumably, he says, they "have all a length?" (259). The duel begins.

Any bout of swordplay involving Hamlet and Laertes is bound to be something more than a fiction, given what Hamlet has done to the family of Polonius. The better the fight is done, the better for the scene, which is apt to be a little ridiculous unless everybody concerned is very careful. Perhaps the most spectacular was the fight of Laurence Olivier and Raymond Massey (1937) which had the look of film duels in the same period by Errol Flynn and Basil Rathbone. Most actors use rapier and dagger as the text requires.

In the first bout Hamlet claims a hit, Laertes denies it, Hamlet appeals to the judges, and Osrick decides in his favour: "A hit, a very palpable hit" (275). The King rises to perform his ceremony. He has planned to back the poisoned rapier with the poisoned cup. Hamlet is the better fencer; Laertes may not touch him, and Claudius is running no risks:

Stay, give me drink. Hamlet, this pearl is thine.
Here's to thy health. Give him the cup. (276-277)

He drinks from the cup first, then draws the pearl from his finger and drops it in (we guess he presses a spring which releases the poison). He directs his attendant to give the cup to Hamlet who says, "I'll play this bout first; set it by awhile" (278).

They engage again. This time Hamlet's hit is so "palpable" that Laertes cannot deny it. Gertrude, happy to see the change in her son, rises from her throne and joins him, offering to wipe the sweat off his face. In a merry mood she seizes the cup and, mischievously parodying the King's phrase, says: "The Queen carouses to thy fortune, Hamlet." Claudius calls out, "Gertrude, do not drink." She insists: "I will, my lord. I pray you, pardon me." The King, aside, points the irony explicitly for us: "It is the poisoned cup. It is too late" (285-286). Meanwhile the thwarted Laertes is whispering to the King: "My lord, I'll hit him now," to get the grim answer, "I do not think't" (289).

The third bout Osrick pronounces a draw: "Nothing neither way" (295). Suddenly Laertes shouts, "Have at you now!" (296) and lunges at the unprepared Hamlet, wounding him with the poisoned foil. In fury at Laertes' treachery, Hamlet leaps at him. They scuffle: Hamlet wrests the poisoned foil from Laertes, forcing on him his own in exchange. The King cries: "Part them, they are incensed." Laertes knows (but Hamlet does not) that he is fighting for his life. The double climax comes suddenly. As Osrick sees the Queen fall: "Look to the Queen there, ho!" Horatio calls out: "They bleed on both sides": the poisoned blade has cut Laertes (297-298).

Hamlet has his death wound but does not know it. Laertes has his and knows it. Osrick's "How is it, Laertes?" starts his confession:

> Why, as a woodcock to mine own springe, Osrick.
> I am justly killed with mine own treachery.     (300-301)

Claudius pretends Gertrude has fainted at the sight of blood. But she says:

> No, no, the drink, the drink! O my dear Hamlet!
> The drink, the drink! I am poisoned.     (303-304)

Hamlet is transformed and stands there, Hamlet the Dane restored.

> O, villainy! Ho! Let the door be locked.
> Treachery! Seek it out.     (305-306)

Claudius is trapped. Laertes reveals the whole grim truth:

> The treacherous instrument is in thy hand,
> Unbated and envenomed ...
> ... Thy mother's poisoned ...
> ... The King, the King's to blame.     (310-314)

Hamlet runs Claudius through at once. The courtiers raise a perfunctory cry of "Treason!" But, though the wounded man cries pitifully "O, yet defend me, friends. I am but hurt," they do nothing. Then Hamlet drops the sword, takes the cup, and chokes the King's mouth open to pour the poison down. At this consummate moment Hamlet has his last outburst of mockery:

> Here, thou incestuous, murderous, damnèd Dane,
> Drink off this potion. Is thy union here?
> Follow my mother. (319-321)

The "union," the pearl, was the poison in the cup; but the union of his uncle with his mother is in death. Ironically, poison began the rottenness in Denmark, and it is poison that now claims the lives of so many victims. Laertes' generosity in death contrasts with the villainy of his plot: he offers to exchange forgiveness, which with Christian charity Hamlet accepts.

Moissi, after an elaborate but anachronistic eighteenth century fight with foils (in a Gothic production), took the poisoned sword by the blade with both hands and stabbed the King in the back! The guards, in diagonally striped cloaks, then closed in on the three bodies, making a background for Hamlet to die against.

Hamlet's dying speeches are carefully calculated in a variety of tempi, volume and colour with a running musical structure that knits them together: "I am dead, Horatio ... Horatio, I am dead ... O God, Horatio" ... "O, I die, Horatio!" (327-346). Part of what he says is a public utterance to the hostile court and to the theatre audience:

> You that look pale and tremble at this chance,
> That are but mutes or audience to this act ... (328-329)

Suddenly, he is surrounded by actors on all four sides. The *play world* reaches out to encompass the theatre audience and sweep it into the play. This is an old effect from the Cycles, but Shakespeare gives it new meaning: the power of the theatre to unify illusion and reality. Here, in a theatre whose name, the Globe, implies the play metaphor, is the last in a series of affirmations of the power of the stage.

But Hamlet is dying: "O, I could tell you" is urgent. Horatio must set the record straight:

> Horatio, I am dead.
> Thou livest. Report me and my cause aright
> To the unsatisfied. (332-334)

Horatio, of all people, the man that is not passion's slave, suddenly resolves not to survive his friend:

> Never believe it.

> I am more an antique Roman than a Dane.
> Here's yet some liquor left.                    (334-336)

But Hamlet's urgent need overcomes his friend's faltering purpose:

> O God, Horatio, what a wounded name,
> Things standing thus unknown, shall I leave behind me!
> If thou didst ever hold me in thy heart,
> Absent thee from felicity awhile,
> And in this harsh world draw thy breath in pain,
> To tell my story.                    (338-343)

Suddenly we hear *"A march afar off"*: Fortinbras' army's drums and fifes, and a shot of salute. Hamlet, dying, calmly orders affairs of state:

> I do prophesy th'election lights
> On Fortinbras. He has my dying voice.
> So tell him ...                    (349-351)

Then, "the rest is silence." As Hamlet dies he receives Horatio's blessing, "Flights of angels sing thee to thy rest!" (354). In Elizabethan stage convention, the catastrophe is just: the villains are hoist by their own schemes; and Hamlet kills Claudius in a way that does not harm his soul. Since he is dying and cannot ascend the throne, he has no self-interest as he kills a murderer: a dying act of public justice. Only Hamlet can restore right; and his own death expiates those of Polonius and Laertes.

The final action is public, and its main theme is Hamlet's reputation. Horatio claims the right to make his funeral oration. He will speak

> Of carnal, bloody, and unnatural acts,
> Of accidental judgements, casual slaughters,
> Of deaths put on by cunning and forced cause,
> And, in this upshot, purposes mistook
> Fall'n on th'inventors' heads.                    (375-379)

This is a startling account. It sounds like the prologue to a conventional revenge tragedy, not a description of Shakespeare's *Hamlet*. Horatio astonishes us by leaving out everything that seems important, reducing all to a stereotype. On that level it is accurate enough, but it is certainly not Hamlet's "story." However, Horatio speaks from a knowledge much inferior to that of the audience, and he is addressing Fortinbras, who is not the kind of man who would be tempted to speculate in the way Hamlet has done.

The play is rich in death. Horatio's tone, echoing Hamlet's fascination with the skulls the Gravedigger unearths, takes us to death in Fortinbras' comment:

> This quarry cries on havoc. O proud Death,
> What feast is toward in thine eternal cell
> That thou so many princes at a shot
> So bloodily hast struck? (358-361)

The future belongs to Fortinbras, whose epilogue pays tribute to Hamlet:

> Let four captains
> Bear Hamlet like a soldier to the stage.
> For he was likely, had be been put on,
> To have proved most royal. And for his passage
> The soldiers' music and the rites of war
> Speak loudly for him.
>     *[Exeunt marching: after the which a peal of ordnance is shot off.]* (389-394)

In the theatre, the final moments have varied widely. Forbes-Robertson died sitting on the throne with the king's crown set on his lap and was then borne off on locked shields. Leslie Howard also was carried off in a great procession to end the play. The poisoning of the Queen is difficult to manage, and Granville-Barker thinks she should play her death scene on the ground, like the pictures of the death of Queen Elizabeth, and not die until Halmet says "Wretched Queen, adieu!" (327). It is ironic for Hamlet to realize at this moment that his mother has died just as his father did. Undoubtedly the King should have poison in a ring, and the audience should see him pour it into the cup. In Tyrone Guthrie's production (1937) the scene was produced for violent melodrama, and the Queen fell from a six-foot platform into the arms of the attendants.

## WORDS, WORDS, WORDS

POLONIUS:    What do you read, my lord?
HAMLET:      Words, words, words.    (II.ii.191-193)
Shakespeare's language in mid-career has no formula. By testing it in rehearsal and performance, he slowly drops artifice and works for a seemingly spontaneous verbal expression. *Hamlet* is a huge leap to this end.

Shakespeare's dramatic verse has several sources. The traditions of the English theatre help him to understand the form and structure of dramatic poetry, but he grows beyond other dramatists even at the start of his career. His early inclination is to the lyric and to expanding it for dramatic use, much as Lyly had done. And he masters the heroic rhetoric. Shakespeare is the greatest dramatic poet of his era because he realizes that speech on stage has to fulfil many purposes: to exhibit character; to tell the story so that it continuously goes on while its background is suggested; and to unify with the action so that the *dramatic verse is jointly word and act.* But he also conceives his poetry as music for the living individual voices of actors whom he knows. Shakespeare speaks through his actors. His aim is to present people talking. When the modern player uses the prevailing rhythm of a passage, the cadence of a line provides its meaning, melody and emotion. There is no one correct way of speaking a passage; Shakespeare writes it so that the actor shares in creating the meaning.

*Hamlet* is a tragedy of character where the tragic is modulated by a strain of comedy. It demands every variety of verse and speed. Shakespeare draws on all his previous styles: he modifies them, subdues them to the theme, and incorporates them in the action and in character. In other words, he makes them completely dramatic: words, action and character are one.

The normal style in the play is as always the open-textured, steady and disciplined iambic pentameter. He can vary this pace by the slow grace of his early lyrical style, as in Horatio's

> But look, the morn in russet mantle clad
> Walks o'er the dew of yon high eastward hill. (I.i.167-168)

which relieves the tension of the Ghost's appearance. The Queen's tale of Ophelia's death, with its elegiac harmony, is lyrical. But it is also intensely dramatic in its placing. Hamlet talks to Horatio in almost the detached rhetoric of his early plays:

> Give me that man
> That is not passion's slave, and I will wear him
> In my heart's core, ay, in my heart of heart ...
>
> (III.ii.81-83)

When the Ghost interrupts Hamlet's onslaught on his mother, he knows that it has come to chide him for being "lapsed in time and passion" (III.iv.108). Yet Hamlet's rant, compared with those in his early plays, has controlled intensity of utterance.

For certain effects Shakespeare creates distinctive verse. The Ghost speaks solemn and spacious poetry made strangely stiff and formal by its repetitive rhetorical structure, while *The Murder of Gonzago* is in archaic, sententious, and monotonous couplets.

Shakespeare puts two or more epithets together for emphasis and dramatic life. He does so both in tragedy where, not content with "Bloody, bawdy villain!" Hamlet adds "Remorseless, treacherous, lecherous, kindless villain!" (II.ii.577-578), and in comedy, like Polonius' "The best actors in the world, either for tragedy, comedy, history, pastoral, pastoral-comical, historical-pastoral ..." (II.ii.395ff.). Or to amplify a meaning he uses a conjunction, as in "slings and arrows" (III.i.58), or a noun used as a adjective, like "ponderous and marble jaws" (I.iv.50) for he was the first to use these two words as adjectives. He reiterates a single significant word which is deeply felt by the person who speaks it, like "Mother, mother, mother!" (III.iv.6) or "words, words, words" to the wordy Polonius.

Shakespeare has previously used predominant image-clusters in specific plays. But in *Hamlet* they are unified and extended into the bowels of the tragedy. Sickness, rankness and rotting flesh are everywhere. With few exceptions, everyone in the play has human weaknesses: human purpose is unstable, and people fail before Fortune. Hamlet begins this theme when he describes how from that single blemish a person's whole character may take corruption. The world is:

> an unweeded garden
> That grows to seed. Things rank and gross in nature
> Possess it merely. (I.ii.135-137)

Hamlet's problems arise from a condition for which he is not responsible, any more than a sick man is to blame for his infection. He has inherited it; he is "born to set it right!" (I.v.189). He would be, the Ghost says,

> duller ... than the fat weed
> That roots itself in ease on Lethe wharf ... (I.v.32-33)

not to revenge his father's murder and his mother's shame. To her Hamlet pictures Claudius

> like a mildewed ear,
> Blasting his wholesome brother (III.iv.65-66)

and instructs her to keep from him and not to
>               spread the compost on the weeds
>       To make them ranker.                    (III.iv.152-153)

Shakespeare emphasizes infection: the running sore, the ulcer, the hidden abscess. Hamlet tells his mother of the "flattering unction" which

>       will but skin and film the ulcerous place
>       Whiles rank corruption, mining all within,
>       Infects unseen ...                       (III.iv.148-150)

and Claudius' "O, my offence is rank. It smells to heaven" (III.iii.36) echoes through the play. The whole image-cluster is made concrete in the smell of the graveyard and the grin of Yorick's skull.

The weeds of Gertrude's sin contrast with the flowers of Ophelia. To her Hamlet is "Th'expectancy and rose of the fair state ..." (III.i.153), and she to Laertes is a "rose of May" (IV.v.159). Hamlet's garden grown to seed is contrasted with Laertes' warning:

>       The canker galls the infants of the spring
>       Too oft before their buttons be disclosed;
>       And in the morn and liquid dew of youth
>       Contagious blastments are most imminent.   (I.iii.39-42)

Ophelia images such danger as a "primrose path of dalliance" (I.iii.50) and gives flowers in her madness. Denmark was a garden when Hamlet's father ruled, but as the Ghost reveals:

>       The serpent that did sting thy father's life
>       Now wears his crown.                       (I.v.39-40)

Gertrude took off "the rose" from the "forehead of an innocent love" and set "a blister there" (III.iv.43-45).

The infection in Demark is alternatively seen as poison. The poisoner is Claudius. The juice he pours into the ear of the old King is a mixture of poison and disease, a "leperous distilment" that curbs "The thin and wholesome blood" (I.v.64, 70). Hamlet says that his "wit's diseased" (III.ii.329-330), the Queen speaks of her "sick soul" (IV.v.17), the King is troubled by "the hectic" in his blood (IV.iii.68), and Laertes thinks revenge will warm "the very sickness in my heart" (IV.vii.54). These images bring a profound feeling of loss: the Ghost talks of his "most seeming-virtuous Queen" (I.v.46,50) and says, "O Hamlet, what a falling off was there." Of Hamlet, Ophelia says,

"O, what a noble mind is here o'erthrown!" (III.i.151). Moral virtues are attacked: Hyperion's throne is occupied by "A king of shreds and patches" (III.iv.103), and Hamlet asks questions like, "Why wouldst thou be a breeder of sinners?" (III.i.121-122).

There is a second image-cluster related to the main one: a gun or a concealed explosion. Laertes tells Ophelia to keep out of the "shot and danger of desire" (I.iii.35). The King compares slander's whisper to the "poisoned shot" of a cannon (IV.i.43), the volley of bad news to that of a "murdering-piece" (IV.v.96), and proposes the poisoned cup if Laertes' sword should "blast in proof" (IV.vii.153). Hamlet talks of "slings" or culverin (III.i.58), of words "too light for the bore of the matter" (IV.vi.25), and says:

> For 'tis the sport to have the enginer
> Hoist with his own petar; and 't shall go hard
> But I will delve one yard below their mines
> And blow them at the moon.              (III.iv.207-210)

Shakespeare hints at the image of the sapper when he calls the Ghost "A worthy pioneer!" (I.v.163). Hamlet associates disease with mines, primarily military but industrial by implication, in his "ulcerous place ... mining all within" (III.iv.148-149). Similarly when Claudius says:

> But, like the owner of a foul disease,
> To keep it from divulging let it feed
> Even on the pith of life. Where is he gone?

to which the Queen replies,

> To draw apart the body he hath killed;
> O'er whom his very madness, like some ore
> Among a mineral [mine] of metals base,
> Shows itself pure.              (IV.i.24-27)

The King's simile of the murdering-piece follows immediately after a double metaphor of infection and pestilence, and his image of the gun blasting is separated from that of the ulcer by only a few lines.

Shakespeare is now sure of what his people say. This enables the director to retain the necessary techniques of stage speech, but in addition, he rehearses the performers in the delivery of spontaneous talk in verse.

## *HAMLET* AND THE ACTOR

It has been said that the characters in Hamlet are not in sharp focus. That may be true for the reader, but it is not so in the theatre. Actors find that even Rosencrantz and Guildenstern, usually thought of as colourless, have individual touches; each new pair of actors discovers their differences. Shakespeare gives every actor enough for a vivid sketch of character in a few words (e.g., Barnardo). The reader may not discover these people, but after all, they were written for acting not reading.

As no Shakespearean hero changes as much as Hamlet, where does the actor begin? The key for the actor lies in Hamlet's reason and intelligence. What he says and thinks of others is true. There is no fault in his logic: his mother is faithless, the prettiness of Ophelia masks a fragile spirit, Polonius is "a foolish prating knave," Rosencrantz and Guildenstern are self-serving flatterers, and Claudius' smooth charm hides a murderer: he is "a damnèd smiling villain." No wonder Hamlet is cynical.

He learns that people are no better than beasts if they do not use reason. The actor must first create *the grieving Hamlet*: he is morbidly sensitive to his mother's degradingly hasty marriage, and he grieves for his father's death. But the villain is his kindly uncle: Claudius, whose crime was evil, now appears healthy and happy. The perplexed Hamlet watches, analyses and probes others. He can even joke about his worries:

> Thrift, thrift, Horatio. The funeral baked meats
> Did coldly furnish forth the marriage tables.     (I.ii.180-181)

Yet his cynicism does not hide his discriminating reason ("'Seems,' madam? Nay, it is. I know not 'seems'" [I.ii.76]) or his contempt for all "actions that a man might play." He has "that within which passeth show," but his sensitivity can quickly turn to the impulsive,

> Haste me to know't, that I, with wings as swift
> As meditation or the thoughts of love,
> May sweep to my revenge ...                    (I.v.29-31)

or the futility of

> Now might I do it pat, now 'a is a-praying.
> And now I'll do't. And so 'a goes to heaven.
> And so am I revenged. That would be scanned.
> (III.iii.73-75)

Fortinbras would not think so precisely nor hesitate.

With the Ghost's revelations, the actor creates *the mad Hamlet,* a man possessed. He never regains a natural spiritual health; he is led into deeper despair which, but for "the dread of something after death," he would happily end. We know this from his soliloquies, but others only see his madness. This, with his reason, isolates him. At court he is the odd man out: the others are uncertain what he will do next, and this terrifies them. He can speak lovingly to his mother at one moment and, the next, in an excess of revulsion, torment her with withering sarcasm. His mind and his emotions change swiftly; others think this volatility madness.

- The nearest the actor can reach to the inner man, *"the normal Hamlet,"* lies in three of his actions: His advice to the Players throws light not only on theatrical art but also on himself; it is typical of him in such a crisis to delight in something irrelevant. He prefers the unreal (the fictional) to the real because he can manipulate it.
- In the soliloquies he sees himself reflected by his conscience — he does, as he tells the Players, "hold, as 'twere, the mirror up to nature" and lapses into despair, reproach, excitement, or grief. The mirror makes him self-conscious; he strikes attitudes like an actor. But he finds he knows nothing of himself at all.
- Horatio is the one person close to him whom he does not despise:

> As one, in suffering all, that suffers nothing,
> A man that Fortune's buffets and rewards
> Hast ta'en with equal thanks.          (III.ii.76-78)

This is what he finds best in a man. When he exclaims to Horatio

> Give me that man
> That is not passion's slave, and I will wear him
> In my heart's core, ay, in my heart of heart,
> As I do thee ...          (III.ii.81-84)

he speaks of his friend's qualities which he himself lacks.

When he returns to Denmark in his sea-cloak he is *the hardened Hamlet.* He is "sane" again; at last he is fit for his task. The transformation has taken much of his sweetness but not his spirit. His nobility shines through his words to Horatio and his apology to Laertes. Now he is resolute: he wants the terrible task fulfilled so that he may be at peace.

*He loves Ophelia.* He cries:

> I loved Ophelia. Forty thousand brothers
> Could not with all their quantity of love
> Make up my sum. (V.i.265-267)

She tells Polonius that he woos her "in honourable fashion," of his giving

> countenance to his speech ...
> With almost all the holy vows of heaven. (I.iii.113-114)

But the lovers never have a chance. Her family conspires against them. She feels Hamlet's love is honourable. But when her father tells her that Hamlet's "holy vows" are

> mere implorators of unholy suits,
> Breathing like sanctified and pious bawds,
> The better to beguile (I.iii.129-131)

she, docile and a good daughter, does as she is bidden and keeps Hamlet away. He, in shock from his mother's adultery, finds his love treated like the lust of his uncle for his mother. When Hamlet and Ophelia are alone, the damage is done. She does not tell him she obeyed her father in keeping him away, as he hides his lost faith in womanhood. So it comes to, "I loved you not," her miserable reply, "I was the more deceived," and his "Get thee to a nunnery ... Where's your father?" (III.i.119-130). She then tells a single lie to a madman for his own good: "At home, my lord." As Hamlet knows that Polonius is hiding behind the arras, so she is now as faithless as his mother: "Go to, I'll no more on't. It hath made me mad" (III.i.147-148). For Ophelia, her lie initiates his madness; she stays silent as the King and Polonius discuss Hamlet callously, but her own sanity is wavering. She puts up a good front at *The Murder of Gonzago* when she suffers ignorantly and pitifully as Hamlet cheapens her before all the Court, squatting at her feet and making dirty jokes at her. We do not meet her again: the insane figure we see later is not Ophelia.

Claudius is a superb part. He should not be played as a villain from the start. If the actor thinks primarily of the state of Denmark, he finds a man to admire: he always has a fine steadiness of purpose. All he does and says looks more like innocence than guilt. "O villain, villain, smiling, damned villain!"

seems incredible. Perhaps it is "a damned ghost" that Hamlet has seen? Burbage and his audience had good reason to doubt its veracity, for Claudius is a consummate hypocrite. He is smooth and smiling; we do not see him as he really is for a long time. His flight from *The Murder of Gonzago* finally convinces Hamlet of his guilt; but only in the "prayer-scene" does Claudius confirm this to us. The earlier aside (III.i.49-54) appears to be a later addition to the play.

The "prayer-scene" is the pivot in acting Claudius, as it is in the whole play. Till now we have only been aware of the smiling mask and the mellifluous speech. Here, in sharp contrast, we see him as he really is. "O, my offence is rank. It smells to heaven" (III.iii.36-72) is one of Shakespeare's greatest dramatic poems: the heart of the man is laid bare. His guilt will not let him pray because he still has the fruits of his crime: "May one be pardoned and retain th' offence?" In this world perhaps; yet "'tis not so above." This is solid Elizabethan theology, yet it reveals an inner Claudius who can face the truth about his deed, its consequences, and himself. The actor presents the man as he would be, as he feels that he is, drawn in sensitive phrases that seem to fall spontaneously into verse. This inner picture of him does most to make Claudius a living person. He rises from his knees knowing he is as hardened in sin as ever, and he continues his villainy with even more clarity of mind. He is in danger, and he must act.

The killing of Polonius allows Claudius to counter-attack, and he is swift and decisive. He may play the role of a grieved stepfather and prudent statesman, but he devises two clever schemes for disposing of his nephew without the suspicion of the Queen and Denmark. The first is Hamlet's "healthful" voyage to England, to be climaxed by the beheading of him there. Then with masterly Machiavellian diplomacy, the King converts Laertes' demand for justice for his father's murderer into consent to the charmingly friendly, but fatal, duel. Both schemes are wonderfully specious, but especially the second which the King designs so as to rule out the unforeseen accidents that upset the first. He wears his smiling mask again, but he lets the instant pass in which Gertrude could be saved. Dosed with his own poison, he meets an ignominious end.

The actor must convey that Claudius is a king and no king: he has a superficial royalty, but his crime is so terrible that his rule is virtually worthless. He is "a thing ... Of nothing" (IV.ii.27,30). Once Hamlet is certain how his uncle gained the throne, he calls him "a vice of kings" and "A king of shreds and patches" (III.iv.99,103). He and Gertrude never themselves refer to their joint passion, but we see them only briefly alone together. Claudius always shows her loving respect. We assume his lust as he is a sensualist; Hamlet tells us that "The king doth wake tonight, and takes his rouse," and that such revels give Danes the name of drunkards. As Claudius and Gertrude are the focus of the Court, its ethos consists of coarse pleasures, and we see moral obtuseness (Polonius), sycophancy (Rosencrantz and Guildenstern), treacherous plotting (Laertes) and social triviality (Osrick). "Something is rotten in the state of Denmark." Evil itself is at large.

At the Globe, Shakespeare's Gertrude could not have been a mature matron, the realistic mother of a man of thirty, as she often is in modern productions. A boy could play the young Ophelia, and the old men could play old women, like the Nurse or Volumnia; but neither could play the charm of ripe womanhood. So Granville-Barker is likely right: she was played "young," a pretty creature who clings to her youth, refusing to grow old.* It is from her pathetic incongruity that the whole tragedy stems; yet in the action she is in Claudius' shadow — she even repeats his words or inverts their order. She is fond enough of Hamlet to know that her own "o'er-hasty marriage" is at the root of his trouble; and he comes to see her as an amiable but shallow creature. In the closet scene she is mostly reactive, but afterwards she does not tell Claudius all. Here begins a rift between them; following her son's advice, she stays conjugally apart, and Claudius feels he has lost her. Later, during the fencing match, she disobeys him and drinks from the cup he has prepared for her son. That gesture is her death: the same death her cheated husband died.

The actor of Polonius must convey to the audience his change in the play. When first with his children, he is a sensible old man whose pious and worldly wise words are clear and pre-

---

* Granville-Barker (1963).

cise. But with his instructions to Reynaldo he takes a comic tone, becoming a glorious character: complacent, opinionated, full of clichés and wise saws, circumlocutory in words but hasty in action — and usually wrong. When he is wrong, as he is about Hamlet and Ophelia, he ungrudgingly admits it, even if he is perfunctory:

> I feared he did but trifle
> And meant to wrack thee. (II.i.112-113)

In his dignified position at Court he is pompous, an advocate of order and degree, and loyal to the powers that be. Privately he is kindly, affable and tolerant. His use of Reynaldo to spy on Laertes is similar to his "loosing" of Ophelia to Hamlet: his intentions are good, but he is insensitive to others. He does not stop to think that it is cruel to use his daughter so; and he ignores her feelings when he and Claudius emerge disappointed from their hiding-place. He meddles: the result is that a sword thrust, meant for Claudius, ends him.

Laertes begins as a conventional figure of a fullblooded and confident youth. But there are suggestions of other things: he is much like his father when he moralizes to his sister; and Polonius hints to Reynaldo of

> The flash and outbreak of a fiery mind,
> A savageness in unreclaimèd blood ... (II.i.33-34)

all of which prepares for the contrast with Hamlet, the pensive idealist. The furious Laertes who thrusts his way to the King and threatens Claudius is like a blast of fresh air after the vacillation of Hamlet. Unlike Hamlet, he faces the King straight out:

> To hell allegiance! Vows to the blackest devil!
> Conscience and grace to the profoundest pit!
> I dare damnation. (IV.v.133-135)

Where Hamlet broods, Laertes is tender in his grief:

> O rose of May,
> Dear maid, kind sister, sweet Ophelia! (IV.v.159-160)

And when his enemy is within his reach, he is ready straightway "To cut his throat i' the church," a strong contrast with Hamlet's refusal to kill the praying Claudius. Yet this "very noble youth" villainously uses a secretly sharp foil and poisons it. The actor of Laertes shows us what moral lassitude really is. Hamlet is not morally unstable. His resolution wavers by "thinking too precisely on the event," but it sharpens his sense of right and wrong. Laertes is not good at reasoning. Like his father, he is suspicious. He is also blind to flattery, rash in action, and morally wrong.

Horatio is a difficult role. He lives in Hamlet's shadow, yet he is very much himself. We know him before ever Hamlet appears. He dominates the first scene and, with Fortinbras, the last moments of the play; he is the figure of stability with which all else contrasts. He reveals himself as a poor and educated gentleman, a level-headed and open-minded scholar with a loyal respect for the old King. At first he thinks the Ghost a "fantasy," but seeing is believing. He does not fear it, yet he is sensitive: he trembles and turns pale when it first appears, and he steadies his nerves for the second sight of it. Hamlet's greeting to him as "good friend" and "fellow-student" shows him a chosen friend. So he remains:

> Horatio, thou art e'en as just a man
> As e'er my conversation coped withal.       (III.ii.64-65)

The actor playing him must be an excellent speaker and narrator, and in such lines as

> But look, the morn in russet mantle clad
> Walks o'er the dew of yon high eastward hill ...  (I.i.167-168)

he must show a gentle and sensitive spirit.

# CONCLUSION

*amlet* is one of humanity's greatest images. This is because the play deals with paradoxes and is, in itself, a paradox. Bradley engagingly put into words the probable reaction of anyone seeing the play for the first time: "But why in the world did not Hamlet obey the Ghost at once, and so save seven of those eight lives?"* Although the hero's delay is a common convention of Elizabethan revenge tragedy, most critics have sought psychological explanations. Is Hamlet too humane to murder in cold blood? Or is he like the Raymond Chandler detective hero who fights corruption and sin? In fact, there is no single answer to the question of Hamlet's delay. There are many combinations of answers, some with varying degrees of emphasis. Shakespeare has left the hero an enduring moral enigma. But in the theatre most of the problems which baffle the critics do not arise. Seen through the eyes of one specific player, *Hamlet* becomes an entity.

When the director and the actors seek a unified view of the play to present to the audience, one central fact emerges: to Hamlet death is the primary fact of nature. Life travels towards the grave, just as love does not survive the loved one's life. If his mother's over-hasty marriage is the trigger that begins Hamlet's troubles, physical death in the grave is the focus of the pain in his mind, and it is suffused through the whole play.

Hamlet does not see the truth as evil. The Prince recalls the truth that existed when Denmark was a garden in his father's reign. Hamlet seeks a return to Paradise. But, like the Garden of Eden, Denmark contained a serpent: Claudius, the adulterer and poisoner. At a symbolic level, *Hamlet* is the story of the Fall.

Here is the universal level of *Hamlet*. It echoes human history. At the beginning of civilization, a similar story was performed and developed over the centuries: Osiris, the good and bounteous King of Egypt, was murdered by his brother Seth who took his throne; it was Osiris' son, Horus, who revenged

---

* Bradley (1978).

him by killing Seth and ruling in his place: "The king is dead; long live the king!" This was a ritual-myth performed at Abydos at about the same time as Aeschylus' *Oresteia,* which had much the same plot, was performed in Athens. In *Hamlet,* the villain begins the sequence of the Fall before the play. As the play starts, the Ghost of the good and bounteous King appears to start the action. Once in motion, the action is both particular and universal.

Photograph by Jane Edmonds, courtesy of the Stratford Festival.

The Stratford Festival stage at Stratford, Ontario, was designed by Tanya Moiseiwitsch with Tyrone Guthrie, and is a modern interpretation of the Elizabethan open stage.

# END NOTES

## ELIZABETHAN WORLD ORDER

hakespeare's England is Christian. The English
Reformation, begun by Henry VIII and continued by his
daughter, Elizabeth I, establishes the Church of England
(Anglican) as the official form of worship. But strong Catholic
forces continue to work against the established church: the
Armada, sent by Philip of Spain to restore Catholicism in England,
is defeated in 1588, about the time Shakespeare arrives in London
from Stratford-upon-Avon. Puritanism is also growing at this time.

Richard Hooker's great work defending the Anglican church,
*Of the Laws of Ecclesiastical Polity,* says that God created the world
according to a perfect plan. Each of his creations has a special
function. As long as this order is preserved, the universe works
beautifully and efficiently, with an orderly and permanent hierarchy, a chain of command from top to bottom. This chain is repeated in each realm of existence: thus God rules over the cosmos, the
sun over the planets, the king over the body politic, the husband
over the wife and family, the head over the other body parts, and
so on. If this universal order is disturbed, chaos results — a great
horror.

This view, derived from the male-oriented cultures of antiquity
(Hittites, Israelites, Greeks, etc.), mixed with those aspects of
Christianity encouraged by the Reformation.

The principle of order appears many times in Shakespeare's
plays, most notably in Ulysses' speech on degree in *Troilus and
Cressida* (I.iii.75-137) and Katherine's lecture to the other women
on wifely submission at the end of *The Shrew* (V.ii.135-178) [see
GENDER, below]. The breakdown of order is an offence against
God: Macbeth's murder of Duncan, Paris's abduction of Helen
from her lawful husband, the rejection of Lear by his daughters,
Bolingbroke's overthrow of Richard II, and so on. The parallel of
"king" to "sun" is used of Richard II, but not of Henry V because
his father was a usurper, although Henry V is continually "golden."

## PERSONALITY

A human being is a microcosm, a little world. His or her physical, mental and moral state resembles the macrocosm, somewhat like a hologram. The macrocosm can be seen as the body politic or as the universe. Both microcosm and macrocosm have four elements (fire, air, water, earth) which in people become four *humours:* blood, phlegm, yellow bile, and black bile. In Elizabethan psychology, they produce different "types" of people. These principles lie behind many comedies of the period (e.g., Ben Jonson's *Every Man in His Humour,* in which Shakespeare played a role), and they are inherent in many of Shakespeare's plays: e.g., Antony's final tribute to Brutus (*Julius Caesar,* V.v.68-75).

### GENDER
Katherine's speech on wifely submission in *The Shrew* (V.ii.135-178) is a traditional Elizabethan view of the male-female relationship. This view is offensive to some modern feminists, but it must be understood in terms of Elizabethan mores. "Man" is the term used by Elizabethans for all human beings; females are clearly lesser beings. There is no reason to think that Shakespeare necessarily subscribed to this belief. It is true that throughout the plays he puts customary beliefs in the mouths of persons in the plays. Yet he often changes the traditional balance of males and females, particularly in the comedies, in which the woman may control the man (e.g., Helena, Rosalind) or be the focus of the action (Isabella, Portia). In this respect, Shakespeare is ahead of his contemporaries. Most of the tragedies, however, picture the female from the perspective of the male hero (e.g., Desdemona, Gertrude). The exception is *Antony and Cleopatra,* in which both have equal weight.

### SOUL AND MIND
The Tudors use Aristotle's division of the soul into the vegetal, the sensible, and the rational faculties. The vegetal is shared by all living creatures and is responsible for the body's growth and generation. The sensible faculty, possessed by animals and people, is the source of feeling and motion. We perceive through the five senses. Perceptions are categorized by "the common sense," filtered through the imagination (fantasy), and ratified by reason.

Lack of imaginative control, as in illness, brings delusions. Delusions can also recur in sleep, when reason relaxes its vigilance, and Queen Mab gallops through the mind creating dreams (*Romeo and Juliet*, I.iv.53-103). Theseus in *The Dream* (V.i.4-22) shows that an unruly imagination is responsible for the erratic acts of lunatics, lovers, and poets. In this play the two pairs of lovers exemplify the delusions of unruly imagination.

## TEXTS

The texts of Elizabethan dramatists were not exactly handled with care. The "Master of the Revels," a court official, examined each written script and often required moral or political revisions. The bookkeeper, or prompter, of the playhouse made the original manuscript (called "foul papers" or "fair copy") into a workable stage script (a "book") in which he wrote the cues, stage business, etc., together with any revisions or deletions made to satisfy the Master of the Revels. There were many such alterations, and sometimes the number of collaborators obscured the original author's intentions. Plays often remained in the repertory for a long time and could be revived periodically. Few plays were printed, because theatre managers were afraid that would reduce box-office receipts. Only forty or so of the two hundred or more plays performed between 1592 and 1603 have survived in print. Yet a reasonable reading public emerged for printed plays, usually in quarto editions.

Before 1623, nineteen of Shakespeare's plays had been published singly (in quarto), most more than once. Those printed from Shakespeare's own manuscripts, or from playhouse copies, are today called "good" quartos, while many "bad" quartos were pirated, often reconstructed from an actor's memory. *The First Folio*, in which Shakespeare's colleagues Hemmings and Condell collected most of his plays in one volume, was published in 1623 in a printing of about twelve hundred copies. It includes the engraving of Shakespeare by Martin Droeshout, a Flemish artist. This portrait is one of only two of Shakespeare known to be authentic; the other is the memorial bust in the Church of the Holy Trinity, Stratford.

## SHAKESPEARE'S LANGUAGE

Elizabethan English is more flexible than the language of today. It has not settled down after its growth from Middle English into a modern form; it is not "fixed." For example, spelling is not uniform: the few existing examples of Shakespeare's signature show he even spells his name in different ways. He is not troubled by rigid rules of correctness, grammar, or definition. In addition to employing the common forms of his period, Shakespeare frequently uses language in his own distinctive way.

Elizabethan pronunciation is a matter of considerable scholarly debate. According to Kokeritz and others,* Shakespeare uses sounds similar to some modern English and American rural dialects: our *let* he pronounces *lit; virtue* as *vartue, nature* as *nater;* and *ea* like our *a* in t*ale,* so he said *speak* as *spake* and *dream* as *drame.* The noun *wind* could rhyme with either *kind* or *pinned.* Shakespeare sometimes makes two syllables of *-tion,* or adds a syllable to *Eng[e]land,* and at times makes a distinct syllable out of a final *-ed,* as in Antony's remark "The good is oft interrèd with their bones" *(Julius Caesar,* III.ii.77).

The verse basis of Shakespeare's plays is the iambic pentameter: iambic because there are two syllables with the accent on the second, and pentameter because there are five of them in a line, thus:

Te-TUM, te-TUM, te-TUM, te-TUM, te-TUM.

"And for I know she taketh most delight ... "

Shakespeare varies the beats in a line, and uses other line forms and prose, for dramatic effect. He uses rhyme more often in his early plays, to show artificiality, and can end a scene with a conventional rhyming couplet.

Renaissance writers have difficulty keeping pace with a language that is growing with the expansion of their social life. Shakespeare invents a vast range of words (e.g., assassination, disgraceful, gloomy, laughable, savagery) and combinations (e.g., falling to blows, an abrupt answer, bright and cheerful, sealing one's lips). More difficult for us are words that have changed their meaning or disappeared since Shakespeare used them. An example is "quibble," a game of "mis-taking the word": comic characters play it for fun, young lovers use it as a screen to hide their feelings

---

* See Kokeritz (1953) and Dobson (1968).

(like Beatrice and Benedick in *Much Ado)*, and it can communicate simultaneously on two or more levels, often with irony.

G. Wilson Knight emphasizes that each Shakespeare play is "a visionary unit bound to obey none but its own self-imposed laws ... as an expanded metaphor, by means of which the original vision has been projected into forms roughly correspondent with actuality."[*] Apart from the time-sequence which is the story, each play is unified in space (the play's "atmosphere") through imagery. Shakespeare's images cluster in groups; thus there are many nature images, particularly those relating to growing things in gardens and orchards, and there are repeated images in individual plays — light and dark in *Romeo and Juliet,* disease in *Hamlet,* animals in action in *Othello,* and so on. But imagery almost always refers to the whole play and cannot be separated from other elements.

## THE PLAYHOUSE

Shakespeare writes for performances in the Theatre, the Globe, and other specific buildings. Information about the playhouses is disappointingly scarce, so modern reconstructions have been mostly conjecture; recent archeological discoveries in London have provided little more data. But we know enough about the *principles* of the Elizabethan and Jacobean theatre spaces to understand *why, what,* and *how* things took place.

### THE "HOUSE" AND THE "PLACE"
The Elizabethan stage evolved from earlier forms. The liturgical drama and the massive medieval Cycles were based on two acting-areas: the "house," a localized space (a Paradise, a Hell, an ark for Noah, etc.); and the "place," a generalized space in front of one or more "houses."

The arrangement differed with the position of the "houses": in a line on a stage, as at Valençiennes; around a town square, as at Lucerne; on wagons wheeled from "place" to "place" ("stations"), as with some English Cycles; or in a circle with the audience in the middle, as in the Cornish and other English Cycles. In all cases, much of the action happened in the "place."

Interlude and Morality plays were normally performed by small professional troupes in the lord's hall. There the screen provided

---

[*] Knight (1957) 14-15.

an upper level, and on the ground level there were two doors on either side. On the wall between the doors was a "house" (sometimes a curtain) for entrances. The floor was the "place" where the actors performed. Single professional minstrels or small acting companies roamed far, performing in public streets, fields, taverns, and great houses. They set up the traditional booth stage of the old street theatre (a "house"), using any area around it as the "place."

In the sixteenth century, innyards were used. A wooden platform was built in the courtyard as a stage (the "place"), on which at least one "house" was probably sited. Spectators stood around, the stables became dressing rooms, and the several tiers of the gallery had seats for prosperous patrons. Some innkeepers in London and elsewhere found it profitable to lease their yards exclusively to theatrical companies. The playhouses used all these traditions, maintaining the localized "house" and the generalized "place."

## THE PUBLIC PLAYHOUSES

In 1576 James Burbage built the Theatre, the first permanent playhouse in London, in the priory of Holywell, between Shoreditch High Street and Finsbury Fields. The site was just north of the city, outside the jurisdiction of the city authorities. In 1577 the Curtain was built nearby. In 1600 the manager, Philip Henslowe, with the actor Alleyn, built the Fortune, also to the north but west of Shoreditch. The Red Bull (c. 1605) was the last built to the north. An increasingly important area was Bankside, the south bank of the Thames, also beyond the control of the London council. On Bankside were built the Rose (c. 1587), the Swan (c. 1595), the Hope (1613), and in 1599 Burbage and his men transferred from the Theatre to the new Globe.

The professional companies were sponsored, but not financed, by prominent nobles. The Lord Chamberlain's Men owned and operated the Theatre and then the Globe; the company included Burbage, his son Richard, the famous actor, and Shakespeare. Their chief rival was the Lord Admiral's Men, managed by Henslowe. The principal actor of this company was Edward Alleyn, who created the role of Marlowe's Tamburlaine. The companies were continually harassed by the London burghers, who thought that the congregating mobs were a hazard to public health and law enforcement, and by Puritan agitators, like Stephen Gosson, who denounced theatres as inciting people to sin.

*Popular stage from ancient times to Shakespeare's day: "house" and "place"*

*Two kinds of "house" and "place" in a medieval performance in the round*

*Interlude player in Tudor hall:
"house" is screen with two doors;
whole floor is "space"*

*Later adaptations to the medieval
hall: balcony at the top of the
screen; "tent" (curtains) set
against the centre of the screen*

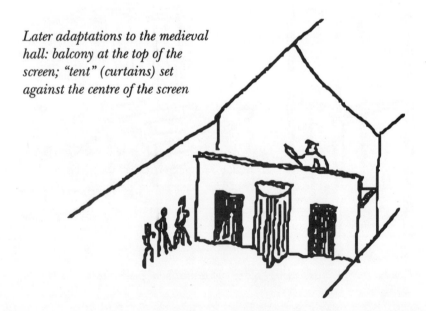

*Conjectural Elizabethan playhouse (based on C. Walter Hodges); note the two doors and curtains for inner stage, plus upper stage, and trap door on the stage ("place")*

The open air Elizabethan playhouse was usually round or polygonal, although the Fortune may have been rectangular. James Burbage, whose Theatre was probably a model for the rest, had previously built bear-pits and may have been influenced by his experience.

The stage area was built on the principle of the "house" and the "place." A bare platform jutted out into an unroofed yard or pit. At the rear of the platform was part of the main building, called the tiring house which had two purposes. Within it, the actors dressed. But the wall that separated the tiring house from the spectators was the façade that backed the stage. This façade had two doors on either side for entries and exits. Between them was either a recess with a draw curtain or a "house," and above was a gallery *(tarras)* where high scenes could be played. Although this was much like the staging for interludes, over the stage area was a roof (the "heavens") for possible descents, for making the noise of thunder, and for protecting the actors from the weather. Under the stage was the hell, or cellarage, from which devils and ghosts could rise through a trapdoor. "You hear this fellow in the cellarage," Hamlet says when the Ghost speaks from below (I.v.151).

Scenery as we know it hardly existed. There were large and small stage properties — a throne for a king, a bed for Desdemona, a tree for Malvolio — which were brought in and out in front of the audience or "revealed" as the rear curtain was drawn. Atmospheric scene changes were done with words:

But look, the morn, in russet mantle clad,
Walks o'er the dew of yon high eastward hill.

*(Hamlet,* I.i.167-168)

Costuming was splendid, but there was little attempt at historical accuracy. The simplicity of the stage allowed the dramatic action to move forward swiftly and continuously and brought a physical closeness between actors and spectators, giving a special force to the aside and the soliloquy.

The groundlings stood in the pit. There were usually three tiers of gallery seats, which cost more. Gallants crowded onto the stage and might behave in a rowdy manner. The size of an Elizabethan audience averaged between two thousand and twenty five hundred. Johannes de Witt, a Dutch visitor who made the famous sketch of the Swan in 1596, said that it could seat three thousand, and there is no evidence to the contrary. Surrounded by gallants on the stage, groundlings in the pit, and the more affluent in the galleries, the actor appeared in the open air between the painted heavens above and the hell below.

## THE "PRIVATE" THEATRES

Plays were also presented at the "private" theatres, often rented halls where more aristocratic artistic and moral traditions existed. Anyone could attend, but they catered to a small affluent group. These halls were roofed, well heated, and artificially lit, so they could be used in bad weather and at night.

Most housed troupes of children. Several London choir schools trained boys into expert actors in their own troupes; they were exploited on the commercial stage. These child troupes are not to be confused with the individual professional boy actors who took female roles in the adult troupes performing in the public playhouses.

When Hamlet asks why the players visiting Elsinore have left the city, Rosencrantz says they are victims of a "late innovation" (II.ii.332) of child troupes that has hurt their business:

> But there is, sir, an eyrie [nest] of children, little eyas-
> es [hawk chicks], that cry out on the top of question
> and are most tyrannically clapped for't. These are now
> the fashion, and so berattle the common stages (so
> they call them) that many wearing rapiers are afraid of
> goose-quills and dare scarce come thither.
>
> *(Hamlet, II.ii.338-343)*

That is, many Londoners did not attend the "private" theatres in case they were satirized by dramatists writing for the children's companies. Shakespeare's company gave winter performances in Blackfriars, a "private" theatre, after 1608.

## THE DRAMATIC WORLD

"All the world's a stage," says Jaques. The comparison of the world with the stage, the *theatrum mundi*, runs throughout Shakespeare's works. He uses it in a variety of ways, changing its meaning from play to play. Although he did not invent the concept, he made it particularly his own.

## DOUBLE MEANINGS

The "theatre of the world," the ancient play metaphor, is of great antiquity: it is used by Pythagoras, Plato, and Augustus Caesar; it occurs in Menander's *The Arbitrants,* and in Plautus and Terence, where characters, and by implication the audience, accept the *play world* as reality.*

In medieval England, the metaphor is used mostly in non-dramatic literature, as with Wyclif. Only in the sixteenth century, when the morality play becomes secular, do dramatists use the metaphor (based on Prudentius' *Psychomachia)* that acting is a disguise: the evil people in Skelton and Lyndsay change their names and clothes to seem honourable to their victims. Once actors are seen as dissemblers confusing honest men with illusion, comments about playing the "knave," or the "part," have a new and sinister quality. John Bale's play, *Kyng Johan* (c. 1539), is full of multiple changes of deceit.

The Vice survives on the Tudor secular stage. In early moralities he is a popular, accomplished rascal, a witty schemer, and a manipulator of the plot. He speaks to the onlookers using questions, insults, and mocking offers, which amuses them and keeps their attention. This brilliant figure joins "actor" to "deceiver," a double meaning taken up by the Puritans who see actors as hypocrites and counterfeits, people who persuade honest men of lies using names and costumes not their own. The Vice's audience address preserves the link between the players and the spectators. Play images cluster to him: in Heywood's *Play of Love* (c. 1532), the Vice pretends love for a woman he knows to be false; in *Ralph Roister Doister* (c. 1550), Merygreeke and Custance plan to gull the braggart by devising a playlet as a dramatist might plan a play; and Diccon, the Vice in *Gammer Gurton's Needle* (c. 1560), makes his mischievous plots dramatic.

Although the aside remains, the Vice's audience address and his clowning make his position in the play ambiguous, particularly when other people cannot overhear him. The final secularization of the theatre and the growth of the play as illusion allow the dramatic metaphor to enter English drama. In Gascoigne's play, *The Supposes* (1566), a character is astonished by a twist to the plot and suggests that "a man might make a Comedie of it" (V.vii.61-62). John Lyly's comedies, performed at court, no longer use the audience address, but prologues emphasize the dream-like nature of the play; the Prologue of *Sapho and Phao* (1584) asks the Queen to wake at the end of the performance. These traditions Shakespeare inherits.

---

* For references, see Righter (repr. 1967).

## THE PLAY-WITHIN-THE-PLAY

The recognition of the theatrical nature of life originated in the medieval tradition and took form between 1550 and the work of Thomas Kyd, when the play establishes itself as illusion. Kyd's *The Spanish Tragedy* (c. 1589) deliberately builds on the metaphor of the world as a stage and creates "the play-within-the-play." Until then, experiments with this device were limited to *Fulgens and Lucres* and the anonymous *Rare Triumphs of Love and Fortune* (c. 1582). Kyd unites the medieval contact with the audience to the device of the self-sufficient play; but he does not use audience address. He relies on "the play-within-the-play" so extensively that the actual audience faces an image of itself: actors who sit as spectators within the play (actual vs. fictional; real Londoners vs. the imaginary court of Spain). This perspective becomes a major device of the time, and Shakespeare relies upon it.

When plays are first given in the new Theatre, the direct link of the audience and stage personages is renewed. Bridges between the real world (audience) and the *play world* are given by prologues, epilogues, and Chorus speeches, while within the play's action a bridge is provided by the aside and dramatic monologues. The audience address becomes the soliloquy; conventionally overheard by the spectators, it is not necessarily directed to them. For over half a century the soliloquy implies a deliberately vague relation of audience to personage, spectator to actor.

Many believe in the power that illusion has over reality. Hamlet says,

> The play's the thing
> Wherein I'll catch the conscience of the king.
>
> (II.ii.602-603)

This belief in the power of illusion is basic to the new relation between actors and audience and to the effectiveness of the play metaphor. It could change people's lives. This belief continues with other dramatists: the citizen's wife of *The Knight of the Burning Pestle* (1607) and Jonson's poor gull in *Bartholomew Fair* (1614) are aware that the play they watch is only shadows, but then they forget. The play holds a mirror up to nature; it reflects the reality of its audience. But illusion affects the audience in many ways: some mistake illusion for reality, while others use the language and gestures of the theatre in the actual world.

## THE METAPHOR IN SHAKESPEARE

Shakespeare combines direct and indirect references to the audience (e.g., *1 Henry IV,* V.iv.124-125; *Measure for Measure,* II.iv.9-10; *The Dream,* II.i.223-226) with the metaphor of the "theatre of the world." Shakespeare's play metaphors work in three related ways: they express the depth of the *play world;* they define the relation of that world to the actual world of the audience; and they show the illusion of ordinary life.

The association of the world with the stage builds itself deeply into his imagination and the structure of his plays. He uses play metaphors to a degree unusual even among his contemporaries.

Allied to the play metaphor is the use of boys for women's parts. In *Twelfth Night* and *As You Like It,* boys play the parts of girls who are acting the roles of boys. Rosalind is very conscious of this inversion, and Viola gently reminds us of gender differences.

A number of Shakespeare's characters function as dramatists within a play; they follow a dramatic plan towards a desired end. They differ in how they do so in two broad types, the actor-dramatist and the director-dramatist, those who act out their own dramatizations and those who manipulate others to perform events, as follows:

- *The actor-dramatist:* The actor-dramatist devises and acts out his own imagined dramas either because of self-delusion (Orsino) or in order to establish his bearings in a vast and chaotic universe (Lear).

  The actor-dramatist may include others in his own dramas, but he almost never forces them to play a part. Petruchio, for example, acts upon the rest of the characters as an actor-dramatist but acts as a director-dramatist when he manipulates Katherine. Othello is more extreme when he makes Desdemona fit into his drama by killing her.

- *The director-dramatist:* The director-dramatist knows what he is doing; he always has a firm goal. This kind of person plots with care before he acts, but, like Iago or Richard III, he often does so only one scene at a time. He functions with equal ease in comedy and tragedy and is related to the Vice, the clever slave servant of classical comedy, and the stage Machiavel. The most extreme kind, like Richard III, is a puppet master. The usual climax of his play is when he compels his victim to accept a new role. He is sometimes a subordinate character who initiates things or keeps them moving, bringing about the comic or tragic sufferings of the protagonists, as Pandarus and Sir Toby. But in *Richard III, Measure for Measure,* and *The Tempest,* he is the protagonist.

## THE PLAYER KING

Queen Elizabeth I said that monarchs, like actors, stand on a stage in the sight of all the world, and the least blemish is visible to both enemies and friends. Shakespeare knew that the actual king sees in the player's performance an aspect of kingship itself. Then the juxtaposition of illusion and reality is enormously powerful and complex. The king at his coronation assumes a dramatic role, a part which he must interpret, but which he may not fundamentally change (Richard III cannot cope with this task). A king is identified with his dramatic role; he cannot be separated from it except by death or violence. He is the timeless and ideal symbol of things, the deputy of God on earth, the representative of the land and a people. He is a paradox: a particular person and the embodiment of an abstract ideal. The pomp and ceremony that surround him are not an idle show; they distance him from the common reality, and they are the outward expression of authority. Form, tradition, ritual, dress, and procession make kingship visible.

The actor who plays the king is a greater paradox: he is a person and a player in the role of a king. In the trappings of royalty, he is a "mock king," like the ancient Whitsun monarch or Lord of Misrule. The Player King is a private man who sees his royalty as dream-like and insubstantial. When he takes off his crown and robes he is separated from his splendour and becomes "ordinary" again. In the history plays the Player King mechanically acts out the gestures of a role for which he is not suited (Henry VI, Richard III, Richard II, John), and he confronts an opposite who aspires to his role and who often helps his cause through the use of conscious role-playing (e.g., Richard Duke of York, Richard of Gloucester, Richmond, Bolingbroke, Faulconbridge).

## THE PLAY AS DREAM

Shakespeare asks the audience to accept that the play is as important in their lives as their own dreams. He often uses "dream" and "play" synonymously; both are illusions. But as people in actual and fictional worlds have dreams, "dream" is a third reality distinct from those in which the audience and players live.

Dreams originate either inside or outside a person's consciousness and can be of natural, diabolical, or divine origin. Sceptics think that dreams have natural, internal causes and do not foretell the future. A dream is caused by a disturbance in the imagination: the bodily spirits of the senses retain some images when they return to the heart, or brain, during sleep; they offer images to the imaginative faculty and produce dreams. According to George Chapman, imagination can be

> stirr'd up by forms in the memory's store,
> Or by the vapours of o'erflowing humours.
> (*The Revenge of Bussy d'Ambois*, V.i.44-45)

Any disturbances in the normal balance of the bodily humours, the mind, indigestion, hunger, nervousness, or fear affect the imagination and are released in dream. Or, says Tourneur, dreams might be caused by

> the raised
> Impressions of premeditated things,
> By serious apprehension left upon
> Our minds. (*The Atheist's Tragedy*, II.vi.29-32)

Hamlet calls dreams "a shadow" (II.ii.69), and Hastings, in *Richard III*, insists they are "the mockery of unquiet slumbers" (III.ii.27). Romeo says that dreamers "do dream things true" (I.iv.52), but Mercutio answers with his Queen Mab speech; dreams, he says, reveal the wishes of the dreamer. They

> are the children of an idle brain,
> Begot of nothing but vain fantasy.
> (*Romeo and Juliet*, I.iv.97-98)

Imagination provides the dream with content, which consists of the events and worries of the actual world. It is memory more than fear or anguish that causes Lady Macbeth to sleepwalk. Richard III's dreams can be thought natural (they originate in Richard's memory), or divine (he is God's agent), or diabolical and supernatural (he is a devilish villain).

For Shakespeare, both malign and benign spirits exist. The malign are "objective evil": spirits, witches, ghosts, devils, demons, who project their power into nature and influence us but cannot change free will. They affect us from without, when they offer us a physical but insubstantial object (as evil spirits offer Macbeth a dagger); or from within, when they interfere with the humours to affect our senses. Dreams from spirits can lead us either to damnation or salvation. If benign, dreams warn us of future events. If malign, they delude us by playing on our desires — they deceive our imagination, fog our reason, and lead us to destruction. Shakespeare is ambivalent about the origin of dreams. He knows spirits exist, and that they affect the universe in storms (as in *The Tempest*), in dreams (as in *Richard III*), or are a mode of communication between the real and the spirit worlds (as in *Hamlet*). People respond to dreams of their own free will. Hamlet and Macbeth are free to accept or reject the advice given in dream. Yet Shakespeare also knows that dreams of any origin are produced by the imagination, and no matter how real they seem, they are illusory.

Shakespeare consistently shows that, when people respond to dreams, their character is revealed by their choice. In the actual world, the *play world*, or the dream world, the individual's response to events tells us of his or her character. Lucullus, in *Timon of Athens*, and Shylock, in *The Merchant of Venice*, are the kind of people who would dream of riches, and they do, but their responses differ. Julius Caesar and Hector respond to their wives' dreams similarly. For Shakespeare, the dream is an imaginative reality. But who we are, and what we do in the actual world can affect our dreams: Hermia wakes up screaming in *The Dream* (II.ii.151-156); Katharine of Aragon, in *Henry VIII*, dreams a masque and responds in sleep with "signs of rejoicing"; and Richard III at Bosworth cries out in the actual world his dream-fears — "Give me another horse! Bind up my wounds! Have mercy, Jesu!" (V.iii.178-179) — that,

> Have struck more terror to the soul of Richard
> Than can the substance of ten thousand soldiers.
>
> (V.iii.218-219)

Dream may affect us in the actual world for any length of time: Christopher Sly, in *The Shrew*, thinks he has been in a dream for fifteen years; he sees his actual experience as dream. Richard II (V.i.18) and Katharine of Aragon *(Henry VIII,* II.iv.71) use dreams to cover a long period of happy time; and they wake to an unpleasant actuality. Similarly Henry V spurns Falstaff:

> I know thee not, old man. Fall to thy prayers.
> How ill white hairs become a fool and jester.
> I have long dreamt of such a kind of man,
> So surfeit-swelled, so old, and so profane,
> But being awaked I do despise my dream.
>
> (*2 Henry IV,* V.v.50-54)

His early adventures with Falstaff are now "my dream" (unreal and insubstantial), and he wakes to the actuality of kingship. This constant interchange of actual to dream, and vice versa, shows their vague boundaries.

Shakespeare thinks of the relation of the *play world* and the actual world much like the relation of the dream world and the *play world*. Hamlet equates the actor's art, and the world that art creates, with dream (II.ii.549); and Theseus says the play as a whole is a dream — "The best in this kind are but shadows; and the worst are no worse, if imagination amend them" *(The Dream,* V.i.208-209). Both figures in dreams and people in a play are shadows. Macbeth says,

> Life's but a walking shadow, a poor player
> That struts and frets his hour upon the stage,
> And then is heard no more.                    (V.v.24-26)

The imagination bridges gaps between "worlds." The poet works imaginatively (as Theseus says) and has this faculty more than others. *Henry V* overcomes the gap between the actual world and the *play world* by prologues in which the Chorus constantly asks the audience to let the players "On your imaginary forces work" (I.Pro.18).

Shakespeare insists on the play's relevance to the lives of the spectators. He says it is a dream designed by the playwright, and the actor is the manipulator of that dream. It is then imaginatively re-created in the actual world by the audience.

The audience must understand that the play is not distinctly different from the actual world. A great play is not just to be enjoyed and forgotten but is a profound imaginative reality as relevant to their lives as their own dreams.

## THE TUDOR MYTH

Elizabeth I was the granddaughter of Henry VII (Henry Tudor), the founder of the Tudor dynasty. As his claim to the throne was weak, two themes of the developing Tudor myth emphasized specific aspects of history. First, Henry VII claimed to be descended from King Arthur, fulfilling the prophecies of Cadwallader, last of the Briton kings — a story told by Leland and other chroniclers, and in Spenser's *Faerie Queene.* But second, Henry VII won the right to the crown at Bosworth, which also ended the tragic Lancaster-York feud in the Wars of the Roses.

This story was told by three main chroniclers: Polydore Vergil, Edward Hall, and Raphael Holinshed, who saw the Wars as a pattern of cause-and-effect, murder-and-revenge, sin-and-punishment. England's guilt, which came about when Bolingbroke usurped the crown from the true king, Richard II, is transmitted down the generations (as in Aeschylean tragedy) until it is expiated at Bosworth where Richmond, before he kills Richard III, prays and sees himself as an agent of God's justice:

> O Thou, whose captain I account myself,
> Look on my forces with a gracious eye;
> Put in their hands Thy bruising irons of wrath,
> That they may crush down with a heavy fall
> Th' usurping helmets of our adversaries;
> Make us thy ministers of chastisement,
> That we may praise Thee in the victory.
>
> *(Richard III,* V.iii.109-115)

But Shakespeare tackles this civil strife in a peculiar order. He writes the plays about the last half first. It is only in the middle of the 1590s that he begins at the beginning. Richard II is the true but weak king who is overthrown by Bolingbroke of Lancaster in 1399; thus England is cursed by God to suffer until the rightful king is crowned. The reigns of Bolingbroke, as Henry IV, and his son, Henry V, follow.

Shakespeare began his early English histories with Henry V's death (1422). The young, weak son of Henry V, Henry VI, after years of factionalism and turbulence, is overthrown by the Yorkists: Edward II and then his brother, the villainous Richard III, killed at Bosworth by Henry Tudor in 1485.

For the Tudors, the break with the medieval line of succession when Richard II is deposed began an era of political disorder. Would a similar disorder happen on Elizabeth's death? Shakespeare focuses on the *role* of king — on the *symbol* of the crown — and he stresses its external theatricality. Henry VI uses it weakly, Richard III wickedly, so that the four early plays are one long tragedy: of England's collapse; of the people who fall; and of a role that no one can fill. The further away we are from Tudor times, the less the audience knows about the historical facts. But these are not of primary importance. Shakespeare sacrifices historical accuracy for dramatic effect to present us with enthralling people.

Each of the eight sequential plays of English history is a single unit. But created by one imagination, they make a coherent whole, often called epic in character — perhaps the only modern work that can be compared to Homer's epics. It has been said that its focus is not a single person but England: the decline and fall of the Plantagenets, with a prologue about King John and an epilogue on Henry VIII. The historical order of the reigns is less relevant to Shakespeare's imagination than the symbolic order. The plays begin with the greatest political confusion and national weakness under Richard II, and end after a great victory by a national hero (Henry VII).

There are differences in quality: only *Richard III* among the early histories compares with the glories of Shakespeare's second group. They have different structures; for each play he creates a new structure to fit a unique historical and political context. There is, for instance, a radical change with *Richard III:* a tighter structure is dominated by a magnetic person, and a whole new idea of the history play comes into being.

Nor does Shakespeare swallow the Tudor myth whole. He accepts the most important issue: Richmond's victory meant that God chose the Tudor monarchs to be his exalted deputies on earth, so obedience to the king is obedience to God. This Shakespeare re-creates as the principle of order in Ulysses' speech on degree *(Troilus and Cressida,* I.iii.75-137), and it is believed by Faulconbridge in *King John* and Richmond in *Richard III.*

But Shakespeare does not accept it completely. His histories have ambiguities, irony, and a dialogic process. His are not plays with "a message," that uncritically put forward specific moral ideas — Shakespeare in the histories is ambivalent about many ideas. His intuition goes beyond the morality of the Tudor myth to question it with sly, subtle ambiguities and even cast doubts on its human truth. He is writing not history but plays for the living stage. His success is evident when we see them today.

**William Shakespeare** was born in 1564 to a prosperous middle-class family in Stratford on Avon. By the age of thirty he was already well established in the London theatre scene. Around 1610 he retired to Stratford, where he died in 1616. The chronology below gives approximate dates the plays were written. From about 1588 to 1600 he wrote mainly history plays and comedies; from 1600 to 1608 tragedies and "dark" comedies, and from 1608 to 1612 dramatic romances.

### Chronology of the Plays:

| | |
|---|---|
| 1588-1591 | *2 Henry VI, 3 Henry VI* |
| 1588-1594 | *The Comedy of Errors, Love's Labour's Lost* |
| 1590-1592 | *1 Henry VI* |
| 1590-1594 | *Titus Andronicus, King John* |
| 1592-1593 | *Richard III* |
| 1593-1594 | *The Taming of the Shrew* |
| 1593-1595 | *The Two Gentlemen of Verona* |
| 1594-1596 | *Romeo and Juliet, A Midsummer Night's Dream* |
| 1593-1595 | *Richard II* |
| 1594-1597 | *The Merchant of Venice* |
| 1597 | *1 Henry IV* |
| 1597-1598 | *2 Henry IV* |
| 1597-1601 | *The Merry Wives of Windsor* |
| 1598-1599 | *Henry V* |
| 1597-1600 | *Much Ado About Nothing* |
| 1599 | *Julius Caesar* |
| 1599-1600 | *As You Like It, Twelfth Night* |
| 1600-1601 | *Hamlet* |
| 1601-1602 | *Troilus and Cressida* |
| 1602-1604 | *All's Well That Ends Well* |
| 1602-1604 | *Othello, Measure for Measure* |
| 1604-1606 | *King Lear, Macbeth* |
| 1604-1608 | *Timon of Athens* |
| 1605-1607 | *Antony and Cleopatra* |
| 1606-1609 | *Coriolanus* |
| 1608-1609 | *Pericles* |
| 1609-1610 | *Cymbeline* |
| 1610-1611 | *The Winter's Tale* |
| 1611 | *The Tempest* |
| 1612-1613 | *Henry VIII, Two Noble Kinsmen* |

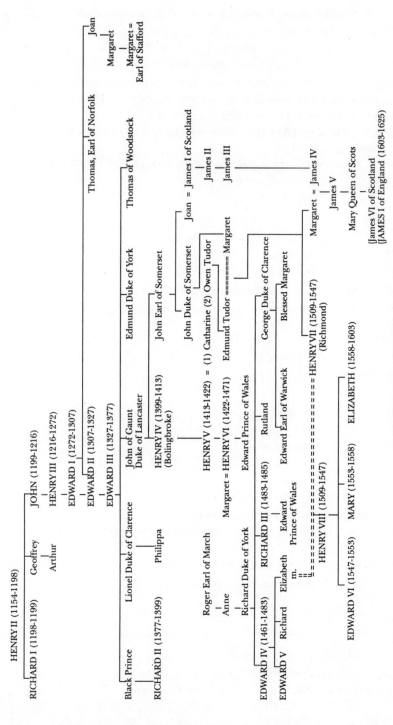

**ENGLISH MONARCHS 1154-1625**

# WORKS RECOMMENDED
# FOR STUDY
## —— ALL VOLUMES ——

Beckerman, Bernard. *Shakespeare at the Globe 1599-1609*. London: Collier-Macmillan, 1962.

Bevington, David. *Action is Eloquence*. Cambridge: Harvard University Press, 1984.

Boas, F. S. *Shakespere and His Predecessors*. New York: Haskell House [1896], repr. 1968.

Bradbrook, Muriel C. *Shakespeare: The Poet in his World*. New York: Columbia University Press, 1978.

Bullough, Geoffrey. *Narrative and Dramatic Sources of Shakespeare*. 8 vols. New York: Columbia University Press, 1957-1975.

Calderwood, James L. *Shakespearean Metadrama*. Minneapolis: University of Minnesota Press, 1971.

Courtney, Richard. *Outline History of British Drama*. Totawa, N. J.: Littlefield, Adams, & Co., 1982.

Dollimore, Jonathan. *Radical Tragedy*. Chicago: University of Chicago Press, 1986.

Dollimore, Jonathan, and Alan Sinfield, eds. *Political Shakespeare*. Ithaca, N.Y.: Cornell University Press, 1985.

Ford, Boris, ed. *The Age of Shakespeare*. London: Cassell, 1961.

Frye, Northrop. *A Natural Perspective: The Development of Shakespearean Comedy and Romance*. New York: Columbia University Press, 1965.

—. *Fools of Time: Studies in Shakespearean Tragedy*. Toronto: University of Toronto Press, 1967.

—. *The Myth of Deliverance*. Toronto: University of Toronto Press, 1984.

—. *Northrop Frye on Shakespeare*. Toronto: Fitzhenry & Whiteside, 1986.

Gaster, T. H. *Thespis: Ritual, Myth and Drama in the Ancient Near-East*. New York: Doubleday, 2nd rev. ed., 1961.

Granville-Barker, Harley. *Prefaces to Shakespeare*. 4 vols. London: Batsford, repr. 1963.

Greenblatt, Stephen. *Renaissance Self-Fashioning*. Chicago: University of Chicago Press, 1980.

—. *Shakespearean Negotiations*. Berkeley and Los Angeles: University of California Press, 1988.

—. *Learning to Curse*. London: Routledge, 1990.

Howard, Jean E., and Marion F. O'Connor, eds. *Shakespeare Reproduced*. London: Methuen, 1987.

Kastan, David Scott, and Peter Stallybrass. *Staging the Renaissance*. London: Routledge, 1991.

Kinney, Arthur F., and Dan S. Collins, eds. *Renaissance Historicism*. Boston: University of Massachusetts, 1987.

Knight, G. Wilson. *Shakespearean Production*. London: Faber, 1964.

—. *Shakespeare and Religion*. London: Routledge and Kegan Paul, 1967.

Kott, Jan. *Shakespeare Our Contemporary*. Trans. B. Taborski. New York: Doubleday [1964], rev. 1967.

Leggatt, Alexander. *Shakespeare's Political Drama*. London: Routledge, 1988.

McGuire, Philip C., and David A. Samuelson. *Shakespeare: The Theatrical Dimension*. Washington: AMS Foundation, 1979.

Muir, Kenneth. *Shakespeare's Sources*. London: Methuen, 1957.

—. *Shakespeare the Professional*. Totawa, N. J.: Littlefield, Adams, & Co., 1973.

Nagler, A. M. *Shakespeare's Stage*. Trans. Ralph Manheim. New Haven: Yale University Press, 1958.

*Oxford Companion to the Theatre* and *Oxford Companion to the Canadian Theatre*. Toronto: Oxford University Press.

Righter, Anne. *Shakespeare and the Idea of the Play*. Harmondsworth: Penguin [1967], repr. 1982.

Salgado, Gamini. *Eyewitnesses to Shakespeare: First Hand Accounts of Performances 1590-1890*. London: Chatto & Windus, 1975.

Sinfield, Alan. *Faultlines*. Trans. Ralph Manheim. Berkeley and Los Angeles: University of California, 1992.

Slater, Ann Pasternak. *Shakespeare the Director*. New York: Barnes & Noble, 1982.

Sprague, Arthur Colby. *Shakespeare and the Actors*. Cambridge: Harvard University Press, 1944.

—. *Shakespearean Players and Performances*. Cambridge: Harvard University Press, 1953.

Sprague, Arthur Colby, and J. C. Trewin. *Shakespeare's Plays Today: Some Customs and Conventions of the Stage*. London: Sidgwick and Jackson, 1970.

Styan, J.L. *The Shakespeare Revolution*. Cambridge: Cambridge University Press, 1977.

Thomas, Brook. *New Historicism and Other Old-Fashioned Topics*. Princeton: Princeton University Press, 1991.

Van Laan, Thomas F. *Role-Playing in Shakespeare*. Toronto: University of Toronto Press, 1978.

Veeser, Aram, ed. *The New Historicism*. London: Routledge, 1989.

Wells, Stanley. *The Cambridge Companion to Shakespeare Studies*. Cambridge: Cambridge University Press, 1986.

Zesmer, David A. *Guide to Shakespeare*. New York: Barnes and Noble, 1976.

# ——— THE EARLY TRAGEDIES ———

Baldwin, T.W. *The Organization and Personnel of the Shakespearean Company.* Princeton: Princeton University Press, [1927], 1961.

Bowers, Fredson. *Elizabethan Revenge Tragedy.* Princeton: Princeton University Press, 1948.

Bradley, A.C. *Shakespearean Tragedy.* New York: St. Martin's Press, [1905], 1978.

Buber, Martin. *I and Thou.* New York: Scribner's, 1958.

Burke, Kenneth. "Dramatism." In *International Encyclopedia of the Social Sciences,* 7. New York: Macmillan, 1968.

Charlton, H.B. *Shakespearean Tragedy.* Cambridge: Cambridge University Press, [1948], 1961.

Charney, Maurice. *Shakespeare's Roman Plays.* Cambridge, Mass.: Harvard University Press, 1961.

Daiches, David. *Shakespeare: Julius Caesar.* London: Edward Arnold, 1976.

Eliot, T.S. *Selected Essays.* London: Faber, 3rd rev. ed., 1951.

Fergusson, Francis. *The Idea of a Theater.* Princeton: Princeton University Press, 1949.

Gilder, Rosamond. *"John Gielgud as Hamlet,"* in Russell E. Leavenworth, ed. *Interpreting Hamlet: Materials for Analysis.* San Francisco: Chandler, 1960.

Hirst, David L. *Julius Caesar.* Oxford: Blackwell, 1971.

Johnson, Samuel, from "Notes on the Plays" (1765), in *Johnson on Shakespeare: Essays and Notes Selected and Set Forth with an Introduction by Walter Raleigh.* London: Oxford University Press, 1908.

Jones, Ernest. *Hamlet and Oedipus.* Garden City, New York: Doubleday, 1954.

Kitto, H.D.F. *Greek Tragedy.* Garden City, New York: Doubleday, 1954.

Knight, G. Wilson. *The Wheel of Fire.* London: Methuen, 1930.

—. *The Imperial Theme.* London: Methuen, 1954.

Knights, L.C. *An Approach to Hamlet.* London: Chatto & Windus, 1960.

Leavenworth, Russell E., ed. *Interpreting Hamlet: Materials for Analysis.* San Francisco: Chandler, 1960.

Mahood, M.M. *"Wordplay* in *Romeo and Juliet,"* in *Shakespeare's Tragedies.* ed. Laurence Lerner. Harmondsworth: Penguin, 1968.

Nagler, A.M. *Shakespeare's Stage.* New Haven: Yale University Press, [1958], 1964.

Ornstein, Robert. "The Mystery of Hamlet Notes Toward an Archetypal Solution," in *Hamlet Enter Critic.* ed. Claire Sacks and Edgar Whan. New York: Appleton-Century-Crofts, 1960.

Sacks, Claire, and Edgar Whan, eds. *Hamlet Enter Critic.* New York: Appleton-Century-Crofts, 1960.

Sanders, Leonard. *The Hamlet Warning.* New York: Scriber's, 1976.

Seward, James H. *Tragic Vision in Romeo and Juliet.* Wilmington, N.C.: Consortium, 1973.

Spurgeon, Caroline F.E. *Shakespeare's Imagery and What It Tells Us.* New York: Macmillan, 1935.

Turgenev, Ivan. *Hamlet and Don Quixote.* Trans. Robert Nichols. London: Henderson, 1930.

Watkins, Ronald, and Jeremy Lemmon. *In Shakespeare's Playhouse: Hamlet.* Newton Abbott: David & Charles, 1974.

Wilson, John Dover. *What Happens in Hamlet.* New York: Macmillan, 1940.

**(Play texts quoted are from the Penguin Shakespeare series,
published by Penguin Books Ltd., Harmondsworth, England.)**

*All's Well That Ends Well*, copyright © 1970; Introduction, copyright ©
Barbara Everett, 1970.

*As You Like It*, copyright © 1968; Introduction, copyright © H.J. Oliver, 1968.

*Antony and Cleopatra*, copyright © 1977; Introduction, copyright © Emrys
Jones, 1977.

*The Comedy of Errors*, copyright © 1972; Introduction, copyright © Stanley
Wells, 1972.

*Coriolanus*, copyright © 1967; Introduction, copyright © G.R. Hibbard, 1967.

*Cymbeline*, not yet in print.

*Hamlet*, copyright © 1980; Introduction, copyright © Anne Barton, 1980.

*1 Henry IV*, copyright © 1968; Introduction, copyright © P.H. Davison, 1968.

*2 Henry IV*, copyright © 1977; Introduction, copyright © P.H. Davison, 1977.

*Henry V*, copyright © 1968; Introduction, copyright © A.R. Humphreys, 1968.

*1 Henry VI*, copyright © 1981; Introduction, copyright © Norman Sanders,
1981.

*2 Henry VI*, copyright © 1981; Introduction, copyright © Norman Sanders,
1981.

*3 Henry VI*, copyright © 1981; Introduction, copyright © Norman Sanders,
1981.

*Henry VIII*, copyright © 1971; Introduction, copyright © A.R. Humphreys,
1971.

*Julius Caesar*, copyright © 1967; Introduction, copyright © Norman Sanders,
1967.

*King John*, copyright © 1974; Introduction, copyright © R.L. Smallwood,
1974.

*King Lear*, copyright © 1972; Introduction, copyright © G.K. Hunter, 1972.

*Love's Labour's Lost*, copyright © 1982; Introduction, copyright © John
Kerrigan, 1982.

*Macbeth*, copyright © 1977; Introduction, copyright © G.K. Hunter, 1977.

*Measure for Measure*, copyright © 1969; Introduction, copyright © J.M.
Nosworthy, 1969.

*The Merchant of Venice*, copyright © 1967; Introduction, copyright © W.
Moelwyn Merchant, 1967.

*The Merry Wives of Windsor*, copyright © 1973; Introduction, copyright © G.R.
Hibbard, 1973.

*Much Ado About Nothing*, copyright © 1978; Introduction, copyright © R.A.
Foakes, 1978.

*A Midsummer Night's Dream*, copyright © 1967; Introduction copyright ©
Stanley Wells, 1967.